CONTENTS

Winning Mind	1
Prologue	3
Chapter 1: The parable of the Lemon:	7
Chapter 2: What is not accounted for, it is managed	14
Chapter 3: Discovering your real self: the path towards success in trading	19
Chapter 4: Developing a Disciplined and Consistent Mindset	64
Chapter 5: Taking responsibility: letting go of ego in trading	80
Chapter 6: What a beautiful rainy day	87
Chapter 7: The evil market: Enemy or ally?	107
Chapter 8: Mathematics is your best friend	118
Chapter 9: Mathematics is your best friend	126
Chapter 10: The exciting adrenaline of danger: The thin thread between trading and betting	129
Chapter 11: Embracing fear: Your best ally	143
Chapter 12: The eternal search for knowledge in trading	159
Chapter 13: The Psychology of Success: Mindset of Abundance and Gratitude	173
Chapter 14: Overcoming Procrastination: Taking Action in the Moment	179

Chapter 15: The Trap of Self-Deception: Focusing on Quality, Not Quantity — 184

Chapter 16: Forging a Winning Mindset: A Guide to Success in Trading and Life — 192

Chapter 17: My commitment. My gift — 198

Acknowledgments — 211

WINNING MIND

Master in Psychotrading : Master your emotions and succeed in trading

Winning Mind

Psicotrading master in your emotions and succeed in trading
First Edition: October 2023
© from the text:
Eduardo Chapellin
Total or partial reproduction of this present work by any means or procedure whether electronic or mechanical, computer processing, rental or any other form or transfer, is prohibited within limits that are stated by law and under the legally established warning of this work without the prior written authorization of the copyright holders.

PROLOGUE

On the pages of this book you will enter the world of traders and discover the importance of cultivating a solid mentality prepared for success. We will focus our attention on trading, however, the principles and techniques that we will explain here will help you with any challenge that comes your way. As a trained economist and an experienced entrepreneur, I have traveled through various paths in the business world and I witnessed first-hand the transformative power that the right mindset can have.

For years, I was the owner of several businesses focused on the sale of mass consumption products, gastronomic establishments, in charge of agricultural projects,, among others. And I have faced both the ups and downs and the challenges inherent to business management. However, more than six years ago my path began to take an unexpected turn when I delved into the study of trading financial assets. It was then that I discovered the exciting and exciting reality of the financial markets.

As I have delved deeper into this new world, I was fortunate to interact with numerous trading professionals and work at an internationally renowned broker. These experiences have provided me with valuable knowledge and insights into the business, but they also revealed an inescapable truth: most aspiring traders focus exclusively on strategies and techniques, neglecting crucial component: mindset.

This is how the inspiration for this book have arisen. I recognized the prevailing need for a guide that would prepare traders mentally, that would help them to understand and to apply methods and approaches that would allow them to achieve that coveted profitability consistently. Because of this, I decided to share my knowledge and experiences on these pages, with the hope that they will be a beacon of light on the path to success in trading financial assets and, even more so, success in your life. Because being successful in any field you dedicate yourself to but being unhappy it should not be called success, it should go hand in hand and be directly proportional to your happiness.

Throughout the chapters we will discover the fundamentals of Forex trading and how the right mindset can make the difference between success and failure. We will learn to set realistic goals and to develop an effective trading plan, as well as to control our emotions and to manage risk intelligently. We will also explore the role of analysis and decision making in the trading process, and how to adapt to constant market changes.

However, this book is not limited to trading itself. It is a call to adopt a long-term winning mentality. I invite you to consider trading not only as a financial activity but as a lifestyle. Whether you are a beginner or you have been in the world of trading for some time, this book will provide you with a clear and concise guide to develop the mindset that will allow you to achieve the desired profitability.

My hope is that this book becomes a valuable tool along your path to profitability in trading financial assets. I encourage you to explore each chapter with an open mind. To reflect on the teachings and to apply the concepts in your own experience. Remember that transformation does not happen overnight but through constant dedication and hard work.

Get ready to discover how a winning mindset brings you closer to your dreams.

Recommendations for Reading

Before delving into the pages of this book, I want to share with you some recommendations that will help you get the most out of its content and enjoy this experience in a unique way.

Freedom to Explore: This book is designed so you can read it in a non-linear way. Feel free to explore the chapters in any order you wish or skip those topics that you consider less relevant to you at this time. Each chapter addresses important aspects of the professional trading mindset, so the order in which you read them does not matter.

Put it into practice immediately: One of the fundamental aspects of this book is that you put it into practice immediately. Every concept, strategy or technique you find on these pages has the potential to transform your mindset and to approach Forex trading. Don't wait to finish the book to start applying what you've learned. The sooner you start implementing what you discover, you can experience the results and fine-tune your path to profitability.

Sincerity and spontaneity: As a writer, I have decided to be sincere and spontaneous in my writing style. You will not encounter excessively formal or pretentious language. You may find profanity and colloquial expressions throughout the book. This is intentional, as I seek to convey the concepts in an authentic and direct way, reflecting the reality of the trading world and fostering a genuine connection with the reader.

Reflect and adapt: As you read, I invite you to reflect on what you learn and how you can apply it to your personal situation. There is no magic formula that works for everyone, so it is essential that you adapt the concepts and strategies to your own experience and personality. Find your own path in the world of trading, using this book as a flexible and adaptable guide.

Remember, this book is a tool to help you to develop a professional and consistent trading mentality over time. Take advantage of the freedom I give you to explore and to jump between chapters, remember to put what you have learned into practice immediately. Enjoy reading and be inspired on your path to profitability in Forex trading!

CHAPTER 1: THE PARABLE OF THE LEMON:

beyond Lemonade

If I told you the phrase: "If lemons fell from the sky", what would you answer? Probably the most common and automatic: "Lemonade". It is an answer that many of us have heard since our childhood, associating the idea of lemons with the preparation of this refreshing drink and, despite whether we like lemonade or not, it is an automatic response that we tend to repeat, perhaps because we hear it from others. And our lazy mind searches its memory bank and takes the answer that it knows will give it the least work, the easiest one. However, this quick and superficial response does not reflect the complexity of the situation or the analytical mindset that we must develop as professional traders.

The truth is that "two lemons fall from the sky" is not the same as having a ton of these falling on you. It is also not the same whether the lemons are ripe or green. Even the day of the week the event occurs, it could influence the response. This simple parable of the lemon teaches us a fundamental lesson:

we should not settle for simplistic and superficial responses and actions.

In the world of trading and life itself, developing an analytical and detail-oriented mentality is essential to stand out and not become one of the crowd, for example, your partner will love that you are more detail-oriented, apart from the consistent profitability over time. If you generally interpret many of the concepts as messages and anecdotes in this book, you will get more sex, more friends, and more time to dedicate to the activities that make you happy. So open your mind and above all force it to work more than it wants. We must train ourselves to evaluate the different scenarios that may arise in each situation. As with lemons, there are a multitude of factors that must be considered before making rash decisions.

The power to adapt is another crucial aspect that we have lost in human evolution. In the modern era, we tend to seek comfort and ease in our lives, even our minds become lazy and reluctant to do mental work. We opt for the simplest and fastest option, instead of the smartest and most strategic one. But being a successful trader requires a different approach.

Every step we take in our activity as traders must be evaluated intelligently and strategically. We cannot limit ourselves to making the first and simplest decision that comes our way. We must carefully consider the implications and consequences of our actions. Making intelligent and well-informed decisions is the basis for achieving our goals in trading and in life in general.

Remember: the world of trading is complex and challenging. We cannot afford to be superficial in our responses and decisions. It is time to delve into the parable of the lemon and to discover how to develop an analytical and detailed mentality that leads us to success.

Returning to the initial question: if I told you the phrase: "If life gave you lemons", what would you answer? Unlike responding automatically, put your mind to work and you will discover that there is nothing more powerful than yourself. mind, where the ability to ask the right questions is essential. An appropriate response would be to question the situation and respond: "it depends." As simple as saying; "it depends", it completely changes the scenarios and it opens up a whole range of responses. In this sense, the power of the right questions lies in our ability to explore all possible scenarios. Not all situations are the same and each may require a unique approach.

Ask ourselves, for example: what type of lemon is it? or are they green or ripe?, leads us to consider the different characteristics and conditions that could influence our decisions.

The analytical and detailed mindset we seek to develop, involves challenging our assumptions and prejudices. We must not be content with simplistic and generalized answers, but we must dig deeper and explore the complexity of each situation. The right questions guide us toward critical thinking and help us to make more informed and informed decisions.

However, it is important to highlight that analyzing the different scenarios does not mean overcomplicating our decisions. We must not fall into the trap of overanalyzing and paralyze us with indecision. The key is to find the balance between deep analysis and the ability to act proactively. To solve this great problem of not knowing when and how to reach a balance of not being paralyzed or acting too much in trading, is to have a clear, proven trading plan or business plan that adapts to your type of person. In the next chapters we will delve into putting together the trading plan.

Simply being aware of our mind's natural tendency toward mental laziness gives us an impressive advantage. Knowing that most people tend to look for quick and superficial solutions allows us to stand out by adopting an analytical and detailed mentality. By being proactive in our approach and pushing ourselves out of our comfort zone, we differentiate ourselves from those who are content to be one of the crowd. I have a hypothesis, this is that the mere fact of having an advantage as powerful as having real and conscious control of your mind and not letting mental laziness dominate you with the famous "don't put off until tomorrow what you can do today", it will already position you within the 5% of the richest population in the world in the short, medium or long term. Because by dominating your mind you already dominate the game. Think about that and put your mind to work.

To give you an example, just by thinking about what business you could develop based on the need you want to cover given the collective laziness of people, just as the majority prefers to have their food delivered to their home and not to have to go to a restaurant. supermarket even if it is less than 100 meters away. They prefer to use their phone and to ask for an application. From that need, the one who identified it put his mind to work on creating companies that will be dedicated to meeting such demand and that is what 95% of successful businesses are like. They start by covering a need that, in most cases, it arises from the mental laziness of people who prefer to pay to have it done.

If you have already had some contact with the world of

trading by taking a paid or free course on the internet, you will have heard of the famous market traps that the big players in the market leave to liquidate the small fish. Do you think they are part of the group of those who just let their lazy minds lead them? No! They understood that human beings tend to repeat and follow patterns. They tend to be repetitive and simplistic, they act in masse. Based on these scoops, they manipulate prices as they see fit. We don't need to beat them, we just have to understand their game and to move accordingly. This is achieved with a lot of discipline and an analytical mind. So if you want to be part of that small percentage that are truly profitable in the world of trading, make a point to eliminate that lazy mind.

The advantage of being analytical but proactive in trading is that it allows us to identify opportunities and to risk that others overlook. While many focus on generic strategies and simplistic approaches, we are trained to consider relevant variables and scenarios. This gives us a broader perspective and it allows us to make more informed and informed decisions.

Remember that trading is a constant challenge, but it is also an opportunity to excel. By developing an analytical and detail-oriented mindset and being proactive in our actions, we position ourselves above those who are still struggling to be profitable in the market. It is our ability to analyze and our willingness to act that will set us apart as successful traders.

The advantage of being analytical but proactive in trading is that it allows us to identify opportunities and risks that others overlook. While many focus on generic strategies and simplistic approaches, we are trained to consider relevant variables and scenarios. This gives us a broader perspective and allows us to make more informed and informed decisions.

— "Are you hungry?"

— "It depends".

In turn, you will be asked: "What does it depend on?"

— He tries to answer: "On what there is to eat "

Another example would be: " Do you want any beer?"

—"It depends".

—"How does it depend?"

—"Yes, it depends on what type of beers they have".

The price reached the range I was expecting to sell, will I sell?

—It depends… on whether it complies with my trading plan, iit has more confirmations, etc.

You start to use "it depends" or some question that opens up the possibilities, but I recommend that you use them carefully because it can be considered obnoxious and irritating to those asking the question and even rude if you don't know how to use it correctly. It could be considered very repetitive that you have never given answers but only just questions, you start today to force your mind to think of questionable answers to possible questions and to evaluate different decisions. You will see that in less than 15 days using this technique you will perceive impressive results in the way you see the world.

The price reached the range I was expecting to sell, will I sell?

—It depends… on whether it complies with my trading plan, has more confirmations, etc.

You start using "it depends" or some questions that open up the possibilities, but I recommend to use them carefully because it can be considered obnoxious ant irritating to those asking the question and even rude if you don´t know how to use it correctly- It could be considered very repetitive that you have never given answers that just questions, but start today to force your mind to think about questionable answers to possible questions and to evaluate different decisions, You will see that in less than 15 days using this technique you will perceive impressive results in the way you see the

Asking yourself and seeking for answers without fear are the fundamental pillars of human evolution.

Most of the time the answers are within you. Remember to put into practice answering with open questions, with questions that open up possibilities and force your mind to be more analytical and not to settle for the most simplistic answer. There is no better person to practice with than yourself, try to force yourself to find creative solutions to everything that causes your curiosity or problems. I find it curious how much energy we spend analyzing, admiring or criticizing other people when the first thing we should admire is ourselves. If what you do or who does not cause you admiration, it is right at that moment that you should ask yourself questions. The power of questions is available to everyone and at any time. But we prefer to avoid them out of laziness, fear or, above all, lack of motivation.

Do not leave for tomorrow what you can do today. Start by asking yourself questions that force you out of your comfort zone.

CHAPTER 2: WHAT IS NOT ACCOUNTED FOR, IT IS MANAGED

The problem is doing something without managing it. There is a phrase that I would like to share with you that I have learned while I was studying economics at the university. The truth is that it is a very simple but powerful and essential phrase so that you can get the most out of this book and of your life. A teacher told me:

— Chapellim what is not accounted for, it is managed

It may seem simple but it makes a lot of sense, returning to the mental laziness that we must try to eradicate from our life. We tend to send goals but we do not set parameters and therefore we can not manage our improvements. If you stop for a moment to think and to reflect about this brief phrase " what is not accounted for, it is not managed", perhaps you will agree with me that unsuccessful people are those who have preferred to live a life managed by others, by the system, by their parents, by the couple, because they were lazy or lacked of courage to take the control of their lives.

Taking control of our lives comes from the simplest things as for instance: to choose or to control what you eat, how long and when you sleep, with whom you spend quality or leisure time, with whom you decide or don't to have relations, what you have chosen to study, what you have decide to focus your energies on, and beyond it, to what you have dedicated your most valuable resource: your time. So we could write a whole book giving details of the quantity of simple or complex things that make up and complement you as a person, you can look up the meaning of success in Google or you can ask your closest person what the meaning of success is and do you know anything? That doesn´t matter. The only thing that matters is what makes you happy and they are all those simple or complex things that surround you and for which two things are fundamental: the first one that you recognize them and the second one that you use them for your advantage. Only in this way will you be able to control or what you have the capacity to control.

Failed people are those who have preferred living a life managed by others

The only meaning that you should pay attention is to your own, and for this it is fundamental that you ask yourself the right questions. But as I have told you, it is fundamental that you use a detailed and analytical mind to ask yourself those ideal questions and to answer them, it doesn´t which they are, the most important is that you start working on them.

A person that is successful as a trader, but he is a disaster in other aspects of his life as for instance at home, selfish with people that love him. If he has people who love him among many other things, he will be a short-lived trader. While a person that is very successful in love , with his relatives and friends, but it is a disaster in his profession, he will have a long life although not complete as the Lion King has taught us, the most important is the balance. So from now on we are going to start working on balancing ourselves and starting from the smallest: we need to feel good and order is a synonym of well-being. You have to, from today on, begin making a list of the things that you do not control and to search the way to control them so that you can manage them, of course you will tell me or think : Eduardo is impossible to control everything, that is true but the ones that you YES can, you must begin to control them.

For instance your food, we are what we eat, to have a healthy boy, gives us a great advantage. Start by controlling the time you sleep, the rest is fundamental to having an energetic and focused mind. Start by organizing your house, being in a tidied environment has a powerful effect on your well-being mind and try to exercise to complement a healthy body and mind. The funny part of all of this is that we know what we fail, referring to the simple things, such as: eating healthy, sleeping, drinking water, being organized, etc. But we are unable to maintain the changes we propose for a long time until we turn them into habits. We say: Monday, I start with exercising. We begin but we finish abandoning them, the same with almost everything. Not to mention the food, it is much easier for us to abandon the diet that we have proposed than maintaining it until it becomes a habit. Then, what can we do?, start by accounting for management.

How can you begin? Write everything on an agenda and stick it in a place where you Friday, I will exercise for 45 minutes, Sunday I will clean the whole house, organize my house and plan my week. From Monday to Friday I will eat healthy food that was sent by the nutritionist, Saturday I will eat everything. It will be my free day for food and drinks, Everyday drink 2 liters of water; everyday I will read 15 minutes before going to sleep; Saturday I will share time with my friends, Fridays and Sundays with my couple; Tuesday I will prepare a dinner for my couple and to get mood going for the week I will order my bedroom everyday before going to work, among other things. This is a simple example and above all, you have to do your own agenda. I recommend you to do it every Sunday, it takes you 30 minutes to plan the whole week and during the week you go managing what you have set out to do and always keeping in mind that the activities are to have a healthy body and mind.

If you have to go to a nutritionist to assign you a diet or to give you ideas about how to improve your diet, it is a very intelligent investment. If you have the possibility to pay a personal trainer at least 3 times a week, it is also an excellent investment. If you don't have the financial possibility, you can use free applications to help you to train with an exercise plan. There are no excuses, your mind is lazy for everything except to give excuses, so you have to prohibit it. Don't make excuses to yourself or anyone, focus on eliminating them. Like every beginning it will be difficult, but work hard until it becomes habitual and when you have mastered it, continue looking for more things that you consider challenging, give a signal to your brain that you are an active person.

When for any reason you are disappointed, come back to your agenda and see how much progress you have made. For that it is very important that each day you carry out those small tasks, tick what you have achieved, granite by granite, step to step you will see the changes, if it were easy it would not be funny, whether this saying is true or not, the important is that it is your life and you must control it and that is the most valuable thing. Maybe there are people around you who complicate the achievement of your goals. I recommend you find the way you get away from them or to talk to them, speaking about your goals and ask them to help you, in any way I do not want you think that I believe that everything is easy, but yes it is possible and it starts for the simplest, for the details, the small changes. It requires that you have great discipline, courage and personality to face them.

◆ ◆ ◆

If it were easy, it would not be funny

◆ ◆ ◆

If you stop for a moment to think and to reflect about this brief phrase" what is not accounted for it is not managed, maybe you agree with me that failed people are those that prefer to live a managed life by others.

CHAPTER 3: DISCOVERING YOUR REAL SELF: THE PATH TOWARDS SUCCESS IN TRADING

This chapter perhaps has some uncomfortable questions, as we have talk¡ked in previous chapters, our mind does not like to ask complicated questions and many times we spend years without asking ourselves question that define us as a person just because we do not want answer or because we do not want to admit that we are lazy and conformist. We prefer

continuing being where we are because the changes imply much energy and they are almost

◆ ◆ ◆

Zombi Mode: Living without passion, without goals, without reasons to get up with energy.

◆ ◆ ◆

Never a path full of flowers, simply we adapt. I call it "zoom mode". Living without passions, without goals, without reason to get up with energy.

The zombie mode is an existence without passion, without goals; it is like a shadow in real life. It is like walking through a gray frog where the colors fade and the feelings dim. In this state, actions are automatic: lacking genuine purpose. It is like being on autopilot, dragging yourself through days without really living them.

Imagine getting up each day without a real re with energy and determination, Without any objective that makes you jump out form the bed with energy and determination. Without goals that inspire you to improve and to challenge your limits. In this zombi mood, life becomes a series of monotonous and boring tasks where time seems to pass without leaving any trace.

What is your passion? Which one?

Passion is the fuel that ignites our souls. It is what drives us to explore, to learn, to create, and to live with enthusiasm. It is like a burning fire that illuminates our path and gives us a deep sense of purpose. Without passion, live becomes a landscape without

nuance, where experiences lack emotions and meaning.

Goals are the lighthouses that guide our journeys. They are the goals that allow us to chart a clear course and keep us moving forward. Without goals, we are adrift, without direction or purpose. Goals challenge us to grow, to overcome obstacles and to reach our heights. They are the engine which drives our personal evolution, and it helps us to build a meaningful life.

◆ ◆ ◆

Live without passion, without goals, it has been dead in life. It is to deny our potential and to waste the opportunity to experience the fullness that life has to offer. In this state, our actions become mechanical and soulless. We become spectators of our own lives instead of being protagonists who shape their destinies.

◆ ◆ ◆

Lack of motivation traps us in a monotonous life without inspiration. It prevents us from growing, learning and evolving. It deprives us of the joy of discovering new horizons and challenging our limits. Motivation is what pushes us to get up when we fall, to persist when we face difficulties and to look for new opportunities inclusively in the darkest moments.

◆ ◆ ◆

They are the objectives that allow us to chart a clear, clear course and keep us moving forward. Without goals, we are adrift, without directions or purpose. Goals challenge us to grow, to overcome obstacles, to reach our heights. They are the engine that drives our personal evolution and it helps us to contribute to a significant life.

They are the objectives that allow us to chart a clear course and keep us moving forward. Without goals, we are adrift, without directions or purpose. Goals challenge us to grow, to overcome obstacles, to reach our heights. They are the engine that drives our personal evolution and it helps us.

Living without passion, without goals is like to be dead in like to be dead in life. It is denying our potential and wasting the opportunity to experience the fullness of our life to offer. In this state, our actions become mechanical and soulness. We become in spectators of our own lives instead of being protagonists that shape our destiny: In this state, our own lives. The lack of motivation.

Lack of motivation traps us in a monotonous routine uninspired without inspiration.it prevents from growing, learning and evolving. It deprives us of the joy to discover new horizons and to challenge our limits. The motivation is what pushes us to get up when we fall, to persist when we face difficulties and to search for new opportunities including the darkest moments.

Summarizing, the zombi mood is a spiritual and emotional

lethargy. It is like leading a half-life, without the passion that gives color and shines, without the goals that give direction without the motivation that drives us. Living like that is to deprive ourselves of the opportunity to experience life in its fullness, to explore our capacities and to build a lethargy that lasts.

Then why settle with this zombi mood when we can select living with passion, with goals and with motivation? Life is a wonderful ephemeral gift and it is our responsibility to make the most of it. Wake up from a zombi mood, ignite the sharpness of passion, set bold goals and find motivation to live each day with enthusiasm and fulfillment.. Do not permit life to pass you by for a while on autopilot. Wake up and live with your whole being because you deceive a full life with meaning and emotion.

Let's go to practice:

Connecting With Your Passion And Purpose

1.1 What are you passionate about?

Reflect anjbout your interests, skills and about what really excites you. Trading and any other activity where you really want to be successful, requires dedication and perseverance. What is important is that you are passionate about what you are doing and what you are doing or starting to do. Through practical exercises and anecdotes, I will guide you so that you can identify what you are really passionate about and how to apply to trading.

To begin, take a moment to reflect about your interests and skills. make a list of the activities that you enjoy and of those ones that you consider yourself proficient at. ut do it for real, stop reading now, open a blog of notes on your mobile or if you prefer, write it down by hand and write down 10 things that make you feel competent, the ones that you like to do alone or with someone. Ask yourself what topics or industries are fascinating for you, and in those ones that you like to dive deep into. Remember, trading involves a wide range of financial tools and markets, for what is important to find an area that you are truly passionate about.

For example, you might be drawn to the foreign exchange market, due to your interest in international economic relations and how they affect the currency. Or maybe a penchant to the stock market because of your fascination for the enterprises and their growth. Identifying the areas of interest will help you to find a specific focus within trading.

Explore your financial passion. A practical exercise that you can do is to do a deep research on a the financing subject that you are passionate about. Read books but with clear goals, count for the quantity of books that you are reading to identify whether you like them or not the ones that are related with trading in a month and in that way you will realize if you feel excitement and curiosity to continue reading. We say OK, I´m going to read FOREX to see whether I like the activity or not, thi is a very vague statement, it is the same to say. I´m going to begin walking to see if I like it or not, it must have parameters. For example: I´m going to up to walk from point A up to point B, on such date at such time, the same with the books or with any other goal that we set, no matter how small or big it is, you must set parameters, strive to meet them and they will be small prizes that you give to yourself. You will already see when you account for it, if you manage it, you will be able to identify much quicklier where you can improve or what things you have to change. If you do not like to read articles and blogs related to this subject, join online or attend seminars and conferences to expand your knowledge. By doing it, you will be able to evaluate the level of enthusiasm and comprehension in this particular area and to determine if trading in this specific field is the right path for you.

Identifying your passions and skills is fundamental to determine if trading is something that really excites you. Remember that dedication and perseverance are essential to success in the financial world. Through the practical exercises and exploring your interests, you will be able to discover which area of trading you are passionate about and how you can apply your skills and knowledge to reach success.

What motivates you to become a trader? Examine your internal and external motivations, Is the desire for financial independence? Is it excitement of market´s challenges ?, make sure that your motivations are genuine and drive you to keep going even in difficult moments,

Example of a question: what are the principal motivations for becoming a trader? Deo you look for financial independence, intellectual challenges, the possibility to work in any part of the world or the opportunity to build a lasting financial legacy?

Motivation is a key factor for success in trading. It is important to examine both internal and external motivations that drive you to embark in this career. Internal motivations are those that come from your own desires and from your personal goals, while external motivations can be influenced by factors such as social pressure or expectations.

It is essential that your motivations are genuine and are

aligned with what you are truly passionate about. If your only reason for becoming a trader is the desire to earn money quickly, it is possible that you may be disappointed easily in difficult moments.. On the other hand, if you find motivation in the process of constant learning, in market challenges and in the possibility of getting financial independence, you will be very well prepared to face obstacles that can arise.

No path is the same, we are very influenced by everything that surrounds us, our childhood, our age, aur relatives, among other things, but you are the owner or your life. No matter what your reality is, by starting to take control of your life, managing every step you take to improve, you will already have an advantage. The trading path can be emotionally challenging and it requires perseverance. Therefore it is important that your motivations are strong enough to keep you focused and committed even when you face difficulties. By understanding your motivations, you will be able to set your realistic goals and constantly work toward them.

Anecdote

I will tell you about a great friend and a professional trader. To write this book I wanted to know what other traders thought and due to the job I had in an international brokerage where I had the opportunity to speak with hundreds of professional traders and experienced market analysts with years in the environment, I took the opportunity to get a clear idea of the mentality that a professional trader should have. I share one of the many stories with you while talking with a friend.

He told me about his genuine motivations: hem, when he

was young, he was a simple aspiring trader, he realized that many persons in his environment looked for becoming traders due to the influence ot he social networks and to the idea of earning money easily. However, he wanted to be sure aht his motivations were genuine and that they were aligned with his personal values

After reflection deep, he identified that what really motivated him was the desire of having financial independence and the opportunity to have a positive impact in other people's life through trading, above in his family since they had limited resources. This genuine motivation gave him th force and the determination to face the market challenges and to persist on his way toward the success as trader and I, while we drank a beers we delved deeply in the subject, I asked him:

—How did you realize that you were successful?- the answer was very simple, he said to me:

—When I could buy my mother the house of her dreams, but above all, when I could take my family to know other countries. Seeing them happy makes me feel happy.

We have explored the importance of examining and understanding our motivations to become traders. Since the desire to achieve financial independence, the yearning of intellectual challenges or any other internal or external motivation, it is essential that our motivations are authentic and they drive us to keep going even in difficult times. it is of no use if you do not make any effort to identify them.

By knowing our motivations, we can set realistic goals and work in a constant way to obtain them. Besides, having genuine motivations gives a solid base to face emotional challenges and market fluctuations, keeping our focus and determination on the way towards the success as traders.

Despite of giving you examples and striving to guide you on the path of self- evaluation I also want you to do your part and strive to ask yourself that help you to achieve those or that reasons that will keep you strong in the moments of turbulence; in the moments when it seems the world is against you. In those moments, what reason will keep you firm to go ahead?, that reason that everyday makes you get up with much energy because you want to begin with your activity. I would also like to clarify that to achieve this reason has not to be overnight, it has not to be immediately, but it is important you set your goal to ask yourself those simple questions: what motivates me to wake up everyday with a winner's mind?

Evaluating Your Commitment

Are you truly committed and willing to invest time and effort in your development as a trader? Reflect about your willingness to dedicate to your education, practice and continued improvement of your skills in trading.

Being a successful trader does not happen overnight. It requires a real and constant commitment to learn and to improve. It is fundamental to valuate tjyour level of commitment before embarking on this activity. It is sure you will have heard the famous saying " soldiers do not die in a war", it is perfectly applied to the mentality that you must have as an entrepreneur.

As a trader, you have to be prepared for war , to go through bad days, but above all to learn from them and to be a better person and professional the following day, knowing that you are in a profession that demands having a strong mind and being completely focused and knowing money will not rain you overnight, to ko¡now that it is not as simple as social networks make it seem to you just to sell the courses.

All of us know that a baby takes 9 months to be born, we all understand that a day has 24 hours and that a year has 52 weeks, everyone understands that a process exists since the profession as a "trader" is ot different from other profession, it takes time, a constant process of improvements, ups and downs. Internalizing that gives an advantage, I give you an interesting data, more than 95% of persons deposit $100USD in a broker, simply they burn the money within a few days, And do you know the first reason why they burn it?, it is because they thought it was going to be easy to multiply it and they thought they would not need any mental effort, simply they would do a couple of transactions and when they get a negative streak , they don't know how to manage those feelings and they end up burning the account.

It is sad because many of them are hopeful persons with many debts and believing that trading will give them the freedom they long for and well asn we already know the result. More than 95% end up burning their account for different reasons, so if you are reading this book, you already have the advantage because you're one of the 5% who has chosen to train, for that I congratulate you and you have to feel proud.

Here I present you some aspects to be considered:

Time: Trading needs a significant investment of time. You must be willing to dedicate time for education and market analysis. This implies reading books, studying charts, conducting research and participating in training programsEvaluate if you are willing to make necessary sacrifices to allocate time for your development as a trader.

Something interesting about time factor is one of the most deceptive and it has a significant weight whether you are profitable or not. What do I want to mean with this? Consciously or unconsciously we want to earn money as quickly as possible. because either we have economical needs,or simply because we feel social pressure to be free financially. It is very curious that most trading aspirants who choose to train independently or through academies, know that trading is another profession, not very different from being a lawyer, an engineer, physician, etc. it is a profession that requires a lot of training and above all a lot of practice. But something within us refuses to accept it and conscious or unconsciously we want to be profitable as quickly as possible.

One of the most common questions of students when they start to make trading is " how long will it take me to be profitable?" and the truth is profitability is not the end of this career, it is the way. It is like a student of medicine asks his professors "how long will it take me to buy a house?", or a student of Law asks: " how long it take me to become millionaire?; the physician will earn money little by little as he performs surgeries or consults, as he practices.The same with lawyers or with any other profession,as they carry out work, they will receive money little by little and in some cases they will lose money, so the same for traders. They must realize that learning an activity then you have to apply it consecutively, and little by little you will receive money and in some cases you will lose but due to your good management, if you subtract losses from the profits, you will end up positive.

Because you are not rentable just once, it is not a destiny and it is precisely at this point I will remind you that you must manage each step you take, because you have to see profitability and manage it correctly. A profitable trader is not one who has managed to do only on a simple withdrawal from a funding enterprise, or who has managed to make a simple withdrawal from $ 10.000 USD to $100.000 USD in a week. No a profitable trader is someone who keeps consistency in time in a positive way and regardless of whether he has a negative streak, looking at it in general it remains positive over the years. If one internalizes the meaning of being profitable in a consistent way, you will remove a weight from your shoulders which is wanting to make a certain amount of money in a determined period of time, And it will lead you to make big mistakes such as overleveraging yourself, taking operations outside from your trading plan among many others.

Education: Constinous learning is key in trading and in your life. You must be willing to invest in your education and to achieve knowledge about technical analysis, trading strategies , risk management and trading psychology. Ask yourself if you are willing to explore new ideas, to attend seminars, courses and to learn from experienced professionals.

Practice: Experience is fundamental in trading. You must be willing to practice and to put your knowledge into play on demo accounts or with small quantities of real money. Practice will help you to develop your skills, to refine your strategy and to familiarize yourself with different sceneries of the market. Evaluate whether you are willing to go through a learning-by doing phase and to make mistakes on the path towards success.

Continuous practice: This is, without any doubt, one of my favorite concepts and I want you to wholeheartedly try to open your mind and to analyze this idea, maybe it sounds receptive thus I have looked for different ways to express it. Trading and the world are constantly evolving, so you must be willing to adapt yourself and to improve your skills. This implies reviewing your last transactions, learning from your mistakes, updating your knowledge and keeping an open mind and new strategies and approaches. Ask yourself if you are willing to commit to constant improvement and to step out of your comfort zone. In a constantly changing world like that of trading, continuous improvement becomes a fundamental pillar for sustainable success. Philosophy behind continuous improvement is simple but deep: each day, in each transaction and decision, we seek to be a little better than we were yesterday. This mindset avoids complacency and it encourages a constant evolution in our skills and approaches.

An emblematic example of the continuing improvement you can find in Toyota's business philosophy, known as the Kaizen method. This Japanese word means "change to improve", and it refers to the constant practice to do incremental improvements in all aspects of an organization. In the trading world, Kaizen´s concept is equally applicable.

Imagine that you are a trader that follows Kaizen´s philosophy in his approach. Each operation is an opportunity to learn, inclusive if the results are not the expected. Instead of mourning losses, you see each loss as a valuable lesson. I wonder what you can learn of this operation, what decisions could have been made in a different way and how to improve your skill next time.

Just as Toyota that it looks for optimizing its processes of production and to deliver higher quality vehicles. Thai implies reviewing your last operations with a critical eye, identifying improving areas and making right decisions to address these areas.

Continuous improvement also requires an open mentality to new strategies and approaches. Just as automobile manufacturers must be willing to adopt new technologies and methods, traders must be willing to explore new strategies and to adapt changes in the markets. This does not mean changing your approach constantly but being willing to adjust when it is necessary and to prove new ideas with a disciplined approach.

Ultimately, continuous improvement in trading helps you to achieve mastery. Each small step that you give in your quest for improvements brings you a little closer to excellence in your operations and decisions making. Just as Toyota seeks to build reliable high quality vehicles, you look for contributing a reliable high quality approach that allows you to achieve your financing goals. So, before you delve into the exciting world of trading, you ask yourself to commit with constant improvement. Are you ready to apply Kaizen´s concept in your approach? Are you willing to f¡learn from your mistakes, to evolve your skills and to maintain your mind open? If your answer is Yes, you are on the right path towards trading success and building a solid base for your financing future.

Imagine a path that stretches infinitely before you, a path that invites you to advance constantly and to surpass yourself in each step. That is the continuous improvement path, a path that leads you towards excellence in trading and in life. Do you dare to tour it?

Look for a momenta Toyota+s philosophy rooted in Kaizen´s japanese word. This word is much more than an expression; it contains a transformative concept. Imagine that each operation, each analysis and each decision are steps of an ascending ladder towards your financing goals. like Toyota´s, fine-tuning its processes to manufacture more efficient and reliable vehicles, you adjust your methods to get more consistent and successful results. Each step you bring takes you closer to the peak of your aspirations.

What stops you applying this same philosophy to your path in trading? Why not take advantage of each winning or lost operation as an opportunity to learn and to grow? It is easy to fall into the trap of complacency and frustration, but constant improvement requires you to rise above those obstacles and keep your eyes on the horizon. Think of an operation that didn't go as you expected. The market has taken an unexpected turn and your profits and your profits have disappeared. Is it a defeat or a learning opportunity? Adopting a continuous improvement mindset means that each experience, inclusive negative ones, become a brick in the building of success.

It is like you were a craftsman working on a masterpiece. Every stroke, every polish, every adjustment contributes to the final beauty. . Similarly, every operation, each analysis, each change contributes to your development as a trader. Continuous improvement is not only a strategy, it is a state of mind. It means that, although you get profits, you never stop in the search of perfection. It also means, inclusively among losses, you find the strength to analyze, to learn and to move forward.

So, reflect for a moment. Are you willing to embrace this path? Are you willing to dedicate yourself to mastery in trading, to constantly move forward excellence? By doing it, you are not preparing to face challenges in the market, but you are building a solid foundation for your long-term financing success.

Imagine for a moment that you are a modern alchemist, transforming every experience in the market into an opportunity to distill knowledge and skill. Thi is the heart of continuous improvement, a philosophy that drives traders towards excellence through the constant evolution and learning.

Consider the history of samurais, Japanese warriors who personified the dedication of continuous improvement. Through the rigorous practice and the constant study, these sword masters reaffirm their skills to achieve unmatched levels of skill. Likewise, as a trader, you can embark on a constant growth trip.

The essence of continuous improvement lies in the recognition that no path towards success is linear. There will be ups and downs, but each challenge is an opportunity to polish your skills and to adjust your approach. How can you apply this to your trading? Imagine that each operation is a training field, each analysis is a mental exercise and each revision is a step towards mastery, The continuous improvement is also like building a skyscraper., It is not built in only one day, but with carefully designed layers, built one over the other one. Each operation that you take, each adjustment you do in your strategy is one of these layers. As you progres, your structure becomes more solid and resistant..

Now think in the learning process of a musician. At the beginning, they may make mistakes, produce discordant notes, but with the constant practice each note becomes in tune and melodious. In trading, each note can look like an individual note, but with time and dedication, these notes come together to create a success symphony.

Continuous improvement is also a way to maintain an open mind to new perspectives and approaches. In an ever-changing market, it is crucial to be willing to adapt and to learn. Imagine you are a painter that uses different brushes and colors in each operation, experiencing and adjusting to build your financial masterpiece.

Continuous improvement is like a garden that you take care of and nurture, it requires constant attention to remove weeds, and to permit flowers to flourish. Likewise, in trading, you must cultivate your skills and knowledge, getting rid of bad practices and allowing your profits to flourish. In this last instance, continuous improvement is a commitment to yourself and with your long-term success. It is the promise that you never stop learning, growing and evolving as a trader. It is an approach that transcends profits and losses and it leads you towards mastery in a constantly changing world.

Continuous improvement is not simply a strategy that applies in your trading, it is a mindset that involves all the aspects of your life. It is the recognition that there is always a margin to grow, to evolve and to improve self-imposed limits. This approach challenges you to look beyond your operation.

Imagine you are the protagonist of your own film of personal improvement. Everyday it is a new chapter in which you have the opportunity to change, to learn, to grow. Continuous improvement is not only optimizing your technical skills, but cultivating your relations, to expand your knowledge and nurturing your mental and emotional well- being.

Think about your life as a white cloth that you can fill with meaningful experiences and achievements. Every time you strive to improve, you are adding strokes of color to that cloth. As an artist works in a masterpiece all his life, you can also look for growing and improving, you become a model to follow for your loved ones. You can inspire your children, friends and colleagues to look for their own path of development and self-improvement. Your commitment with continuous improvement can be a beacon that leads others towards excellence.

The Greek philosopher said: " The only constant is change". Continuous improvement is the embodiment of this universal truth. In a constant evolving world, those who refuse to be left behind are the ones that prosper. Embarrassing continuous improvement is to embarrass the essence of the same life, where challenge becomes an opportunity and each step forward to your best self.

The Greek philosopher Heráclito said: " The only constant is change". Continuous improvement is the embodiment of this universal truth. In a constant evolution world, those who refuse to be left behind are the ones that prosper. Embarrassing continuous improvement is to embarrass the essence of the same life.

In the last instance, continuous improvement is an exciting journey that transcends limitations and reminds us that we are capable of achieving more than what we imagine. Then do you dare to embark on this journey? Are you willing to commit yourself with constant improvement not only in trading, but also in each aspect of your life? The decision is in your hands. Continuous improvement is not just a choice, it is a way of living.

The Legacy of continuous improvement

Imagine that you are in the twilight of your life, looking back on all the experiences and decisions you have made. What would you like to see? A marked life by complacency and conformity or a life of constant pursuit of growing and improvement? The choice is yours and every day you live is an opportunity to write your legacy through continuous improvement.

Think about the successful stories that you have listened to: the inventors that have persisted in spite of failures, leaders that have challenged conventions and the entrepreneurs that have transformed entire industries. What do they have in common? All of them have embarrassed the continuous improvement. They have dared to challenge the status quo and to look for ways to constantly improve and to move forward.

It is not just an accumulation of richness or material achievements but the deep satisfaction of knowing that you have given your best of yourself in each step of the path, continuous improvement allows you to see every challenge as a learning opportunity and every mistake as a springboard towards future success. It pushes your to get out of your comfort area and to explore new horizons.

Think in a tree that grows over the years. As it expands, it develops deep roots that maintain it strong and stable in any climate. Similarly, continuous improvement allows you to develop deep roots of skills, knowledge and resilience. You become an unbreakable force that can face and storm and to continue growing.

There is a tree that I would like you to keep in your mind when things become difficult: bamboo: it is incredibly strong and useful, part of the success of the evolution of Asian countries is due to the quantity of uses that they give bamboos. But there is a feature that I like about this wonderful tree; despite being very thin, it does not break easily, it bends but it does not give up, be like a bamboo: bend but never give up. To surrender you they have to kill you.

Continuous improvement is also an act of gratitude towards yourself and towards life. It is recognizing that you have the ability to evolve and to improve, and that everyday it is a gift that you can make the most of. By living with that mindset, you can find the meaning and the purpose every step of the way, even in the most challenging moments.

So I invite you to contemplate a trip with your eyes. Face each day as an opportunity to grow and to evolve. Accept the challenges as steps towards your success. Embarrass the power of continuous improvement in all the aspects of your life and watch how your reality is transformed. At the end of the day, continuous improvement is not just a focus, it is a trip that takes you to be the best version of yourself, and to leave a lasting legacy in the world. Are you ready to start?

Remember that the commitment with your development as a trader does not imply time and effort but also perseverance and resilience, the path may be challenging, for those that are really committed, have a better chance of achieving success.

◆ ◆ ◆

Imagine you are in the twilight of your life, looking back on all experiences and decisions you have made. What would you like to see? A life marked by complacency and conformity or a life of constant pursuit of growth and improvement? The cession is yours, and each day you live, is an opportunity to write your legacy through continuous improvement.

◆ ◆ ◆

Anecdote: In my research and curiosity to compare my experience in this field, I have always taken the opportunity to ask those who, in my opinion have the most experience in an area and more importantly, what I saw as happy and reflecting success, Speaking with an analyst of the market I asked him how he has gained confidence in his analyst and he told me that in his beginnig when he was an aspiring trader, he realized to have success in trading it is needed unwavering commitment. He has assessed his disposition and he decided to dedicate each morning to study and to analyze markets before starting his work day. He even made sacrifices such as reducing sleep hours and giving up some social activities to invest time in his development as a trader.

As time passed, he has faced obstacles and he has experienced losses in his first trades. However, his commitment and dedication kept him focused on his goal. He kept learning from his mistakes, adjusting his strategy and looking for opportunities for improvement. Over time, his commitment has led him to become a successful and respected analyst. I asked him the reason he was more inclined to be an analyst and not to operate his own accounts, and he commented to me he liked more analysts. He realized he got up very early and he reviewed every daily news and he evaluated the charts before everyone else. When he arrived at his office everybody related to asking him what they could expect during the operating session that made him feel special, he felt more useful than properly operating.

The world trading is much more open than just looking at charts selling or buying. It has many more extremely interesting fields. I invite you to investigate and to evaluate what makes you happiest and, of course, what is more profitable and beyond, what best suits your type of person.

It is extremely important to evaluate your commitment before entering the world of trading. Time, practice and continuous improvement are key aspects that require a real and constant commitment. Those that are willing to invest time and effort in his development as traders, have a greater chance of achieving success in the medium and long term. Before making a decision to become a trader, reflect about your level of commitment and be sure of being willing to make the necessary sacrifice. Remember that trading is a journey of learning and growth, the commitment with your development is fundamental to achieve your goals in this field.

2.2 Are you willing to accept and to learn from your trading mistakes?

Reflect about mindset and willingness to correct and to improve from your mistakes instead of getting discouraged. Trading is a field in which mistakes are inevitable. Even the most experienced traders make mistakes in any moment of their career, I would dare say professional traders make mistakes every day and several times. Mistakes are not a problem, the problem is the mismanagement of our feelings, emotions and capital. As we have mentioned before, what is not accounted for, it is not managed; you have to strive to be as organized as possible, keeping track of each operation and measuring the risks of each action so that you can make the difference before a successful trader and one who remains stagnant. It is the ability to learn and to grow from those mistakes. If you do not keep a diary of your operations because you believe that you have the best memory in the world, you believe that you are capable of remembering each operation that you took throughout the week, during the month or during or year, you will be responsible for staying stagnant.

By keeping a diary, a control of your actions in the market, you will be able to make reviews and to adjust where you're falling, and just at that moment, you will stop being a simple aspirant to become a professional trader.

Here you have some key points to consider:

Learning Mindset: The first step to accept and to learn from your mistakes is to adopt a learning mindset. Recognising your mistakes are opportunities to grow and to improve your skills, instead of seeing them as failures, you should see them as valuable lessons that will permit you to strenght yourself as a trader.

Analyzing mistakes: After making mistakes in an operation, take your time to analyze what has happened. Examine the decisions you have made, the signals you have overlooked and the emotions that have influenced your behavior. identify where you have made a mistake and what you could have done in a different way.

Keep a track of your mistakes: Keep a detailed register of your operations and mistakes. thai is going to allow you to carry out a follow up of your recurrent mistakes and to detect patterns you must correct. Ask yourself if you are willing to take a record and to be honest with yourself to analyze your mistakes.

When I refer to keeping a record, I 'm not talking about extremely sophisticated work, it is important that it will be practical, it can be a simple excel spreadsheet. For example, your trading plan of three operations per day, imagine all the time and how easy it would be to keep the result of such operations daily and in a week you will have between 10 to 15.

Make sure that the way you keep your records is simple and practical. In addition to posting the result and the data of the transaction, you also attach a detailed explanation; why you have taken that transaction, how you have felt before, during and when closing it. All of this data is what you can later manage.

Establish an action plan: Once you have identified your mistakes, develop a plan of action to correct them. What specific steps can you take to avoid making the same mistakes in the future? define clear goals and concrete measures that help you to improve in those specific areas. It is not enough just to know the concept of continuous improvement, you have to put them into practice; that's what all these tools are for, but they are not useful if you use them rigorously.

Practice with exercises: To help you to improve in problematic areas, you can do practical exercises. For example, if you have difficulties managing the risk properly, you can run trading simulations and practice the risk management in different sceneries. Ask yourself if you are willing to spend time on these exercises and to develop new skills.

Seek feedback: Do not be afraid of seeking feedback from other traders or trading professionals. Share your mistakes and ask for advice on how you can improve. The external feedback can provide a fresh perspective and to help you to identify improvement areas that perhaps you have not considered before.

Keep a positive mindset: Learning from mistakes can be challenging and sometimes frustrating. It is important to keep a positive mindset and not to let mistakes get you down. Focus on the progress you are making and the lessons learned instead of focusing on mistakes made.

The Powerful Force Of A Positive Mindset

Life, as the financing market, is full of ups and downs. Profits and losses, successes and failures, are inevitable parts of our existence. In this constant flow, our mentality plays a crucial role. It is a beacon that lights the path through the fog and it leads us towards the shore, no matter how rough the sea is.

Positive mindset does not mean to ignore obstacles or fooling yourself into believing that everything is good. Instead, it is a commitment to face challenges with courage and resilience, it is to understand that mistakes are opportunities to grow and that each problem is a puzzle we can solve. It is not about being blind in front of reality but choosing to see it as a lens that empowers us.

Imagine facing a series of losses in your operations of trading. Positive mindset could lead you to blame yourself, feel defeated and question your skills. In contrast, a positive mindset would permit you to analyze what has happened, learn from your mistakes and adjust your strategy to improve in the future. It would encourage you to stay focused on progress and in lessons that are gaining in each step.

Positive mindset does not only influence your relationship with trading, but also in every area of your life. Have you realized how people with a positive attitude tend to be magnetic?They attract others due to his contagious energy and his willingness to face challenges with positivism. This quality also benefits interpersonal relationships since nobody wants to be near someone who constantly radiates negativity.

In a society where frequently negative aspects are emphasized, cultivating a positive mindset can seem a challenge. But it is a challenge worth facing. Just as an athlete that trains his body to perform at his best, you can train your mind to embrace positivity and resilience, You can achieve it by practicing gratitude, challenging yourself to find the positive in every situation and surrounding yourself with people who inspire you.

Positive mindset is your ally on the path towards success , it helps you to overcome obstacles with determination, to learn from your mistakes and to keep a constructive attitude towards life. It is not denying problems but to face them with an optimistic vision and certainty that each challenge is an opportunity of growth. So are you ready to embrace the positive mindset and to let it light toward success? The election is yours.

Elevating Your Flight Of Your Spirit

The power of a positive mindset lies in its ability to elevate the flight of your spirit even in the darkest moments. Imagine a bird that faces strong winds while it is flying; if it gave in to fear and adversity, it could be swept ashore by the storm . But if you adjust your wings and use the wings to your advantage, you can soar to unimaginable heights.

In a similar way, when you face challenges in your life and in trading, a positive mindset acts as your wings, they propel you upwards, they give you the strength to face headwinds and they allow you to find opportunities even in the midst of adversity. It is a beacon that leads you through a storm, and it reminds you that you are the captain of your ship.

A positive mind is not limited to repeating empty statements. It goes beyond "everything is good" when things are not, It implies a deep connection with your capacity for adaptation and resilience. It helps you to understand, independently what you face, you have the choice of how to react to it. You can choose to be a victim of circumstances or you can choose being the owner of your answer.

In trading, a positive mindset allows you to stay calm when the market becomes volatile. It helps you to resist the temptation of making impulsive decisions in times of stress and to stick to your strategy. It reminds you each operation is an opportunity to learn and to improve, and that losses are an integral part of the path towards success. But how to cultivate this mindset? Just like a garden, it requires constant care, your mind also needs nourishment and attention. Practice nutrition and attention. Practice daily self-reflection, celebrate your achievements, even small ones, and learn from your challenges without judging yourself. Surround yourself who inspire you and drive you forward.

In your journey as a trader and as a human being, a positive mindset is your compass. It leads you towards light, it gives you force to overcome obstacles and it connects you with fundamental truth which has the strength to choose who to face each situation. So are you available to embarrass this mindset and to permit you to lift your spirit to unexpected heights? Remember, the bird is not afraid of the storm, it learns how to fly.

Practices To Cultivate A Positive Mindset

Daily Gratitude: Spend a few minutes every day reflecting about things for which you are thankful for. It can be something so simple as the Sun shining outside or a kind gesture from a friend. Gratitude helps you to focus on the positive and to appreciate what you have instead of regretting what is missing.

Positive Visualization: Spend time to visualize success and overcome challenges. Close your eyes and imagine in detail how you feel when you achieve your objectives. This practice not only motivates you but it also programs your mind to see possibilities instead of obstacles.

Control of Negative Thoughts: Maintain constant vigilance

about your thoughts. When you realize you are having negative or self-critical thoughts, stop and change them to more constructive and realistic thoughts. For example: if you are thinking " I will never succeed"M change it to " I am working hard to achieve my goals and every step counts".

Affirm your successes: Instead of focusing on your mistakes, focus on your achievements. Keep a journal where you write your victories, no matter how small they are. This will remind you constantly what you are capable of doing and what you are making. When you face difficult moments , remember your achievements to regain confidence.

Practice self -acceptance: Nobody is perfect, and to make mistakes is part of human experience. Instead of beating yourself up for your mistakes, embarrass them as opportunities of learning. Let you be human being and learn to laugh at your own mistakes. This reduces the pressure and it allows you to face challenges with a quicker mind.

Remember to cultivate a positive mindsets is a constant and gradual process. Do not expect radical changes overnight, but with perseverance and constant practice, you will see how your perspective begins to change. By adopting these practices in your daily life, you will be strengthening your capacity to face challenges with courage, to keep your focus and to continue moving toward your goals.

Practical exercise: Identify three mistakes you have made in last transactions and analyze them in detail. Reflect about the decisions you have made, signals you have overlooked, and emotions that have influenced your actions. Then, develop an action plan to correct those mistakes and establish concrete measures to avoid repeating them in future.

Remembering, accepting and learning from your mistakes is fundamental for growth and success in trading. To be willing to correct and to improve will allow you to move forward your goals and to become a more skillful and profitable trader. There is an expression that has become famous recent years and the truth is very cute and inspiring. Apply it. Be 1% better each day. It starts with being humble and accepting we have to work to improve. You will see not only do you improve in trading, you also have to be 1% better each day. Start being humble and accepting we must work to improve. You will see not only improvements in trading, you also have to work in your body, mind and it is very important in relations with your loved human beings. You also work to improve a 1% each day in your relations.

Evaluating Your Tolerance To Risk And Emotions

3.1 Which is your tolerance to the risk in trading?

Reflect on how you feel about assuming financing risks and how it affects you emotionally. Assess your capacity to handle pressure and fluctuations of the market without giving it to fear or greed.

The tolerance to the risk is a crucial aspect to consider in trading since the financial market is full of uncertainty and volatility. Evaluating your tolerance to the risk will help you to understand your emotions better and to make decisions more fundamental in your operative.

Here you have some key points to consider:

Emotional self-awareness: Reflecting about your emotions in relation with financing risk. Are you comfortable assuming risks or do you find it stressful? How do you react to losses? Are you prone to being carried away by fear or greed? Being aware of your emotions will permit you to make more rational decisions and to prevent emotions affecting your operations negatively.

Identification of risk limits: Establish clear risk limits you are willing to assume in your operations. Define a maximum percentage of your capital you are willing to invest in only one operation or in a determined period. This will help you to manage your risk exposition and to keep your emotions under control.

Testing strategies with different risk levels: Carry out practical exercises in which you tes different strategies with different risk levels. This will permit you to experience and to evaluate how you feel emotionally in front of different risk levels. See how it affects your confidence and making decisions.

Analysis of your last emotional reactions: Reflec how you have reacted in your last operations emotionally. Have you let yourself be carried out by fear and have you closed positions too soon? Have you given in to greed and kept trading for too long ? Analyze these situations and look for patterns which help you to understand better your emotional risks to risk

Risk scenario planning: Before entering an operation, carry out a detailed plan of the different scenarios that could happen. Visualize how you would feel emotionally in each one of those scenarios. This will help you to prepare yourself emotionally and to have a more controlled answer in any outcome.

Real time emotional monitoring and management: During your operations, keep a constant monitoring of your emotions. If you feel yourself getting carried away by fear or greed, take time to breathe, to evaluate the situation and to remember your strategy. Apply emotional management techniques, such as meditation or breathing control to keep calm and to make more rational decisions.

Learning and continuous improvement: As you operate and you face different risk emotional situations. try to learn from your experiences. Reflect about what it didn't work and what it did and look for ways to improve your risk tolerance and emotions management. Be open to learn from other successful traders and look for educative resources that help you to strengthen your mentality.

Remember that evaluating and working on your risk tolerance and emotional management is an ongoing process. More conscious you are of your emotions and how they affect trading, the more you will be able to help you to adapt yourself and to make fundamental decisions. Practice these exercises and spend more time to reflect about your emotional risk answers and you will see how your capacity is improved to manage the fluctuations of the market and to make decisions more consistent with your objectives.

3.2 How do you relate with money? Reflect about your beliefs and attitudes towards money. Identify whether you have an abundance or scarcity and how that can influence your financing and trading decisions.

The way in which you relate with money has a significant impact on your success as a trader. Here you have some aspects to consider to evaluate your relation with money.

Beliefs about money: Examine your deep - rooted beliefs about money. Do you believe that it is hard to come by or that is only available to a few? Do you believe that money is a source of security or freedom? Your beliefs about money can influence your financing decisions and how you face the risks in trading.

Abundance or scarcity mentality: Identify if you have an abundance or scarcity mentality in relation to money. An abundance mentality is believing that money is plentiful and that there are always opportunities to earn more. On the other hand, a scarcity mentality is believing that money is limited and that you have to compete for every penny. Having an abundance mindset can open you up to more possibilities and allow you to make riskier but informed decisions.

Attitudes towards money: Reflect on your attitudes towards money. Do you see it as a means to achieve your goals and dreams or do you perceive it as something that controls you and causes you concern? Your attitudes towards money can influence how you deal with profits and losses in trading. If you are afraid of losing money, you may make more conservative decisions and miss out on valuable opportunities.

Practical exercise: Write your beliefs and attitudes regarding money on paper. Identify those beliefs and attitudes that may be limiting your ability to achieve trading success. Then, write down a more positive and constructive version of those beliefs and attitudes. For example, if you have a scarcity belief like "money is hard to come by," you can replace it with "money is available in abundance if I am willing to look for and take advantage of opportunities." And apart from that, if you are one of those who like to have conclusive evidence, look up the history of money printing in the world in the last 10 years and you will realize that there is money in quantities and every day there are more and more ways to get it. The United States has been responsible for printing rivers and rivers of money. Thinking that it is scarce because you heard it from your parents or because you are in an environment where you have had little contact with money, does not mean that it has to be your only reality, I invite you to investigate, study more about money, both in form of real data, how to understand the operation of the economic machinery and you will understand that there is a lot of money.

Abundance Visualization: Do a guided visualization in which you imagine yourself enjoying financial abundance. Visualize how you feel, what achievements you have achieved, and how your financial and trading decisions are aligned with an abundance mindset. This practice will help you reinforce a positive mindset towards money and attract financial opportunities to you.

Cultivating Abundance Through Visualization

Imagine a moment when you find yourself in front of an idyllic landscape. The sun shines softly, the birds sing melodies in the air and a feeling of calm and contentment envelops you. Do you realize that this image is as real in your mind as any other experience you have had? This is the power of visualization, a tool that can transform your thoughts into reality.

Visualization is not just a passive act of imagining pretty things; It is a powerful practice that engages all your senses and emotions. The science behind this is fascinating: when you visualize a situation with enough detail and emotion your mind cannot distinguish between reality and imagination. This means you can train your mind to accept abundance as a reality, rather than a distant dream.

Creating abundant reality through visualization

Build the scene: Find a quiet, comfortable place to sit. Close your eyes and begin to build a scenario of abundance in your mind. Visualize your ideal financial space: what does it feel like to be surrounded by wealth and opportunity?

Incorporate details: Add specific details. Where are you? What are you doing? Who do you share your achievements with? The more details you can incorporate, the more real your visualization will become.

Feel the emotion: Don't limit yourself to just the images. Feel the emotion of abundance in every cell of your body. Emotion is the key to activating your brain's emotional response and making visualization more effective.

Use the focus effect: This effect is a powerful technique that involves concentrating your mind on what you want to achieve. Imagine that you are using a magnifying glass to focus sunlight on a specific point. Do the same with your thoughts and emotions: focus on abundance and allow your mind to focus on that goal.

Create a daily routine: Set aside time each day to do your visualizations. It can be in the morning when you wake up or before going to sleep. Consistency is key to training your mind in the desired direction.

The power of visualization in financial abundance

Visualization is a bridge between your goals and your reality. When you practice visualizing financial abundance consistently, you are sending clear signals to the universe and your subconscious mind about your intentions. You are reprogramming your mind to believe that you deserve abundance and that you are on the right path to achieving it.

Remember, visualization is not a magic pill that gives you

instant wealth. It is a tool that strengthens your mindset, helps you maintain focus and make decisions aligned with your financial goals. Combine this practice with concrete actions, such as constantly learning, applying your trading plan and being disciplined in your decisions. By doing so, you will be creating a solid bridge between your aspirations and the financial abundance you deserve.

The Spotlight Effect And The Reality You Create

Imagine for a moment that you are in a dark room with a flashlight in your hand. This flashlight is your mind, and the light it emits is your focus. As you direct that light into different areas of the room, you illuminate what you choose to see and experience. Likewise, the focus of your mind can illuminate the aspects of life you focus on.

The spotlight effect is a powerful tool that reminds us that what we focus on is what we amplify in our lives. There will always be challenges and obstacles, but the key is deciding where you direct your focus and how you interpret what is happening around you.

The Focus Effect In Trading And Abundance

In the world of trading, the focus effect is especially relevant. Imagine that you have had a series of losing trades. Your mind can lean towards negativity and feed the fear of failure. However, if you apply the focus effect, you can choose to focus on the lessons you have learned, how to improve your strategies, and the opportunity for growth that each mistake gives you.

In the search for financial abundance, the focus effect

becomes a vital ally. Do you focus on the lack or the chances of winning? When you keep your focus on abundance, you attract more of it into your life. Your subconscious mind, which is like a magnet for your experiences, works to manifest what you believe and visualize.

The Science Behind The Spotlight Effect

Neuroscience supports the idea of the spotlight effect. Our neurons connect through synapses, and these connections become stronger with frequent use. When you focus on a certain belief or perspective, you are strengthening those neural connections. This means that the more you focus on abundance, the more natural it will become for your mind to see opportunities and possibilities.

Practice: Applying the focus effect in your life.

Self-awareness: Start by being aware of your thoughts. Where does your mind usually focus? In the positive or in the negative?

Perspective shift: When you notice negative or lacking thoughts, challenge them. Shift your focus toward possibility and abundance.

Guided Visualization: Take time to visualize your financial goals in detail and emotion. Feel as if you have already achieved what you want.

Power Words: Use positive, powerful affirmations to reinforce your focus on abundance. Repeat phrases like "I am worthy of prosperity" or "I always attract financial opportunities."

Focused Gratitude: Focus on what you already have and feel

gratitude for it. Gratitude is a source of positive energy that attracts more blessings.

Focus Decides Your Reality.

Remember: every day you have a choice about what you focus on. Your focus not only influences your perspective but also your reality. By applying the focus effect and directing your thoughts towards abundance, you are sowing the seeds of a prosperous life full of achievements. Develop this practice, watch it grow, and be surprised by the results it can bring to your financial and personal life.

Financial education: Invest time in learning about personal finances and trading. The more knowledge you have about how money and financial markets work, the more confidence and security you will develop. Financial education empowers you and allows you to make more informed and conscious decisions in your operations.

Remember that changing your beliefs and attitudes towards money takes time and effort. However, by being aware of how you relate to money and working on developing an abundance mindset, you can improve your financial decision making and increase your chances of trading success.

Don't underestimate the power of a positive mindset and a healthy relationship with money!

I am striving so that each paragraph, each chapter, each sentence has a valuable message, but it is essential that you do your part by using, internalizing and analyzing the ideas that I present to you in a more general way but also applied to your reality. Since it is not a secret that each person is different and has or has a different environment in which they develop. And since I wish with all my heart to give you tools that help you achieve the mind of a winner. The truth is that what I want most is to give you tools that teach you how to think. Let's work together to transform our lazy mind into a proactive, curious and brave mind; It won't be an easy job but we're not looking for it to be. It will surely be a path that will give us pride when we look back.

Defining Your Goals And Objectives

4.1 What are your short and long term financial goals? Setting clear and realistic goals is essential to maintain focus and motivation on your path as a trader. Here are some aspects to consider when defining your financial goals:

SMART Goals: Use the SMART approach to set specific, measurable, attainable, relevant and time-bound goals. For example, instead of saying "I want to make a lot of money," set a specific goal like "I want to earn a 10% monthly return for the next six months." This clarity in your goals will allow you to have a sense of direction and measure your progress more effectively. Remember: what is not accounted for is not managed, do not leave your future to chance, start having control of your life.

SMART goal setting is a methodology for defining objectives. This is an English acronym through which the basic characteristics of SMART objectives are explained. These must be Specific, Measurable, Achievable, Realistic and Time-bound.

Short-term goals: Define financial goals achievable within a period of 3 to 6 months. These goals can be related to your trading skills, your trading performance or the growth of your account. For example, you could set a goal to complete a trading course in the next three months or achieve consistent performance during a given month.

Long-term goals: Set long-term financial goals spanning 1 to 5 years. These goals may include annual income goals, the size of your trading account, or the ability to live exclusively off of it. When setting long-term goals, it is important to keep in mind that trading is a constant journey of learning and development, and that results may vary. These long-term goals have to be composed of your short-term goals, for example, if your short-term goal is to have a profitability of between 5% and 10% per month for the next three months, the annual goal has to be composed of your short-term goals. Four quarters maintaining profitability will give me a year with a certain result. Remember that you have to design achievable short-term goals to achieve big goals.

A castle is built from the foundations, from the first stone. If a castle is made up of 100,000 stones and I place 100 stones every day, I will have the castle ready in two years and seven months. But if I only think about the 100,000 stones I need to move, I will try my best to never start because it would seem like an eternity. But if I divide it and focus on putting 100 stones a day in the best possible way, in the blink of an eye there will be a beautiful castle. Remember this message.

Stone by stone, mountains are made

♦ ♦ ♦

Planning the path: Once you have established your goals, develop a strategic plan to achieve them. Identify the specific steps you'll need to take and set a realistic timeline for achieving each milestone along the way. For example, if your long-term goal is to double the size of your trading account in three years, set quarterly milestones to measure your progress.

Review and adjust: Regularly review your financial goals and make adjustments as necessary. Trading is a dynamic field and your circumstances can change. As you gain more experience and knowledge, you may want to review and modify your goals to reflect your growth and aspirations. Always remember to manage. It is not just drawing up the plan and putting it in a place to collect dust, it is carrying it out and following it up; and if something needs to be modified, it is modified and we move forward.

Here I want you to have a clear message: the person who works the hardest is not the one who earns the most money. The one who makes the most money is the one who works in the smartest way possible. This is very important to keep in mind when achieving your goals, but it is even more important when you are going to invest and manage them. Along the way you will be able to find ways to do what you had planned in a better, faster, more efficient way. If you are always curious about how you can improve to reach your goals in a better way and without ceasing to live in other aspects such as giving quality time to your loved ones, you will be able to adapt your goals, objectives and achieve them.

Remember that our goal is not only to be successful in one

area. Our mission is to be and feel happy with what we do because we have planned it that way and if at any time our plans change and something happens that disorganized us, we will not have problems because we understand and know that we are in control of our lives.

The person who works the hardest is not the one who earns the most money.

The one who makes the most money is the one who works the smartest way.

It is not a sheet to carry dust

Practical exercise: Write your short and long-term financial goals in detail. Describe specifically what you want to achieve and why it is important to you. Then break each goal down into smaller steps and set deadlines for achieving them. This will help you have a clear roadmap and stay focused on your goals.

Remember that your goals should be realistic and aligned with your level of experience, resources and available time. Don't compare yourself to other traders or set unrealistic goals that can cause frustration. Maintain a gradual and constant focus on growing and developing your trading skills.

4.2 What type of lifestyle do you want to achieve through trading?

Think about how trading can contribute to your ideal lifestyle and how you would like to balance your personal and professional life. Here are some aspects to consider when defining your desired lifestyle:

Identify your priorities: Reflect on what your priorities are in life. Do you value time freedom or financial stability more? Do you want the flexibility to travel or spend more time with your family? Identifying your priorities will help you establish goals and strategies that bring you closer to your desired lifestyle.

Balance between personal and professional life: Think about how you want to balance your personal and professional life. Do you prefer to have flexible schedules or establish more structured routines? How much time would you like to dedicate to trading and how much time to recreational activities, leisure and rest?

Being clear about this balance will allow you to make more conscious decisions in your approach and dedication to trading.

Work style: Define what type of trader you want to be. Do you prefer to operate full-time or part-time? Are you more comfortable working independently or collaborating with other traders? Also consider whether you would like to diversify your income sources and explore other trading-related opportunities such as teaching or account management.

Financial goals: Set specific financial goals to help you achieve your desired lifestyle. Do you want to generate consistent and substantial income through trading? Do you have a long-term savings or investment goal? Define how much money you need to maintain your lifestyle and create a plan to achieve it taking into account your trading goals.

Wellness priorities: Don't forget to consider your physical and emotional well-being priorities in your desired lifestyle. Do you want to have time to exercise, relax, or spend time outdoors?

Incorporate these activities into your lifestyle plan and make sure you maintain a healthy balance between trading and your overall well-being.

Practical exercise: Write a detailed description of your ideal lifestyle as a trader. Describe what you would like your daily routine to be like, your income, your personal relationships, and any other relevant aspects. Then break down the steps necessary to get closer to that lifestyle and set realistic deadlines to achieve each of them.

Remember that your desired lifestyle must be realistic and achievable. Don't get carried away by unrealistic expectations or comparisons with other traders. As you define your ideal lifestyle, make sure it aligns with your values and brings you long-term satisfaction.

This chapter has been designed to help you reflect on who you are and what you want to achieve as a trader. By asking yourself these questions and taking the time to explore your motivations, goals, and values, you will be better prepared to make informed decisions and stay on the right path to trading success. Remember that authenticity and self-knowledge are essential to achieving your goals and building a rewarding career in the world of trading.

CHAPTER 4: DEVELOPING A DISCIPLINED AND CONSISTENT MINDSET

In this chapter, we will delve into the importance of cultivating a disciplined and consistent trading mindset. Being a successful trader requires more than just technical knowledge and analytical skills; It involves having the ability to maintain discipline and consistency in your decisions and actions.

The Importance Of Discipline In Trading

Why is discipline crucial in trading? We will analyze how discipline helps you follow your trading plan, manage your emotions and maintain consistency in your decisions. We will also address the consequences of a lack of discipline and how it can negatively affect your results.

Discipline is the ability to consistently follow your trading plan and maintain consistent behavior in your decisions and actions.

Follow your trading plan: Having a solid plan and following it in a disciplined manner is essential to achieving long-term success. Your trading plan should include clear rules on when to enter and exit trades, how to manage risk, and set realistic goals. Discipline will allow you to adhere to these rules, avoiding temptations to deviate from your strategy due to emotional impulses or market events.

Manage your emotions: Trading is full of intense emotions such as fear, greed and impatience. Discipline will help you maintain emotional control and make rational decisions instead of getting carried away by your feelings. By being disciplined, you can avoid making impulsive decisions based on fear or momentary euphoria, which will protect you from potentially costly mistakes.

Maintain consistency in your decisions: Discipline allows you to maintain consistency in your trading decisions. Avoid jumping from one strategy to another or making sudden changes to your approach. On the other hand, if you continue to apply your trading plan consistently this will allow you to accurately evaluate the results and make gradual improvements. Consistency in your decisions will also help you build confidence in your process and make informed, analysis-based decisions rather than reacting to emotional impulses or the latest market news.

Consequences of lack of discipline: This can have negative consequences on your trading operations. You can fall into bad habits such as excessive trading, ignoring your rules or letting emotions dominate your decisions. This can lead to significant losses and a lack of consistency in your results. Discipline is what will keep you focused on your trading plan and help you avoid these costly mistakes.

Remember, discipline is not something innate but a skill that you can develop over time and practice. It is important to establish a disciplined mindset from the beginning and constantly work on strengthening your discipline throughout your trading journey. With solid discipline, you will be in a favorable position to make informed and consistent decisions, thus increasing your chances of trading success.

It is curious that the word discipline and its meaning is something that we all know, know and accept as the fundamental basis of success in any field. Discipline can transform the ordinary into extraordinary, it can make you achieve any goal you set for yourself and the funny thing is that we all know it. Now, what is the reason why you are not disciplined? What is the most powerful reason that prevents you from being disciplined? I can't answer you. You have the answer. But it's not enough for you to answer it, you have to work on changing that weakness. Without discipline it is not possible to be successful, it is in your hands whether you achieve it or not.

You can read millions of books, you can even read this book a million times, take the courses you want, dedicate time and money to it. But, if the change does not start in you, you will not achieve it. And the first change you must make is to forget, eliminate the idea that you are a person who has no discipline, eliminate that thought, repeat and believe that you are the most disciplined person you know and that you work every day to continue being that way; then everything becomes a habit and positive results will begin to come steadily. Discipline is a word that we all know very well but few of us apply it to our lives. If you are not disciplined with your own rules or your goals, you have no right to complain about the results. Discipline is essential to achieve success, it is black or white, there are no grays. And it is easy to understand the idea, but you must have a will of steel to really carry it out. I believe in myself, you should believe in yourself too. You have to take control of your life, your present, your future and you must give importance to discipline. To achieve your dreams you only need discipline to follow your action plan.

◆ ◆ ◆

If you are not disciplined with your own rules or your goals, you have no right to complain about the results.

◆ ◆ ◆

How To Develop Discipline In Trading

I will give you practical advice that has helped me develop discipline in trading. We will discuss the importance of setting clear rules and adhering to them, how to maintain consistency in your trading, and how to manage distractions and temptations that may come your way.

Establish clear rules: It is essential to establish them for your trading operations. Define specific criteria for entering and exiting trades, risk limits and profit targets. These rules will act as guides that will help you make decisions based on analysis and logic instead of being carried away by emotions or momentary impulses.

Keeping a Trading Journal: Keeping a trading journal is an invaluable tool for developing discipline. Record all your operations, including the reasons behind each one, the results obtained and the lessons learned. Analyzing your past trades will allow you to identify patterns and areas of improvement and will help you maintain a disciplined and goal-oriented approach.

Practice consistency in execution: Being consistent in the execution of your trades is essential to developing discipline. Make sure you follow your trading rules consistently, no matter the circumstances or emotions of the moment. Avoid making impulsive decisions or letting yourself be carried away by fear or greed. Consistency in execution will help you avoid costly mistakes and maintain a disciplined approach over the long term.

Manage distractions and temptations: Trading can be an activity that presents many distractions and temptations.It is important to learn to manage them to maintain your discipline. Identify what external or internal factors may interfere with your focus and establish strategies to overcome them. This may include time management, setting limits on technology use, or seeking support and accountability from a community of traders.

Learn from mistakes and adjust your approach: Mistakes are inevitable in trading, but the most important thing is to learn from them and adjust your approach. Focus your attention on learning and continuous improvement instead of regretting mistakes made. Reflect on them, identify the lessons they have taught you and make adjustments to your trading plan to avoid making them in the future.

Practical exercise: Create a set of clear and specific rules for your trading operation. Write them down and keep a copy on hand while you trade. Then, keep a detailed diary in which you record all your operations, emotions and reflections. At the end of each week, review your journal and analyze whether you have remained disciplined in executing your rules. Identify areas where you can improve and set clear goals to work on.

Remember that developing discipline in trading takes time, effort and commitment. Don't be discouraged if you encounter difficulties along the way. With practice and perseverance, you can strengthen your discipline and increase your chances of success. It is important that when developing your plan and clear rules you also take into account external factors, for example, the schedule that you decide to operate, if we talk about that you have to propose to be and feel comfortable with your plan, it does not make sense for you to set a schedule in the early morning that will cause you to lose valuable hours of sleep, therefore, it will change your mood, your health and it will be a lot for you. more difficult to follow among other things; When you put together your plan you have to evaluate that it adapts to the lifestyle you want to lead, that it is balanced with your mind and body. Perhaps when you start you will have other activities such as a job in which trading is impossible. In cases like these it is important that you adjust your plan for a shorter time operation but that does not affect your mental health, that respects your dream schedules, your family sharing times, etc. It won't be easy and you will have to make sacrifices, but do your best to make your plan as balanced as possible.

Overcoming Emotional Challenges

I will try to explain to you the emotional challenges you will face as a trader and how to overcome them to maintain a disciplined and consistent mindset. Trading is an activity that involves intense emotions such as fear, greed and frustration. Learning to manage these emotions is essential to avoid impulsive decisions and maintain discipline in your operations.

Recognizing and understanding your emotions: Firstly, it is important to be aware of your emotions and understand how they affect your decision making. Analyze what emotions arise during your operations and how they influence your behavior. For example, do you feel anxiety when opening a trade or euphoria when you make profits? Understanding your emotional patterns will allow you to take steps to manage them effectively.

Developing emotional management techniques: You require practical techniques to manage your emotions in trading. These techniques include meditation and conscious breathing to calm the mind, visualization to reinforce a positive mindset, and using affirmations and mantras to maintain self-confidence. Practical exercises will help you identify and challenge your limiting beliefs and develop a more resilient and balanced mindset. Trading can be an emotional roller coaster and it is crucial to have effective techniques to manage your emotions and maintain a balanced and resilient mindset.

Meditation and conscious breathing: Both are powerful tools for calming the mind and reducing stress. Take a few minutes before starting your trading session to practice meditation and focus on your breathing. This will help you focus on the present moment, distancing yourself from negative thoughts and emotions that may influence your decisions.

Practical exercise: Dedicate at least 5 minutes a day to practice meditation and conscious breathing. Sit in a quiet place, close your eyes and focus on your breathing. Breathe in and out slowly; It is important that you fill your lungs as much as you can when you inhale, force yourself to fill them as much as you can, repeat this breath for five minutes. There are many courses on the internet and books that give more details about these techniques, I will recommend the way I do it and it makes me feel much better and more comfortable.

I inhale gently but deeply until I fill my lungs and count in my mind while I inhale for 10 seconds, hold the air for 20 seconds and then gently release it for 10 to 15 seconds. I last 10 seconds without inhaling and then repeat the process for 5 minutes. I invite you to do it, it is magical. Try to focus on what your body feels, listen and feel your heartbeat, try to feel your organs, imagine that you are traveling inside your body to the ends of your hands, your feet, observe how your mind calms down and becomes still. . This exercise will help you cultivate calm and mental clarity, which can be especially helpful before facing stressful moments in trading.

Visualization: Visualization is a powerful technique to reinforce a positive mindset and visualize your goals as a trader. Spend time each day visualizing your successful trades, imagining how it feels to make good decisions and profit. This practice will not only boost your confidence but will help you program your mind for success.

Practical exercise: Before starting your trading session, close your eyes and imagine a successful trading day. Visualize each trade going your way, feel the thrill of winning and the confidence in your disciplined approach. This visualization will help prepare your mind to face the day with a positive and determined attitude.

Affirmations and mantras: Both are positive phrases that you can repeat to maintain self-confidence and encourage a positive mindset. Create affirmations that increase your strengths as a trader and help you overcome doubts and fears that may arise along the way.

Practical exercise: Write at least three positive statements related to your skills and strengths as a trader. For example, "I am a disciplined and consistent trader", "I trust my analysis and make informed decisions" or "I learn and grow with each trade". Repeat these affirmations out loud every day, especially before starting your trading session.

Identifying and challenging limiting beliefs: These are negative, self-limiting thoughts that can sabotage your success as a trader. It is important to identify these beliefs and actively challenge them. Reflect on thoughts like "I'm not good enough," "I'm always losing money," or "The market is against me." Question the veracity of these beliefs and look for evidence that contradicts them.

Practical exercise: Keep track of your thoughts during your trading sessions. If you identify limiting beliefs, write them down and then look for evidence to disprove them. For example, if you think, "I always lose money," look for past trades where you made profits and remember the times you made good decisions. By challenging your beliefs, your limiting beliefs, you can change your mindset and generate a more positive and confident approach.

Remember that trading is as much an emotional as an analytical activity. By developing emotional management techniques and challenging your limiting beliefs, you will become a more resilient and balanced trader. These tools will help you maintain the discipline and focus necessary to achieve your goals as a trader and face challenges with confidence and determination.

Creating a supportive environment: Recognize the importance of surrounding yourself with people who support you on your journey as a trader. Find a community of like-minded traders with whom you can share experiences, advice, and emotional support. Participating in discussion groups, online forums, or attending trading-related events and conferences can provide you with a valuable support network.

Evaluating and adjusting your strategies: As you gain trading experience, you will have the opportunity to evaluate your strategies and make adjustments when necessary. If you notice that certain situations or assets trigger negative emotions or lead you to make impulsive decisions, consider adapting your approach. For example, you can limit your exposure to certain assets or implement stricter rules for entering and exiting trades.

Practical exercise: Conduct a daily reflection on your emotions and how they affect you in your operations. Keep a journal where you record your thoughts and feelings before, during, and after each operation. Identify recurring emotional patterns and look for specific strategies to manage them more effectively. Additionally, develop an action plan to deal with challenging situations and practice relaxation and visualization exercises to strengthen your mindset.

Remember, developing a disciplined and consistent mindset requires practice and perseverance. Don't be discouraged if you encounter obstacles along the way. As you work on strengthening your discipline and managing your emotions, you will become a more confident and successful trader.

The Importance Of Consistency In Trading

Why is consistency crucial in trading and how can you develop it?

Consistency refers to the ability to apply your trading plan in a constant and disciplined manner without getting carried away by emotions or momentary impulses.

The advantage of consistency: Being consistent allows you to more accurately evaluate the performance of your strategies, identify areas for improvement, and build confidence in your decision-making process. Additionally, consistency helps you build a reputation in the market and generate predictable results in the long term.

Developing a solid trading plan: A well-defined plan is the foundation for consistency. It is essential to develop a trading plan that includes clear rules for entering and exiting trades, risk management and trading objectives Profits. It is also extremely important to keep a detailed trading journal to continually evaluate and adjust your plan.

Trading plan: The route to consistency in trading

Trading without a trading plan is like having a business without a business plan, flying a plane without having experience, driving a ship without a route, it is literally like driving blind. But you will not be irresponsible, you will make your trading plan like a professional.

Developing a solid trading plan is essential to achieving

consistency and success in the world of trading. Next, I will guide you in creating a trading plan that will help you make informed decisions and manage your trades effectively. It is important to clarify that I will give you brief information about how and what your plan should contain, however, you have to be the one to develop it since each trading plan is specific to each individual and must be adapted to the type of trader they are, the type of asset, the time in which it operates and its strategy, etc.

Set your clear objectives: Before starting to trade, define your short- and long-term financial objectives. How much do you want to earn in a given period? How much are you willing to invest per operation? Setting clear goals will give you a sense of direction and allow you to measure your progress over time. In this first step it is essential that your objectives go hand in hand with your working capital.

Define your trading strategy: What trading approach are you going to use? You can opt for technical, fundamental analysis or a combination of both. Define the indicators and tools that you will use to identify entry and exit opportunities in the market. Your strategy must be clear and based on data, avoiding impulsive or emotion-based decisions. I give you some advice: try to make your strategy understandable by a 5-year-old child, and make it as simple as possible.

Trading, unlike many beliefs, is an activity in which the strategy only represents between 10% to 15% of success, everything else is made up of the variables that we have exposed and will continue to expose, such as: discipline, mental control of your emotions, perseverance, working capital, time, among internal factors and apart from external factors such as the brokers and their conditions, the economy of your country, the internet, etc. There are many factors that influence your results and I dare say that one of the reasons why more than 90% of aspiring traders fail is that they focus a lot of energy on finding the perfect strategy and neglect other more relevant aspects such as having a good trading plan, discipline, order, etc.

Entry and exit rules: Establish clear rules for entering and exiting trades. Define specific criteria to identify entry opportunities and when to close your positions to secure profits or limit losses. This will allow you to act with discipline and avoid making hasty decisions.

Risk Management: Risk management is essential to preserve your capital and maintain consistency in trading. Set a maximum risk percentage per trade, for example, risk no more than 2% of your capital on a single trade, and use stop loss orders to protect your positions from significant losses.

Define your schedules and the number of maximum operations per day, per week or per month. It is important that you be organized with your time and especially in your exposure to the market.

Keep a trading journal: Keeping a detailed journal is an essential practice for evaluating and improving your trading plan. Record every trade you make, including the reason for entering the trade, your strategy used, the results, and how you felt emotionally during the process. This will allow you to identify patterns and areas of improvement in your operations.

Practice discipline: This is key to following your trading plan consistently. Avoid making impulsive decisions or deviating from your established rules. Patience and consistency in execution are essential to achieving your goals.

Evaluate and adjust your plan: Periodically review your trading plan and make adjustments as necessary. If you notice that certain strategies aren't working or that your goals have changed, adapt accordingly. Flexibility and the ability to learn and improve are essential for growth as a trader.

Remember that trading success does not happen overnight. It takes time, practice, and the ability to learn from your experiences. With a well-defined trading plan and a disciplined mindset, you will be on the right path to achieving your financial goals and becoming a consistent and successful trader. Stay focused, keep learning, and enjoy the journey to trading excellence!

The importance of discipline in execution: Discipline is key to being consistent in your trading execution. We'll look at how you can maintain discipline by following your entry and exit rules, respecting your risk limits, and avoiding impulsive trades. We will also discuss the importance of patience and perseverance in trading.

Evaluating and adjusting your approach: As you gain trading experience, it is important to regularly evaluate your approach and make adjustments if necessary. We will discuss how you can identify patterns in your trading, evaluate your performance, and make incremental improvements to your trading plan. In addition, we will provide you with practical exercises to evaluate your consistency and detect areas for improvement.

Practical exercise: Perform a detailed analysis of your past operations to evaluate your consistency. Review your trading journal and analyze whether you have consistently followed your rules and objectives. Identify areas where you can improve your consistency and set clear goals to achieve it. Practice executing trades according to your trading plan and record your results to track your progress.

Remember, consistency is not achieved overnight. It requires time, practice and constant discipline.

As you strive to be consistent in your trading, you will be closer to achieving long-term success in trading.

Overcoming Challenges And Maintaining Discipline

Common challenges traders face and how you can overcome them to maintain discipline in your trading. Have practical strategies and reflections that will help you face obstacles and maintain focus on your goals.

Maintain discipline in times of volatility: Market volatility can generate intense emotions and test your discipline. It is crucial to stay calm and follow your trading plan even when the market is choppy. Reflect on how emotions can influence your decisions and look for emotional control techniques, such as deep breathing and rational analysis of market data.

Avoid the influence of news and market noise: These can be a constant source of distraction and temptation to deviate from your strategy. Develop a disciplined approach to filter and evaluate relevant information and avoid making decisions based on rumors or speculation. Keep your attention on your trading plan and the fundamental and technical indicators you use.

Manage the pressure of losses: Losses are an inevitable part of trading and the way you handle them can influence your discipline. Accept that losses are part of the process and focus on learning from them instead of getting carried away frustration or fear. Develop risk management techniques, such as setting stop losses and using stop loss orders, to protect your capital and maintain discipline during bad times.

Cultivate a learning mindset: Discipline not only involves following rules, but also being open to learning and continuous improvement. Develop a learning mindset in which you view experiences, both gains and losses, as opportunities for growth and development. Reflect on your operations, evaluate your decisions, and constantly look for ways to improve your decision-making process.

The importance of perseverance: Trading can be a path full of challenges and obstacles. Perseverance is key to maintaining discipline over time. Accept that there will be difficult times and setbacks, but remain determined and focus on your long-term goals. Find ways to stay motivated, whether through visualizing your goals, finding support in a community of traders, or celebrating your achievements.

Reflection: Take a moment to reflect on your own trading challenges and how you can apply the strategies mentioned above. What obstacles have you faced in the past and how have you managed to overcome them? What actions can you take to strengthen your discipline and face future challenges? Write your reflections in your trading journal and use them as a constant reminder of your commitment to discipline.

Remember that discipline is a skill that is strengthened with practice and perseverance. As you face and overcome challenges, your discipline will become stronger and bring you closer to your goals as a trader. Stay focused, maintain discipline and enjoy the path to trading success.

CHAPTER 5: TAKING RESPONSIBILITY: LETTING GO OF EGO IN TRADING

One of the biggest obstacles traders face: ego. Taking responsibility and working on humility are essential to overcome this challenge and achieve success in trading.

Admit mistakes: Accepting that we all make mistakes in trading is the first step to freeing ourselves from the control of the ego. Making wrong decisions is a natural part of the learning process, but the problem arises when we don't want to admit it and look for justifications instead of learning from our mistakes.

I see my worst enemy every day in the mirror. He knows me too much and I know him very little. Work on mastering your ego and thus you will take away the strength of your greatest enemy.

Practical exercise: Reflect on past operations in which you

have made mistakes. What could you have done differently? What lessons can you draw from those situations? Write down your conclusions in your trading journal and be sure to apply what you learn in your future trades.

Embrace humility: Recognizing that you will not always be right and that the market is unpredictable is an important step in controlling the ego. Learn to be open to different scenarios and outcomes, without stubbornly clinging to your analyzes or forecasts.

Practical exercise: During your next trading session, when you face a situation where the market behaves unexpectedly, take a deep breath and recognize that it is normal to make mistakes. Accept that the market is bigger than any individual trader and that you need to adapt to its movements.

Learn from other traders: Listening and learning from other more experienced traders is a great way to develop humility and improve your skills. Participate in trading communities, attend seminars or workshops and seek advice from successful traders.

Practical exercise: Research and select some traders that you admire or who have a similar trading approach to yours. Observe how they make decisions and how they manage their emotions. Learn from their experiences and mistakes to enrich your own approach.

Take responsibility: Accept that you are the only one being responsible for your trading actions will empower you to make informed decisions and to learn and grow as a trader.

Practical exercise: Make a list of your objectives as a trader and the steps you need to take to achieve them. Commit to yourself to take responsibility for following your trading plan and not to blame external factors for your results.

Create a positive mental environment: Fostering a positive mental environment is essential to overcome ego and maintain confidence in your decisions.

Practical exercise: Practice gratitude and self-affirmation daily. Every morning, spend a few minutes recognizing the things you are grateful for in your life and reminding yourself of your strengths and accomplishments as a trader. Adopting a prosperous mindset will help you stay focused on your goals and overcome adversity.

Practical exercise: Identify situations in which your mentality has led you to be more perseverant and successful in trading. How could you cultivate a prosperous mindset in all areas of your life and in trading?

Remember that trading is a constant learning journey and ego can be a significant obstacle. Working on humility, taking responsibility, and creating a positive mental environment will allow you to make more informed decisions and stay calm in challenging situations. Get rid of the weight of ego and focus your energy on becoming a more resilient and successful trader.

The ego, that internal voice that seeks constant validation and that drives us to always want to be right, can become our worst enemy in the world of trading. Throughout our lives, ego may have crept in in subtle ways, making us reluctant to admit mistakes, learn from experiences, and face reality when things don't go as we expected.

Imagine a trader who, full of confidence and pride, enters the market with an arrogant and not very humble attitude. Convinced that his analyzes are infallible, he dismisses any warning signs and proceeds with risky trades. In a short time, those unfortunate trades lead you to lose a large amount of money. However, instead of acknowledging his mistakes, he makes excuses, blames the market or external factors, and clings to the idea that he will recover his losses in the next trade.

This story, sadly, is not uncommon in the world of trading. The ego can blind us and lead us down a path of denial and self-destruction, but taking responsibility is a liberating act that allows us to break the chains of the ego and take control of our lives and results as traders. It is important to identify at the moment what is happening, for example, you have an open operation that goes against the analysis you had done, at once you have to accept and close or wait for it to reach its stop loss; but a voice comes to you that tells you to let it run, that the price is going to go in the direction you expected, to move the stop loss, that you are a very well, the market has to go back. It is just at that moment that you are blinded by your ego of not accepting a loss, like this example there are thousands and you have to identify and correct them immediately. Stick to your trading plan even if your ego speaks to you.

Trading is not about being right or wrong. It's about flow with the price.

The reality is that everyone makes trading mistakes, even the most successful traders. But what sets us apart is how we face and learn from those mistakes. Successful traders are not afraid to admit their mistakes and, instead of seeing them as failures, they see them as opportunities for learning and growth.

How can you overcome ego and take responsibility in trading? Here are some practical tips:

Be honest with yourself: Reflect on your past trades and honestly ask yourself what you could have done better. Learn to listen to that little inner voice that tells you when you are making impulsive or emotion-based decisions.

Practice humility: Recognize that the market is unpredictable and that no one has all the answers. Being open to learning from other traders and hearing different perspectives will help you broaden your horizon and make more informed decisions.

Keep a trading journal: Keeping a detailed journal will allow you to evaluate your decisions and emotions objectively.

Record your thoughts before, during and after operations to identify patterns and areas for improvement.

Accept losses as part of the process: Losses are inevitable in trading and taking responsibility for them will allow you to free yourself from the emotional burden they can generate. Learn to see losses as an opportunity to learn and improve.

Cultivate a prosperous mindset: Instead of focusing on what you've lost or your past mistakes, focus on your achievements and what you can learn and improve. Maintain a positive mindset focused on growth.

Remember that in trading and in life, ego can be a significant obstacle to success. Taking responsibility, working on humility and putting aside your ego will allow you to make more informed decisions and manage your emotions more effectively. Get rid of the weight of ego and free yourself to become a more resilient, flexible and successful trader. At the end of the day, the market is not our enemy, the enemy is our own ego. Learn to leave it behind and face the path to consistency in trading with an open and humble mind.

Throughout our lives the ego can manifest itself in various ways. It not only affects our trading decisions but also our personal and professional relationships. We often find it difficult to admit our mistakes and prefer to protect our image rather than face reality. However, by recognizing and working on our ego problems we can free ourselves from its control and open ourselves to new opportunities for growth and success.

Ego in trading can lead us to make impulsive and poorly informed decisions. When we let ego direct our operations, we are more likely to ignore warning signs and take unnecessary risks. The fear of admitting mistakes can also lead us to hold on to losing positions, hoping that the market will turn around in our favor, even when all signs point in the other direction.

On the other hand, by letting go of the ego and taking responsibility we can develop a more balanced and resilient mindset. Accepting our mistakes will not only help us learn and improve, but will also allow us to maintain a more objective and realistic perspective on our abilities and expectations. By learning to manage our emotions and stay calm in challenging situations, we will be able to make more informed decisions based on analysis and logic.

One of the practical exercises to work on the ego is meditation. Meditation is a powerful tool to calm the mind and free ourselves from thoughts and emotions that can influence our trading decisions. Take a few minutes a day to sit quietly, focusing on your breathing and observing your thoughts without judgment. As you practice meditation, you will notice greater mental clarity and a greater ability to recognize and let go of selfish impulses.

Taking responsibility and letting go of ego is essential to achieving consistency and success in trading. Working on humility and a prosperous mindset will allow us to face challenges with courage and learn from our experiences without fear of making mistakes. By freeing ourselves from the emotional burden that ego can impose, we will be able to make more informed and balanced decisions and reach our potential as traders and as human beings. Let's accept the challenge of leaving our ego behind and find true freedom to prosper in the world of trading.

CHAPTER 6: WHAT A BEAUTIFUL RAINY DAY

Imagine a beautiful rainy day. The drops fall gently from the sky, painting the landscape with their dew and fresh aroma. For some people, this day represents an opportunity to enjoy a cozy and relaxing atmosphere at home, reading a good book or sharing moments with the family; We could write a whole book about the different perceptions we can have regarding a beautiful rainy day. It will depend on each person, there is a saying that I really like and it says "every head is a world". However, for others, this very day may be perceived as a gray and boring day, full of sadness and melancholy.

This simple illustration shows us how perception can shape our experience and how different people can have opposite reactions to the same situation. The same thing happens in the world of trading. Every day, every trade and every market event can be perceived differently by traders.

In trading, clearing our mind of thoughts that do not affect us is essential.

Our perception of the market and our own abilities can drastically influence our decisions and results. If we allow ourselves to be carried away by fear and uncertainty, our operations can be affected by doubt and indecision. On the other hand, if we adopt a positive, learning-focused mindset, we will be more open to taking calculated risks and facing challenges with courage.

Change is a choice and it is ours to act based on our perception. We can decide to see each loss as an opportunity for learning and growth rather than a failure. We can choose to view each operation as a valuable experience, regardless of the outcome, and learn from it to improve in the future.

Perception and risk are also intrinsically linked in trading. Every trade involves a certain level of risk and our perception of that risk can influence our decisions. If we view risk as a threat, we are more likely to feel overwhelmed and make impulsive decisions to avoid potential losses. However, if we understand that risk is an inevitable part of trading and that we can manage it intelligently, we will feel better able to make informed and controlled decisions.

The power of association also plays a crucial role in our perception in trading. Our mind tends to search patterns and associations to understand the world around us. If we have experienced losses or failures in the past, our minds may associate trading with negative emotions and make us fear facing similar situations in the future. However, by changing those negative associations to more positive and empowered thoughts, we can change our perception of trading and increase our confidence in our abilities.

I want you to remember this chapter as "What a beautiful rainy day", that way you can remember and associate these valuable lessons and reflect on the dynamics of perception in trading. Our way of perceiving the market, our skills and our experiences can significantly influence our decision-making and results. Clearing our mind of negative thoughts and learning to see situations from different perspectives allows us to develop a more flexible and balanced mentality in trading. Change is a choice, and we can choose to act based on a positive and constructive perception that allows us to take advantage of each day and each operation as an opportunity to grow and prosper in the exciting world of trading.

In the history of trading and finance, we can find numerous anecdotes that illustrate how perception and attitude can make a difference in the most challenging moments. One of the most notable examples is the 1929 "Crash" on Wall Street that marked the beginning of the Great Depression in the United States.

During that dark period, many investors gave up and sold their stocks at rock-bottom prices, afraid of losing even more money. However, there were financial leaders who saw opportunity amid the chaos. One of them was Bernard Baruch, a successful investor and advisor to several US presidents.

Baruch maintained a positive and calm attitude in the face of the crisis. Instead of panicking, he continued buying shares in companies he considered solid and undervalued. His optimistic vision and ability to remain calm during difficult times allowed him to take advantage of the unique investment opportunities that arose during the crisis. Over time, his investments proved extremely profitable and established him as one of the most successful financial leaders of his time.

Another inspiring example of the importance of perception and attitude in trading comes from legendary investor Warren Buffett. In the 2008 stock market crash, many investors were overwhelmed by market uncertainty and volatility. However, Buffett maintained a different perspective.

In the midst of the crisis, Buffett made a famous statement:

"When others are greedy, I am afraid. When others are afraid, I have greed." This quote encapsulated his approach of seeking opportunities in times of adversity and shows how his perception of the market drove him to make bold and strategic decisions.

Buffett saw the market crash as an opportunity to invest in solid companies at discounted prices. Through his courageous attitude and long-term approach, he managed to achieve exceptional returns and became one of the most successful investors of all time.

These historical examples teach us that our perception and attitude can greatly determine our success in trading. If we give in to fear and pessimism, we are likely to miss valuable opportunities and make impulsive decisions. On the contrary, if we adopt a positive and resilient mindset, we will be more open to seeing opportunities in the midst of adversity and making informed and informed decisions.

In the world of trading, we constantly face challenges and moments of uncertainty. Our perception of these situations can influence how we react to them and the decisions we make. By learning to see situations from different perspectives and maintaining a positive and courageous attitude, we can develop a more balanced and successful mindset in trading and in our lives. As historical financial leaders they have shown us that the right perception and attitudes can make the difference between success and failure.

The importance of controlling our perception not only applies to trading, but encompasses all aspects of our lives. The way we perceive the world and the situations we face can determine our success in any field and gives us a powerful advantage in the best and worst of circumstances.

An inspiring example of how perception can be a determining factor in success is the story of Sir Richard Branson, the founder of Virgin Group. In the 1990s, Virgin Atlantic, Branson's airline, was in financial trouble and faced stiff competition from more established airlines.

In the midst of the crisis, instead of giving in to pessimism and defeat, Branson maintained a bold and positive outlook. At a press conference, he declared that he was going to keep his bet on Virgin Atlantic and that if the airline did not survive he would shave his head. This striking and defiant statement captured the public's attention and generated a wave of support and confidence in the airline.

Branson's bold and optimistic insight not only inspired his team and Virgin Atlantic employees, but also attracted investors and customers. The airline was able to overcome the crisis and, over the years, it has become a leading brand in the aviation industry.

Another notable example is that of Nelson Mandela, who faced extremely difficult conditions during his time in prison. Despite hardships and oppression, Mandela maintained a sense of resilience and hope. His resilient attitude allowed him to maintain his integrity and principles, and he became a symbol of the fight against injustice.

Mandela's perception of himself and his cause was a was a key factor in his success as a leader. His determination and commitment to the fight for equality and freedom made him an inspiring and unifying leader for the South African people.

In the business world, Steve Jobs was also a leader known for his insight and bold vision. Despite challenges and criticism,

Jobs stayed true to his vision and created innovative products that revolutionized the technology industry.

His insight into what was possible and his ability to think outside the box led him to create iconic products like iPhone and iPad that changed the way we interact with technology in our daily lives.

These examples demonstrate how perception can be a decisive factor in the success of leaders in various fields. How we see the world and how we see ourselves can influence our decisions and actions, and ultimately our success.

In trading, mastering how we want to see the world gives us the advantage to face challenges with confidence and courage. If we can maintain a perception of a winner, we open ourselves to seeing opportunities in the midst of uncertainty and making informed and strategic decisions.

Controlling our perception also helps us deal with losses and mistakes more constructively. Instead of letting ourselves be overcome by defeat and frustration, we can see each experience as an opportunity for learning and growth.

Perception is a powerful tool we have in our hands. If we can master how we want to see the world, we can influence our actions and decisions in positive ways. By maintaining a bold and optimistic attitude, we give ourselves the opportunity to achieve success in trading and in every other aspect of our lives.

Let's look at some inspiring stories of leaders and entrepreneurs who achieved their goals despite obstacles and adversities thanks to their attitude and determination:

Thomas Edison: He is known as one of the most prolific inventors in history. Edison attempted thousands of times to create a functional incandescent light bulb but faced numerous failures along the way. Instead of becoming discouraged, he saw each failure as a learning opportunity and proof of what wasn't working. Finally, after countless attempts, he managed to invent a functional incandescent light bulb that revolutionized the world and changed the way we live and work.

Elon Musk: The founder of Tesla, SpaceX and other innovative companies has faced many challenges and skeptics throughout his career. When SpaceX launched, many considered it an impossible goal and crazy. However, Musk maintained an optimistic and persevering attitude, overcoming numerous obstacles to achieve success in space exploration and the creation of reusable rockets.

Henry Ford: The founder of Ford Motor Company revolutionized the automotive industry with his innovative approach to chain production. Although he faced many challenges and rejections before achieving success, Ford maintained a resilient attitude and never stopped believing in his vision. His introduction of mass production reduced manufacturing costs and made automobiles affordable to the middle class.

Oprah Winfrey: The renowned presenter and businesswoman has overcome obstacles and difficulties since her childhood. Despite facing poverty and adversity, Oprah maintained a positive attitude and believed in herself and her dreams. Her determination and passion led her to become one of the most influential women in the world of entertainment and philanthropy.

The truth is that there are thousands and thousands of stories and they are not very far from us, if we start to detail our surroundings, we will find fantastic people around us, from the bakery owner who always strives to have excellent products for his customers, Despite the crisis that you may be experiencing in your life or in the country, you continue to make an effort looking for the positive, even family members, taxi drivers, There are thousands and thousands of examples, you just have to change the glass of your lenses and start seeing the details and work on changing your perception.

These stories highlight the importance of maintaining a positive and persevering attitude on the path to success. All of these leaders and entrepreneurs faced criticism, rejection, and failure, but they refused to give up. They saw failures as opportunities to learn and improve, and used each obstacle as a springboard to achieve their goals.

In trading, it is also essential to maintain a resilient and optimistic attitude. Financial markets can be volatile and challenging, but if we can see each experience as an opportunity for growth and learning, we can move toward success. Like these leaders and entrepreneurs, we can use our failures as a drive to improve and move forward with determination and confidence towards our goals. Attitude is a powerful tool that we can use to face challenges and to achieve success in any field, whether in the world of trading or in any other area of our lives.

Controlling our perception and focusing on eliminating negativity from our minds are fundamental aspects of leading a full and successful life. Our mind is like a garden and negative thoughts are like weeds that can stifle the growth of positive and constructive thoughts. Here are some strategies to clear our minds of negativity and develop a more positive and optimistic attitude:

Practice gratitude: Instead of focusing on what you lack or

the negative, focus on what you have and the positive things around you. Keep a gratitude journal and write down three things you are grateful for daily. This will help you shift your focus and appreciate the good things in life.

Change your thoughts: Identify negative thought patterns and replace them with more positive and constructive thoughts. If you find yourself thinking about the worst thing that could happen, change it to thinking about the opportunities you could find in each situation.

Surround yourself with positive people: The people we interact with can influence our attitude and perception. Seek to be around optimistic and positive people who inspire you and motivate you to see the good side of things. Remember the famous saying, "you are the average of the five people you surround yourself with." I'll tell you a secret: when I was a teenager, my mother repeated that saying to me a lot and the truth is that, due to my immaturity and rebellion, I refused to accept it, to understand it. But as the years went by and I reflected on the depth of that saying, I realized that it is totally true. So be careful who you spend your time with; and it doesn't mean that you abandon your oldest friends simply because they think differently. No, but it is important that you have priorities to achieve your goals.

Here you must work on saying "I CAN'T"; It is something that was particularly difficult for me, whenever they invited me or asked me for favors I said yes, although I knew it was harming me I always prioritized my friends, to fulfill my friendship, but the truth is you have to have priorities and understand that not You will be a bad friend, for saying: sorry but "I CAN'T". Just as you must put into practice the questions of questions, also put into practice the "I CAN'T" and give priority to your goals. Give value to the greatest resource you have, your time. It doesn't mean that you will become a hermit, but it does mean that you can't be there for everyone at any time. You must have a balance and if they really love you they will surely support you and I tell you something else, as time goes by they will even admire you because giving priority to our goals is a quality that not many people possess and those who have it will become role models. Paradoxically, by saying "I CAN'T", you are also helping your loved ones, giving them a clear message that if you can be disciplined with your goals, they can also be disciplined with theirs.

Practice self-compassion: We all make mistakes and face challenges in life. Instead of blaming or judging yourself negatively, be kind to yourself and treat your mistakes as opportunities for learning and growth.

Find the positive side in challenges: Facing challenges is a part of life, and instead of seeing them as insurmountable obstacles, try to see them as opportunities to grow and improve. Learn to see challenges as experiences that make you stronger and more resilient. It is crucial that you use the techniques we mentioned in "The Parable of the Lemon" and "What a Beautiful Rainy Day." You can use questions that open your mind to seek a solution to the challenges that arise instead of just complaining, getting frustrated or self-sabotaging; You have to ask yourself questions that put your lazy mind to work.

Instead of worrying, get busy.

◆ ◆ ◆

Facing challenges is part of life; We all have them, whether big or small. But instead of seeing them as insurmountable obstacles, what if we saw them as opportunities to grow and improve?

When we face a challenge we have two options: we can give up or we can try to overcome it. If we choose to give up, we stay stagnant, we will not learn or grow. But if we choose to try to overcome the challenge, we will force ourselves out of our comfort zone and that is where the magic will happen.

When we leave our comfort zone, we learn and grow. We become stronger and more resilient, and realize that we are capable of achieving more than we thought.

So the next time you face a challenge, don't see it as an obstacle, try to see it as an opportunity.

10 Techniques To Work Your Mind Outside Your Comfort Zone

Dare to get out of your routine: Do new and different things; Try things you would never have done.

Set challenging goals: Set goals that are difficult, but achievable; This will help you get out of your comfort zone and grow.

Surround yourself with positive people: Positive people will inspire you and motivate you to get It will motivate you to get out of your comfort zone.

Accept failure: This is part of the learning process, don't get discouraged if you don't get it the first time, keep trying.

Learn from your mistakes: When you make a mistake, don't be angry with yourself, learn from it and move on.

Ask for help: Don't be afraid to ask others for help, you never know who can help you overcome challenges.

Be patient: Don't expect changes overnight, leaving your comfort zone takes time.

Be persistent: Don't give up, keep trying and eventually you will succeed.

Celebrate your successes: When you manage to overcome a challenge, celebrate your success, this will help you stay motivated.

Enjoy the process: Getting out of your comfort zone can be challenging but it can also be a lot of fun, so enjoy the process and learn from it.

One of your enemies is your lazy mind. He is always trying to keep you in your comfort zone by telling you things like: "Don't try, you won't be able to do it" or "It's too hard" or "We'll do it later, there's still time." But don't listen to her, your lazy mind just wants to keep you safe. But if you want to grow and improve you have to overcome it, you have to get out of your comfort zone.

So the next time your lazy mind tells you not to try it, say yes. Tell him you're going to get over it, that you're going to get out of your comfort zone, and then do it. Stepping out of your comfort zone can be challenging, but it can also be very rewarding. When you step out of your comfort zone, you learn and grow, you become stronger and more resilient, and you realize that you are capable of achieving more than you thought.

Here are some real-life examples of how lazy we humans are to act and think outside the box:

We are afraid of change: When we face change, we resist it, we prefer to stay in our comfort zone even if it is more uncomfortable than leaving it and facing the unknown.

Don't leave for tomorrow what you can do today.

We are procrastinators: We are too lazy to do things, so we leave them until the last minute. This can cause us a lot of stress and anxiety and can lead us to make bad decisions. The truth is that it is sad to know that we ourselves waste our most valuable resource: our time.

We are conformists: We tend to conform with what we have, even if it is not what we want. We don't want to work hard to get what we want so we settle for what life gives us.

We are mentally lazy: We don't want to think too much, we prefer to go with the flow and do what others do. We don't want to think for ourselves, so we let ourselves be carried away by the opinions of others.

These are just some examples of how lazy we humans are to act and to think a little further. If we want to improve our lives, we have to overcome our laziness and start acting. We have to start thinking for ourselves and making our own decisions. We must leave our comfort zone and face change, only then can we grow and improve.

Here are some tips to overcome our laziness and start taking action:

Start with small steps: Don't try to change your life overnight, start with small steps and little by little you will move forward.

Surround yourself with positive people: Positive people will inspire you and motivate you to act.

Celebrate your successes: When you achieve something, celebrate your success, this will help you stay motivated.

Don't give up: It is normal to have relapses, but don't give up, keep trying and eventually you will succeed.

Overcoming our laziness is not easy, but it is possible: If we want to improve our lives, we have to start acting. We cannot wait for things to change on their own, we must take the initiative and make things happen.

Reflect on your challenges and find solutions: I leave you some questions that can help you put your mind to work. As I have told you, I want you to stay with the general idea, but it is you who, depending on your personal case, must delve deeper into the idea, analyze and find the best questions that will help you get out of that famous comfort zone.

What is the problem? What is the specific challenge I am facing?

Why is it a problem? What are the negative consequences of the problem?

What are my options? What are the different things I can do to solve the problem?

What are the advantages and disadvantages of each option? What are the pros and cons of each option?

Which is the best option? Which option is most likely to solve the problem?

What do I need to do to implement the best option? What are

the steps you need to follow to implement the best option?

What obstacles can I face? What are the things that may prevent you from implementing the best option?

How can I overcome obstacles? How can you deal with the things that may prevent you from implementing the best option?

What makes me feel comfortable? What are the things that make me feel comfortable making a decision?

What makes me feel uncomfortable? What are the things that make me uncomfortable when making a decision?

What is most important to me? What are the most important factors I should consider when making a decision?

What I am going to do? What decision am I going to make?

These are just a few questions that can help you reflect on your challenges and find solutions. It is important that you take the time to think about these questions and to consider all the options available, only then can you make a decision that is best for you.

I give you one of my favorite questions: How do I solve it?

I give you one of my favorite questions: How do I solve it? simple but powerful. You also have the rude option: How the hell do I solve it? In any case, the "how" opens up the possibility and makes you think.

Here are some additional tips that may help you overcome your challenges:

Don't be afraid to ask for help: If you're not sure what to do, don't be afraid to ask for help from other people who could offer you advice and support.

Don't give up: It is normal to have relapses, but don't give up, keep trying and eventually you will succeed. Winner's mind.

Celebrate your successes: When you achieve something, celebrate your success, this will help you stay motivated.

Overcoming challenges is difficult, but it is possible: If you follow these tips, you could overcome any obstacle that comes your way, it all depends on you. Among the questions you should ask yourself, it is also valid to ask yourself if it is worth solving it or not; What I mean is that sometimes we take challenges too proudly, we get blinded by our ego, and sometimes there are wars you shouldn't fight. The bravest is not the one who wins the most wars but the one who knows and acts when he should act. Fighting and winning the wrong war can be worse than losing the right war. Analyzing whether or not the effort is appropriate depending on the reward is also valid.

Fighting and winning the wrong war can be worse than losing the right war.

Practice meditation and mindfulness: These practices will help you calm your mind and be more present in the moment. Meditation will allow you to observe your thoughts without judging them and cultivate greater awareness of your mental state.

Surround yourself with nature: Spending time outdoors and in contact with nature can have a positive effect on our mood and perception. Enjoy walks outdoors, observe the landscape and connect with the beauty of the world around you.

By clearing our mind of negativity and developing a more positive and optimistic attitude, we will not only improve our quality of life, but we will also attract the people around us. A positive attitude is contagious and attracts others, while negativity pushes people away and can affect our personal and professional relationships. Controlling our perception allows us to face life's challenges with an open and resilient mind, making us happier and more successful people on our path to success in trading and in all areas of our lives.

Focus on solutions, not problems: Instead of getting caught up in problems and worries, focus on finding solutions. Embrace challenges as opportunities to develop problem-solving skills and creativity. When you face an obstacle, ask yourself, "What can I do to overcome this?" or "What is the best way to address this situation?"

Instead of worrying, get busy solving it and if there is no solution, there is nothing to do.

◆ ◆ ◆

Practice self-reflection: Take time to reflect on your thoughts and emotions. Identify limiting beliefs or negative thought patterns that may be affecting your perception and work to change them. Self-reflection will help you become more aware of your thoughts and make more informed and positive decisions.

Celebrate your big and small successes: Recognize your achievements and merits, even the smallest ones. Celebrating your successes will help you stay positive and motivate you to keep going. Appreciate your efforts and recognize that each step, no matter how small, will bring you closer to your goals.

Learn to let go: Sometimes, negativity can arise from holding on to the past or things that are out of our control. Learn to let go and let go of those situations or people that cause you stress or anguish. Accept that some things are beyond your control and focus on what you can change. This feeling is very common in trading after making a trade and it goes negative, you are left thinking about the loss, or if you win and the price continues in the estimated direction, you also stay clinging to it because you closed so soon. Either way it is useless and wears you out, the worst thing is that you live in the past; Staying attached to any situation, whether positive or negative, is like a time machine: it will transport you to the past and you will live in the past. You have to master those thoughts that make you cling to the past. It won't be easy, but start by identifying and using tools that help you get those thoughts out of your mind, such as going to the gym, doing some physical activity, dancing, singing, doing some activity that brings you back to the present.

Surround yourself with inspiration: Look for sources of inspiration that

◆ ◆ ◆

> *Staying attached to any situation, whether positive or negative, is like a time machine: it will transport you to the past and you will live in the past.*

◆ ◆ ◆

They motivate and fill you with positive energy. They can be books, movies, music or people you admire. Inspiration can be a powerful tool to maintain a positive attitude and help you get through difficult times. Sometimes the inspiration can be your own fears of failure. Be very afraid of not achieving your goals and use that fear as fuel to get up every morning and fight to achieve it.

Be aware of your inner language: Pay attention to how you speak to yourself in your mind. If you find yourself being self-critical or negative about yourself, replace it with affirmations and words of encouragement. Talk to yourself as you would with a close friend and support yourself in times of difficulty. Make an effort to eliminate those words that don't add up from your mind.

By practicing these strategies and adopting a more positive and optimistic, you will notice significant changes in your life. You will feel more empowered to face the challenges of trading and everyday life. Clearing your mind of negativity will allow you to make more informed and objective decisions, which will help you be more consistent and successful in your trading operations.

◆ ◆ ◆

The inspiration can be your own fears of failure. Be very afraid of not achieving your goals and use that fear as fuel to get up every morning and fight to achieve it

Being positive does not mean living in the clouds and not realizing mistakes, being positive means that despite making mistakes you focus on the solutions and not on the error itself. It's a delicate game between just complaining or being frustrated to taking control of those emotions and moving forward. I dare say that trading is one of the professions where the most mistakes are made and each mistake can cost thousands of dollars, but it is also one of the professions that can give you the most freedom. It will be worth the fight. If it were easy it would stop being what it is, but it is not true that it is super difficult either, it is a matter of perspective.

Remember that our perception of the world and ourselves can influence our emotions, actions and results. Controlling our perception is a powerful tool that gives us the advantage in difficult situations and allows us to find opportunities where others may see only obstacles.

With a mind clean of negativity and a positive attitude, you will be able to face any challenge with courage and determination, you will achieve greater success, greater happiness in trading and in all areas of your life.

CHAPTER 7: THE EVIL MARKET: ENEMY OR ALLY?

The truth behind the "evil market" and how we must change our perception to make it an ally in our trading operations. It is common to hear novice and experienced traders refer to the market as an implacable enemy, but it is time to see beyond this false belief and understand how we can flow with the market instead of fighting against it.

The market is not your enemy: It is important to understand that the market does not have a personal agenda against individual traders. The market is simply an entity that reflects the supply and demand of financial assets in real time. It has no knowledge or intention of the individual trades that traders make. Therefore, instead of seeing it as an enemy, we should see it as an opportunity to take advantage of fluctuations and trends in our favor.

Embrace uncertainty: The market is inherently uncertain and volatile. Instead of feeling stressed by this uncertainty, you should accept it as a natural part of trading. Instead of trying to predict every market move, focus on developing a solid strategy and sticking to it even when things don't go as you expected. Learn to flow with uncertainty and make informed decisions based on your trading plan.

The market is dominated by supply and demand: Market forces are driven by the supply and demand of financial assets. Large institutions, banks and investment funds play an important role in forming market trends and movements. Instead of fighting these actors, we must learn to follow in their footsteps and adapt to their movements. Observe the signals that the market offers us and adjust to them instead of trying to resist.

Flow with the market and manage risk: Instead of trying to beat the market, we must learn to flow with it. This involves having a flexible and adaptive mindset that allows us to adjust our strategies according to changing market conditions. Furthermore, success in trading largely comes from proper risk management. Sticking to our trading plan and not letting emotions affect us will allow us to maintain a more balanced and coherent attitude in our operations.

The real profit is in capital management: Rather than trying to win each individual trade, the key to success in trading lies in proper capital management. Controlling position sizes, setting loss limits, and locking in profits are essential to maintaining balance and long-term profitability. A successful trader focuses on preserving his capital and maintaining a long-term perspective rather than obsessing over individual trades.

By changing our perception of the market and recognizing that it is not our enemy, but a source of opportunities and natural fluctuations, we can free ourselves from stress and uncertainty. Flowing with the market and focusing on proper capital management will allow us to find consistency and success in our trading operations. Let's remember that the key is to constantly adapt and learn as well as maintaining a resilient and optimistic attitude in this exciting world of trading.

Imagine for a moment the immensity of the foreign exchange market, also known as Forex. Every day, trillions of dollars move in this decentralized global market, where different currencies from around the world are bought and sold. The average daily trading volume in the Forex market is estimated to exceed $6.6 trillion, making it the largest and most liquid financial market in the world. Do you realize the magnitude of that figure? It's just amazing.

So that you can understand the immensity of the $6.6 trillion dollars that are traded daily in the Forex market, allow me to give you an illustrative example:

Imagine that you have a $100 dollar bill in your hands. It's just a ticket, but it has significant value. Now, if we could place those bills one after another, forming a long chain of $100 dollar bills, how many times do you think we could make around planet Earth?

To calculate how many times $6.6 trillion in $100 USD bills could go around the planet Earth, we need to know the total length of the $100 USD bills and then divide that length by the circumference of the Earth.

First, let's calculate the total length of the $100 USD bills:

$6.6 trillion dollars = 6,600,000,000,000 dollars. Each $100 USD bill has a length of approximately 15.6 cm (0.156 meters)

Total length = 6,600,000,000,000 USD × 0.156 meters/USD Total length = 1,029,600,000,000 meters

Now, we are going to calculate how many times around the planet Earth we can make with that total length:

Circumference of planet Earth = approximately 40,075 km =

40,075,000 meters

Laps around planet Earth = Total length / Circumference of planet Earth = 1,029,600,000,000 meters / 40,075,000 meters = Laps around Earth = 25,674 laps

Therefore, with $6.6 trillion dollars in $100 USD bills, approximately 25,674 complete revolutions could be made around planet Earth. It is an incredible amount that highlights the immensity of the volume of money that is traded in the Forex market every day!

This example shows us the immense amount of money that moves in the Forex market every day. It is an astonishing amount that exceeds our mind's ability to imagine it. The Forex market is an ocean of opportunities and, at the same time, a reality that demands prudence and knowledge to navigate successfully.

Now, with this information in mind, consider the position of an individual trader in this vast financial ocean. A trader's capital is just a drop in that immense sea of money in motion. Compared to the trillions of dollars flowing into the market, a trader's capital is insignificant in terms of its impact on market prices and movements. This does not mean that we cannot make profits, but it does help us understand that we cannot control the market or significantly influence its direction.

It is important that traders understand that the Forex market is a complex system and that it is driven by various economic, political and social factors at a global level.

The market is not aware of the individual position of each trader or their expectations. There is no enemy behind market fluctuations but a dynamic interaction of supply and demand, of decisions made by large financial institutions, governments and economic actors.

This is where the importance of maintaining a balanced and realistic mindset as a trader comes into play. We can't control the market, but we can control how we react to it. The key is to have a solid strategy and to react to it. based on fundamental and technical analysis, and to apply adequate risk management to protect our capital. Instead of seeing the market as an enemy that we must defeat, we must adopt an attitude of respect and adaptation. Flowing with the market and acting based on the signals it gives us will allow us to make more informed and coherent decisions.

It is important that a trader does not feel overwhelmed by the magnitude of the market, but rather learn to find his or her place within it. Remember that we are not alone on this journey, that even the most successful traders face losses and challenges on their path to consistency. The key is to constantly learn, improve our skills and maintain a realistic perspective. Take advantage of the opportunities that the market offers you, but also be aware of its risks.

The Forex market is neither an enemy nor an ally, it is simply a financial reality that we can approach with a balanced and humble mindset. Understanding the magnitude of the market and our position in it will help us make more informed decisions and maintain a resilient and optimistic attitude in our trading operations. The key to success lies in constant learning, risk management and focusing on our own strategies without trying to beat a market that is beyond our control.

Imagine that you are a ship captain sailing in an immense and choppy ocean. The Forex market is like that vast ocean full of currents, tides and unpredictable forces that can change in a matter of seconds. As a trader, your ship is your capital and your trading skills; You will be faced with the task of navigating through market fluctuations and volatilities.

◆ ◆ ◆

The only constant in the market is change.

On this journey, it is essential to recognize that the market does not have a personal agenda against you. He is not harsh on you or trying to make you lose money. In reality, the market is just a manifestation of the interaction between buyers and sellers, the only constant in the market is change. As a trader, your success depends on how you adapt and respond to this constant change.

A realistic perception of the market will allow you to move away from the mentality of "beating" the market and will help you focus on making well-informed decisions based on analysis and strategies. You will learn to understand that in the market you don't always win, but you don't always lose either. As in any business, there are profits and losses, the key is to ensure that the profits exceed the losses in the long term.

Many traders become frustrated when their trades do not go as planned. However, instead of seeing the losses as failures, it is important to see them as learning opportunities. Losses are a natural part of the learning process in trading. Each loss can provide us with valuable information about our decisions, strategies and will allow us to adjust and improve our approach in the future.

An inspiring example of perseverance in the midst of adversity is found in the story of Thomas Edison, the famous inventor of the light bulb. Edison made thousands of attempts before finally managing to invent a working light bulb. When asked about his many "failures," he replied, "I didn't fail, I just found 10,000 ways that didn't work." This attitude is fundamental in trading: seeing each loss as an opportunity to improve and grow.

To maintain a balanced and resilient mindset in the market, it is essential to develop a conscious attitude towards your emotions and thoughts. Learning to recognize and control emotions such as fear and greed will allow you to make more rational and objective decisions in your operations. Practicing meditation and conscious breathing will help you stay calm and mentally clear, even in times of high pressure.

It is also important to surround yourself with a community of traders or mentors who share your values and provide support in your moments of difficulty. Sharing experiences with other traders can be enriching and can help you maintain a balanced perspective on the market.

The Forex market is a challenging and complex environment, but it is not our enemy. The key to success lies in developing a realistic perception of the market and maintaining a balanced and resilient mindset. Learn to flow with the market, adapt to changes and see losses as learning opportunities. With a conscious and objective attitude, you will be better prepared to navigate this vast financial ocean and achieve your goals as a trader.

Participating in market movements following the main

trend is how to flow with the current in that vast financial ocean. When you navigate in tune with the trend, you find yourself in an advantageous position, taking advantage of the force of the market instead of fighting against it. It's like surfing the waves of the market and taking advantage of its momentum to lead your operations towards success.

A useful analogy to understand this is that of a surfer. Imagine that you are a surfer on a beach with large, constant waves. What would you do if you wanted to surf successfully? The first thing you would do is wait for the right moment, when the wave is at its maximum strength and power. At that moment, you would launch yourself with skill and grace towards her, following her direction and letting yourself be carried away by her momentum. And there will be days, many days when the sea simply does not have the necessary conditions for surfing, what does a surfer do? He simply relaxes and remains an observer. You as a trader do not always have to take trades; If the parameters for you to execute following your trading plan are not met, simply remain calm, as an observer and take advantage of making strategy reviews. The key is in the way you see your work, it is not mandatory to operate every day.

The same applies in trading. You must wait for the right moment to enter a trade, when the main trend is clearly defined and at its optimal point of strength. By following the trend, you join the force of the market and position yourself for greater odds of success.

Once you are in the wave (the operation), it is essential to maintain concentration and balance. Don't get carried away by impulse and excessive enthusiasm. Stay calm and follow the direction of the main trend. Remember that the money is not yours yet, it is in motion in the market. Your goal is to stay focused and make sure you're on the right wave.

Finally, as every surfer knows, eventually the wave comes to an end. You must be prepared to get out of the wave at the right time. Don't hold on to an operation longer than necessary. The money is yours once the trade closes with profit. Don't fall into the trap of greed and overoperation. There will always be new opportunities in the market, it is better to be prepared for the next wave rather than getting stuck in the current one.

Overoperation is like trying to surf every wave you see without clear criteria. You will end up exhausted and without a sense of direction. In trading, this can lead to disastrous results and the loss of your capital. Stick to your trading plan, carefully select trades and maintaining discipline are essential to avoid over operation.

Being a successful trader means flowing with the market, and following the principal trend and leaving at the right time.

◆ ◆ ◆

The money is yours once the trade closes with profit.

Taking advantage of market strength and being aware that money is still on the line while the trade is open will keep you focused and disciplined. Avoid the trap of overtrading and remember that there will always be new opportunities in the market. As a surfer in the financial ocean, keep your balance, be patient and prepare to surf to success.

Once an owner of a large food company told me a phrase that stuck with me, I will share it with you: "The money you lose cannot be recovered." When he told me that, I disagreed, but he clarified: "You can make more money but what you already lost, you lost and it won't be recovered." That phrase is very true; When you lose money in a business or trading, it is already lost money and that's it. You have to close the chapter and move on, it's a clean slate. You can make more money, but it is not correct to want or think about recovering something you lost, because the truth is not the same, they are totally different operations.

The trader's true enemy is not the market, but the internal obstacles that must be overcome on the path to success. Ego, lack of discipline and the inability to follow the trading plan are the main adversaries that a trader faces.

The ego can be an ally or an enemy in trading. If it is under control and in harmony with your trading plan, it can give you confidence and determination. However, if the ego takes control, it can lead to impulsive decision making, overoperation, and refusal to admit mistakes. The ego makes us feel that we are always right and that we can beat the market, which leads us to ignore the signs and take more risks than we should.

Overcoming ego is a constant challenge, but it is essential to success in trading. Humility and the ability to learn from mistakes are essential to grow and improve as a trader. Admitting that we can make mistakes and adjusting our approach is a strength, not a weakness. Ego can be the enemy that blinds us to opportunities and prevents us from learning from past experiences.

Lack of discipline is another trap that many traders fall into. Sticking to the trading plan, following the rules and avoiding making impulsive decisions is key to staying on track and not deviating from the established objectives. Discipline is what allows us to maintain focus and consistency in our actions, even when emotions threaten to take over.

A solid and well-defined trading plan is like a map that guides us through the market. Without it, we are lost and at the mercy of our emotions and ego. The discipline to follow our plan even when things don't go as we expect is what sets us apart as successful traders.

Facing and defeating the real enemy in trading requires a combination of self-discipline, self-knowledge and emotional control. Identifying the areas in which we falter and working to strengthen them makes us more resilient and capable of overcoming the challenges that the market presents us.

It is essential to remember that the market is not personal. It is not there to punish us or to reward us according to our desires. The market is simply an ever-changing environment, dominated by supply and demand and economic and political forces. Our job as traders is to adapt to that environment and make decisions based on fundamental and technical analysis, not on emotions or selfish desires.

The real enemy in trading is our ego, lack of discipline and inability to follow our trading plan. Overcoming these internal obstacles is essential to succeed in the financial market. Humility, self-discipline and the ability to learn from our mistakes are the weapons that will allow us to defeat the internal enemy and achieve our goals as traders. Keep your focus, stay true to your plan and remember that the market is not your enemy, but a challenge that you must face with intelligence and perseverance.

CHAPTER 8: MATHEMATICS IS YOUR BEST FRIEND

The importance of mathematics in trading and how it can be your best ally to efficiently manage your capital. Success in trading does not depend on guesses or hunches, but on making decisions based on data, analysis and probabilities.

The mathematics of capital management: One of the fundamental pillars to survive and prosper in trading is proper capital management. It is vital that you define how much you are willing to risk in each operation. A commonly used and highly effective approach is to risk only a small percentage of your capital on each trade, such as 1% or 2%. This will allow you to maintain a margin of safety to weather potential losses.

Example: Imagine that you have a trading account with $100 USD and you decide to risk only 1% ($1 USD) on each trade. Even if you have a streak of losing trades, your account will not suffer big losses and you will have a chance to recover with winning trades.

Think in terms of probability: Trading is not an exact science, but a matter of probabilities. No matter how good your analysis is or how much you have studied the market, there is always the possibility that a trade will result in a loss. The key is to increase the odds of success through sound strategies and risk management.

Random results, consistent results: It is normal that, at times, the market behaves unpredictably and leads to random results. However, if you maintain discipline and follow your trading plan based on mathematics and probability, you will see consistent and favorable results in the long term.

Let's look at a mathematical example that demonstrates how a trader can be profitable with only 40% effectiveness and a risk/reward ratio of 1 to 3.

Suppose a trader makes 100 trades in the Forex market, with a strategy that has a risk/reward ratio of 1 to 3. This means that for every trade he loses, he risks $1 and for every trade he wins, he gets $3.

Winning trades: 40 (40% effective)

Losing trades: 60 (60% effective)

Now let's calculate the financial result:

Earnings per winning trade: $3. Losses per losing trade: $1

Total profits (40 winning trades): 40 trades x $3 = $120

Total losses (60 losing trades): 60 trades x $1 = $60

Total winnings: $120 - $60 = $60

In this example, even though the trader is only 40% effective (40 winning trades out of 100), he manages to obtain a positive result of $60 USD at the end of the 100 trades. This is due to the 1 to 3 risk/reward ratio, which allows profits to exceed losses even with a relatively low hit rate.

It is essential to understand that profitability in trading does not depend solely on the success rate, but on how operations and capital are managed. Good risk management, combined with a favorable risk/reward ratio, can lead a trader to obtain positive results despite having more losing trades than winning ones.

Let's analyze another scenario where the trader is 30% effective, applying the rules I mentioned before:

Rules:

Maximum risk per trade: 1% of capital (i.e. $100 USD per trade)

Maximum 3 daily operations.

Initial capital: $10,000 USD.

The sample size that we will evaluate is that the trader performs 1,000 operations in total.

To maintain a risk benefit of 1 to 3, for every trade you lose ($100 risk), you must make $300 profit.

Effectiveness: 30% (300 winning trades, 700 losing trades)

Now let's calculate the financial result for the scenario with risk benefit 1 to 3:

Earnings per winning trade: $300

Losses per losing trade: $100

Total profits (300 winning trades): 300 trades x $300 = $90,000

Total losses (700 losing trades): 700 trades x $100 = $70,000

Total earnings: $90,000 - $70,000 = $20,000

After carrying out 1,000 operations with an effectiveness of 30% and a risk-benefit of 1 to 3, the trader obtains a positive result of $20,000 UD.

Now, let's analyze the financial result: I want to highlight that it is only 30% effective, which is actually not good at all since it only wins 3 times out of 10. Its strategy can be improved, apart from that we do not apply compound interest which would have given us greater profit, but with that and everything he came out a winner. It is essential that you internalize this lesson so that you understand that if you follow your trading plan perfectly and use mathematics to your advantage, you will dominate profitability consistently.

These examples illustrate how a trader can be profitable even with low effectiveness, as long as he has adequate risk management and a favorable risk/reward ratio. It is essential to understand that the focus in trading should be on the process and capital management, rather than on the hit rate.

Mathematics is a powerful tool that will help you make informed decisions and properly manage your capital in trading. By thinking in terms of probability and applying sound mathematical strategies, you can stay focused and control emotional risk. Remember that the secret is in the statistical approach, consistency and discipline to achieve success in the world of trading.

Harnessing the power of leverage: This is a powerful tool in the Forex market, but it can also be double-edged if not handled properly. It is important to understand how leverage works and how it can affect your trading. The key is to use it responsibly and always consider the risk it entails.

Example: Let's say you have an account with $1,000 USD and your broker offers a leverage of 1:100. This means you can trade up to $100,000 USD in currencies with just $1,000 in your account. If you decide to use all available leverage and the market moves against you by 1%, you will lose all your capital. For them, it is essential that before opening a transaction you have already calculated the possible loss you may have, the exposure to the market according to the lot you select and have already placed your respective stop loss.

The 2% rule: One of the best-known rules in capital

management is the 2% rule. This rule suggests that you should not risk more than 2% of your total capital on a single trade. By adhering to this rule, you will protect your account for devastating losses and will give you the opportunity to recover from losing streaks.

Example: If you have an account of $5,000 USD, following the 2% rule, you would only risk $100 USD on each trade. This will allow you to have a margin of safety and ensure that a series of losing trades does not significantly affect your capital.

The risk/reward factor: Another key mathematical concept in trading is the risk/reward. When evaluating a trade, you should consider how much you are willing to risk compared to the potential reward. A proper risk/reward ratio will allow you to be profitable even if you don't win on all your trades.

Example: Suppose you decide to risk $50 USD on a trade and have a target profit of $150 USD. In this case, your risk/reward ratio would be 1:3, meaning you are willing to risk $1 USD to win $3 USD. Even if you only hit 40% of your trades, you will still be profitable due to the favorable risk/reward ratio.

Keep a trading journal: Keeping a detailed journal is an essential practice to improve your skills as a trader and analyze your results. Write down each trade you make, along with the reasons for entry and exit, the size of the position, the risk assumed and the results obtained. This will allow you to identify patterns and improve your mathematical and probabilistic approach.

Example: If you keep a record of your operations during a month and analyze your results, you will be able to identify if you are properly following your trading plan, if your strategies are giving consistent results and if you are respecting capital management. With this information, you can adjust your approach and improve your chances of success in the future.

Mathematics is your best friend in trading, as it provides you with tools and strategies to manage your capital efficiently and make informed decisions based on data and analysis. By understanding and applying mathematical concepts such as capital management, leverage, risk/reward ratio, and maintaining a trading journal, you will be in a much stronger position to achieve profitability in the Forex market.

Manage expectations: It is essential to be realistic and have appropriate expectations when trading. Don't expect to win on every trade or avoid every loss. Learn to accept that there will be ups and downs on your path to success. Maintain patience and discipline to continue applying your math and probability-based approach.

Always keep in mind that each trade is an opportunity to apply your strategy and mathematical approach. Don't feel discouraged by losses, as they are part of the process. Instead of worrying about individual trades, focus on the overall performance of your strategy over the long term.

Managing expectations is a crucial skill in both trading and life in general. A winning mentality managing expectations means being realistic, objective and flexible in the face of the results that arise. Here are some important aspects to consider in developing a winning mindset in managing expectations:

Focus on the process, not the result: Instead of obsessing over the end result of a trade or situation, a trader with a winning mentality focuses on following their trading plan and properly executing each trade. Recognize that results may vary and that the most important thing is to maintain consistency in your approach and risk management.

Understand the nature of the market: A trader with a winning mentality understands that the market is unpredictable and there is always a degree of uncertainty. He is not surprised or discouraged by occasional losses or periods of lower profitability. Instead of seeking certainties, it focuses on adapting to the changing environment and making decisions informed by data and analysis.

Accept losses as part of the process: A trader with a winning mentality does not fear losses and sees them as learning opportunities. You know that every loss can be a valuable lesson in improving your strategy and focus. You learn to take responsibility for your decisions and strive to constantly learn and improve.

Define realistic expectations: A key aspect of managing expectations is having achievable and realistic goals. A trader with a winning mentality avoids setting unrealistic or unfounded expectations in his trading plan. Instead, it focuses into goals that are consistent with your strategy and your level of experience.

Practice patience and persistence: Being patient and persistent is essential in managing expectations. A trader with a winning mentality understands that trading success is not achieved overnight, but requires time, effort and dedication. Maintaining a positive attitude and persevering through difficult times is essential to achieving long-term success.

Flexibility and adaptability: A trader with a winning mentality is willing to adjust his approach and strategy according to changing market conditions. He knows that there will not always be a single way to approach trading and is open to learning and adapting to new circumstances.

A winning mentality in managing expectations involves being realistic, objective and flexible. Accept that there will be ups and downs along the way, but stay focused on the process and constant improvement. A trader with this mindset is more likely to stay calm, make informed decisions, and ultimately achieve trading success. This same attitude can be applied in life in general, allowing us to face challenges with resilience and grow in each experience.

CHAPTER 9: MATHEMATICS IS YOUR BEST FRIEND

In the fascinating world of trading, hope can be a dangerous trap. Often, novice and experienced traders fall into the trap of hope, imagining that the market will move in the direction they want, instead of basing their decisions on hard data and objective analysis. However, this mentality can come at a high cost both financially and emotionally. of even greater losses. It can also lead you to hold losing positions much longer than you should, waiting for the market to change direction.

Discipline and objectivity are the best weapons against the hope trap in trading. Successful traders understand that emotions and hopes must leave room for logical, data-driven analysis. This doesn't mean you should be cold and unemotional, but it does mean that your decisions should be backed by solid rationale and objective analysis.

As in life in general, working with objectivity and discipline in trading can seem boring and repetitive at times. But it is precisely that consistency that will lead to long-term success. Sticking to your trading plan, basing your decisions on real data and analysis, and avoiding falling into the hope trap will make you a more confident and profitable trader.

Remember, hope is a powerful tool in the spiritual and emotional life, but in the world of trading, its cost can be high. As you advance on your path as a trader, cultivate objectivity, discipline, and confidence in your analysis. Let hope be left out of your financial decisions and allow yourself to make informed decisions that will lead to sustainable success in trading and in life.

Imagine for a moment that you are standing on the edge of a cliff. You can feel the breeze on your skin, the emptiness under your feet and the immensity of the horizon in front of you. At that moment, your thoughts may wander to what might be on the other side what could await you. But in that very moment, you know that it is objectivity and awareness of your surroundings that keeps you safe.

Similarly, in trading, hope is that precipice where your emotions can cloud your judgment and make you forget the firm ground of objectivity. When you expect the market to behave in a certain way, you are actually creating illusions in your mind. But here is the crucial point: illusions are not data, they are not analysis, they are not foundations.

The mentality of a professional trader is objective and grounded. It is based on the concrete reality of graphs, indicators, economic data and historical trends. This mentality does not seek to guess, but to analyze. He doesn't wait for things to happen, but instead prepares for all possibilities. It is like a chess player who anticipates the opponent's moves and plans his strategies accordingly.

As you progress on your path as a trader, it is essential that you become aware of your own tendencies towards hope and illusion. Are you basing your decisions on concrete facts or uncertain desires? Are you operating with the discipline and objectivity of a professional or are you letting emotions guide you?

The objective mindset is not cold or emotionless. Rather, it is a mix of emotional control and informed decision making. It allows you to face challenges with your head held high, knowing that you are doing everything in your power to achieve success. And if, despite your efforts, things don't go as you expected, you can face the situation with the peace of mind of knowing that you have done everything possible with the information you had.

Separating the mentality of hope from objectivity will not only benefit you in trading, but is also a valuable lesson for life in general. Learning to make decisions based on data and analysis, instead of being carried away by illusions and desires, makes you a stronger and more resilient individual.

So, as you face the financial markets and life's challenges, remember that hope has its place in your emotional world, but not in your financial decisions. Cultivate objectivity and discipline as your most reliable allies. Keep your feet firmly on the ground of facts and make informed decisions. At the end of the day, it will be that mindset that will lead you to achieve your goals and successfully overcome obstacles.

CHAPTER 10: THE EXCITING ADRENALINE OF DANGER: THE THIN THREAD BETWEEN TRADING AND BETTING

The world of trading can be fascinating and exciting, full of opportunities to make profits and achieve financial freedom. However, there is a dark side that we must take into account: the danger of falling into the trap of vice and gambling. It is essential to understand the difference between being a professional trader who operates with strategy and discipline, and becoming a gambler who seeks the excitement and adrenaline of risk without taking into account the consequences.

When we confuse trading with gambling, we expose ourselves to significant risks that can jeopardize our financial and emotional stability. It's like walking on a thin thread, where one wrong step can lead us to perdition. It is important to approach this issue seriously and responsibly so that we can make the most of the opportunities that trading offers us without falling into the trap of uncontrolled emotion.

In many ways, trading and betting may seem similar, as they both involve taking risks in search of a favorable outcome. However, it is crucial to understand the fundamental differences between both activities:

The element of chance vs strategy: The fundamental difference between chance and strategy in trading is that, in chance, the results depend largely on unpredictable and random events, while in strategy, the results are based on analysis , planning and informed decision making.

In the case of the bettor, the outcome of a bet is mainly subject to chance. For example, in a roulette game at a casino, the player can bet on a specific number, but the winning number is completely random and cannot be predicted with certainty. The player has no control over the outcome and his bet is based on the hope that chance will work in his favor.

On the other hand, in trading, although there are elements of uncertainty, it is about making decisions based on technical, fundamental and/or statistical analysis. Professional traders develop well-defined strategies that include entry and exit criteria, risk management and profit objectives. Although they cannot predict with certainty the outcome of each individual trade, their success generally relies on the consistency and adherence to their strategy over time. An example to illustrate the difference between chance and strategy in trading could be the following:

Suppose a trader and a bettor are participating in a coin toss game. The gambler bets on heads or tails while the trader uses an approach based on probability and analysis. The bettor simply chooses at random their option, while the trader could have done prior research and observed historical release patterns to make more informed decisions.

As more rolls are made, the bettor will rely on chance to make profits, while the trader will rely on their strategy and ability to make informed decisions. Over time, the trader is likely to have an advantage due to his probability and strategy based approach, while the gambler will be at the mercy of chance and ultimately more likely to experience losses.

It is important to note that although trading is based on strategy and analysis, there are still elements of uncertainty and risk. However, the key to trading success is maintaining a long-term probabilistic advantage, meaning that well-defined and consistent strategies will allow the trader to make profits over time, even if there are some losses along the way.

Time and patience: Successful trading requires time, patience and consistency in applying a strategy over time. Bets are usually short-term events with immediate results.

Let's imagine a graph that shows the performance of a professional trader and a gambler over time. On the horizontal axis is time and on the vertical axis is performance in terms of profits and losses.

The professional trader follows a well-defined and consistent strategy over time. Your graph shows fluctuations and ups and downs as the market is inherently uncertain, but as time passes, its yield curve tends to show a constant and gradual growth upwards. This is indicative of his probability and strategy based approach, where he knows that in the long term his mathematical and probabilistic advantage will allow him to make consistent profits.

On the other hand, the bettor's chart shows a series of much steeper peaks and valleys. Their results are more influenced by chance and uncertainty. Sometimes you can make a significant profit on an isolated event, but you are also subject to large and abrupt losses. As time progresses, your performance curve tends to become bumpier and less predictable.

The key difference here is temporal focus and patience. The professional trader understands that successful trading is a long-term activity and that it is normal to have ups and downs along the way. He focuses on maintaining consistency in his strategy and is not influenced by the results of a single trade or day.

On the other hand, the bettor is more focused on immediate results and can fall into the trap of being short-termist. If you have a losing streak, you may be tempted to increase your risk and look to recover what you lost quickly, increasing your exposure to chance and risk.

The key message here is that time and patience are essential in trading. Maintain a long-term perspective allows the professional trader to maintain an advantage over chance and be consistently profitable. On the other hand, the bettor who seeks immediate results and allows himself to be influenced by the emotion of the moment can put his capital at risk and compromise his long-term success.

It is important for the trader to understand that trading is a marathon and not a sprint. Consistency and patience are key to success in this profession. It is always essential to keep your mind focused on long-term goals, follow a well-defined strategy and maintain discipline even in difficult times.

The professional trader's chart is a gradual and consistent growth curve, while the gambler's is more irregular and volatile. This highlights the importance of patience, consistency and long-term focus in trading. A successful trader understands that time is on their side, and with a winning mindset, well-defined strategy, and a disciplined approach, they can overcome challenges and achieve success over time.

Risk Management: Professional traders understand the importance of risk management and apply clear rules to protect their capital. Gamblers often ignore risk management and can put their entire capital at risk in a single play.

Imagine two real life stories:

Story 1: The Professional Trader

I met a professional trader named Alex. He was a calm and focused man who had been trading in the financial markets for over a decade. Alex had a well-defined strategy based on technical analysis and solid fundamentals. His focus was always long-term and he understood that successful trading required patience and consistency.

Once, during a particularly volatile period in the markets, Alex experienced a series of consecutive losses. It was a difficult time for him, but instead of panicking and increasing his risk, Alex stuck to his risk management plan. He had set a daily loss limit of 0.3% of his capital and stuck to it strictly.

As the days passed, Alex continued to trade according to his strategy and his patience finally paid off. Market conditions began to favor his strategy and he began making profits again.

Its performance graph over time showed ups and downs, but overall, it was on an upward trajectory.

Story 2: The Gambler

I met a man named John at a casino. He was a gambling enthusiast and got a great thrill from betting large sums of money on games such as roulette and blackjack. John had a great drive to win and his sense of adrenaline was addictive. However, his lack of risk management led him down a dangerous path.

John had a streak of good luck and he won large sums on his first visits to the casino. But, over time, everything changed and he began to lose. Instead of stopping and rethinking his approach, John got caught up in the emotion of the moment and increased his bets in a desperate attempt to recover what he lost.

Unfortunately, this only led to him losing even more, to the point where he compromised much of his capital. Its performance graph over time was a steady decline, with sharp peaks followed by even deeper valleys.

The difference between Alex and John was their approach to risk and capital management. While Alex applied clear rules to protect his capital and maintained a long-term perspective, John was carried away by the emotion and urgency of winning quickly.

Trading is a profession that requires a calculated and disciplined mindset. Risk management is an essential part of the process as it protects the trader from significant losses and allows them to trade consistently over time. Professional traders understand that it is not about winning on every trade, but about maintaining a long-term mathematical advantage and protecting your capital to be able to trade another day.

The exciting adrenaline of danger can be tempting, but those who confuse trading with gambling put themselves at risk of losing all their capital and compromising their long-term success. The successful trader has a winning mentality based on discipline, long-term focus and proper risk management. The thrill of adrenaline may be short-lived, but the satisfaction of a successful trading career can last a lifetime.

The biggest challenge a trader faces is controlling their emotions and not getting carried away by irrational impulses in times of losses or bad streaks. When operations do not go as expected, it is natural for emotions such as frustration, fear and impatience to arise. However, it is in these crucial moments where the trader's true discipline is tested.

The fine line that separates the trader from the bettor is marked by the way they react to losses. The bettor, driven by emotion and the desire to recover what was lost quickly, may increase the size of his trades without following his risk management plan, in a desperate attempt to achieve quick profits.

On the other hand, the disciplined and professional trader understands that losses are a natural part of trading and that not all trades will be successful. Instead of getting carried away by the emotions of the moment, you stick to your trading plan and continue to apply your strategy consistently. Understand that trading is a game of probabilities and that you cannot win on every trade.

Furthermore, the successful trader understands the importance of protecting his capital at all costs. You know that proper risk management is essential to preserving your capital and continuing to operate in the future.

He does not get carried away by the urge to win quickly, but rather takes a long-term perspective and focuses on maintaining a mathematical advantage.

A disciplined approach and a focused mindset are the key to staying on the trader's path and avoiding falling into the gambler's trap. The trader must be aware of his emotions and learn to manage them effectively. This involves being honest with yourself, recognizing when you are feeling emotionally affected by an operation, and taking steps to regain calm and focus.

An effective strategy to manage emotions is to have a well-defined trading plan and follow it rigorously. The plan should include clear rules on the amount of risk per trade, profit targets, and maximum losses allowed. By having a solid plan, the trader will feel more secure and confident in their approach, which will help them avoid the temptation to act impulsively.

Another useful technique for controlling emotions is the use of meditation and conscious breathing. Taking a few minutes to meditate before trading can help calm the mind and reduce emotional stress. Additionally, practicing conscious breathing during trading can help a trader stay centered and calm during stressful times.

The trader's challenge is to stay on the right path and avoid crossing that fine line that separates the trader from the bettor. The key to achieving this is to have a disciplined and focused management of emotions effectively. By doing so, the trader will be on the path to long-term success in the world of trading.

Long-term approach: Successful traders take a long-term approach where consistency and discipline are key to achieving sustainable financial goals. Gamblers tend to look for quick results and can fall into a spiral of risk addiction.

The long-term focus is one of the distinguishing characteristics of a successful trader compared to a gambler. While the bettor seeks quick results and gets carried away by the emotion of the moment, the professional trader understands that success in trading requires time, patience and consistency in the application of a strategy over time.

An example of a long-term approach can be seen in the story of Warren Buffett, one of the most successful investors of all time. Buffett is known for his long-term investing mindset and focus on valuing strong companies. Throughout his career, he has resisted the temptation to follow trends or make decisions based on the short term. Instead, he has maintained a consistent focus on his investing principles and had the patience to wait for his investments to reach their true value over time.

For the trader, this means avoiding the urge to win quickly and being willing to accept that not all trades will be successful. Trading is an endurance race and not speed. It is important to remain patient and not get carried away by the emotions of the moment.

A useful exercise to work on long-term focus is to keep a detailed trading journal. In this journal, the trader can record every trade they make, including the reasons behind the entry and exit, the results, and the lessons learned. By regularly reviewing the journal, the trader could identify patterns and areas of improvement, which will help them adjust their approach and maintain consistency over time.

Another effective tool for developing long-term focus is to set clear and realistic financial goals. By having long-term goals, the trader could stay focused on the big picture and not get carried away by the daily ups and downs of the market.

Additionally, the trader could use visualization techniques to reinforce their focus and maintain a positive mindset. Imagining achieving your financial goals and trading success could strengthen your determination and keep you motivated even in difficult times.

It is important to note that the long-term approach does not mean being inflexible or stubborn in your strategies. Markets are dynamic and changing, so the trader must be willing to adapt and adjust their approach according to market conditions. However, you should always keep your long-term vision and avoid falling into the trap of looking for quick, emotional results.

The long-term approach is essential for trading success. Maintaining patience, discipline and consistency over time is the key to achieving sustainable financial goals. By learning to control emotions and maintain a long-term vision, the trader can separate himself from the gambler and build a successful and profitable career in the world of trading.

It is essential to recognize that the financial market is not a casino and that operating with the mentality of a gambler can lead to disastrous consequences. Some strategies used by casinos to dominate the minds of customers and encourage addiction can also be applied to those who confuse trading with gambling. Some examples include:

Intermittent reinforcement: Casinos often offer random rewards to keep players hooked. Likewise, a trader who makes a significant profit occasionally may feel the excitement and desire to continue risking more.

Illusory sense of control: Casinos create an environment where players feel they can control the outcome of their game, making them more likely to continue gambling. A trader may fall into the illusion that he can predict the market and make impulsive decisions instead of following his strategy.

Loss of perspective: The thrill of adrenaline can cloud judgment and cause a trader to make reckless or risky decisions without considering the long-term consequences.

To avoid falling into the trap of vice and gambling, it is essential to have a professional and focused mentality long term. Here are some key practices to keep the focus on trading as a profession and not a bet:

Have a solid trading plan: Develop a clear and well-defined plan that includes entry and exit rules, risk management and long-term financial objectives.

Practice discipline: Maintain discipline in the application of your strategy, even in times of volatility or uncertainty in the market.

Risk management: Limit risk per trade and per day to protect your capital and avoid significant losses.

Stick to the rules: Avoid making impulsive or emotion-based decisions and follow the rules established in your trading plan.

Continuous learning: Be open to constantly learning and improving, always seeking excellence in your trading approach and skills.

Remember that trading is a serious profession with the potential to achieve financial freedom, as long as you approach it with responsibility, discipline and a winning mentality. Don't let the exciting adrenaline of danger divert you from your long-term goals and always keep in mind that the key to success lies in managing emotions and making informed decisions.

In the pursuit of excitement and adrenaline, some people may engage in dangerous activities that can have serious consequences, not only for themselves but also for their loved ones and their long-term success. Next, I will mention some examples of these activities:

Compulsive gambling: There are those who are attracted to the excitement of games of chance such as casinos, slot machines or sports betting. Although the thrill of winning can be intense, this type of behavior can lead to addiction and the loss of large sums of money, seriously affecting financial stability and emotional well-being.

Extreme Sports: Thrill-seeking through extreme sports, such as skydiving, rock climbing, or dangerous water sports, can provide a high dose of adrenaline, but they also carry a high risk of serious injury or even death.

High-speed car or motorcycle racing: Participating in high-speed car or motorcycle racing can be an exciting experience, but it is also extremely dangerous and it can have fatal consequences in the event of an accident.

Drugs and alcohol: Seeking altered emotions and sensations through drug or alcohol use can lead to health problems, addictions, and damage to personal and professional relationships.

Dangerous or irresponsible trips: Some people seek thrills from dangerous or irresponsible trips such as climbing mountains without proper preparation or visiting unsafe places. This can put their safety and that of those accompanying them at risk.

It is important to keep in mind that the emotions and

adrenaline that these activities can provide are temporary and ephemeral. In many cases, the negative consequences far outweigh any exciting moment they may have experienced.

In trading it is also crucial to avoid falling into the trap of seeking intense emotions and making impulsive decisions based on the excitement of the moment. The financial market can be volatile and challenging; Seeking excitement can lead to risky trades and significant losses. It is better that you accept and say that trading is quite boring, but it has many benefits and you can look for fun activities outside of it since one of the great advantages is that it gives a lot of free time to do other activities.

It is essential to develop a professional mindset and focus on the long-term approach. Just like in life, success in trading requires discipline, patience and responsibility. Avoiding extreme emotions and maintaining composure, even in volatile situations, is essential to making informed decisions and achieving consistent results.

It is always important to remember that our actions and decisions not only affect ourselves, but also our loved ones and our relationships. Being aware of the impact of our actions and seeking a balance between emotion and responsibility is key to maintaining long-term success in trading and in life in general.

Responsible Adrenaline: Keep Trading And Emotion Separate

In the world of trading, it is common for traders to be attracted by the excitement and adrenaline that can arise when operating in the financial markets. However, it is essential to understand that trading and emotion must be kept separate to ensure long-term success.

It is a serious business that involves managing risk and protecting capital. On the other hand, high-risk and exciting activities can be found outside of trading, such as extreme sports, adventurous travel, or any other adrenaline-pumping activity.

The main reason why it is important to separate trading from emotion is that emotions can cloud judgment and lead to impulsive and poorly informed decisions. When traders trade under the influence of emotion they are more likely to fall into traps such as overtrading, irresponsibly increasing risk, or chasing losses to recover. These impulsive actions can be detrimental to the trading account and take the trader away from their long-term financial goals.

Another recommendation is to establish clear times and limits for trading sessions. It is important to establish specific times to operate and respect those limits. After finishing the trade, the trader can look for exciting activities outside of trading that will give him the adrenaline he is looking for. Doing so creates a healthy balance between emotion and discipline in the life of the trader.

If the trader feels the need to experience emotions and adrenaline, it is recommended that they seek these experiences outside of trading. During trading, it is essential to maintain discipline and follow the established trading plan. By separating trading from emotion, the trader can maintain objectivity and ensure that their decisions are based on sound and logical strategies. By following this recommendation, the trader will be in a stronger position to achieve long-term success in the world of trading.

CHAPTER 11: EMBRACING FEAR: YOUR BEST ALLY

This is undoubtedly one of my favorite chapters, I invite you to take notes and delve into the simple ideas that I present to you. I apologize if I repeat some concepts during this chapter. I am trying my best to make the message I want to convey clear to you and in my heart I know that if you only keep a small percentage of what I tell you, you will be able to develop a winning mind in all of them. aspects of your life.

Fear, that primal sensation that has accompanied humanity since its beginnings, is a powerful and complex topic. In the world of trading, fear can be both an ally and an enemy, depending on how we face and use it. In this chapter, I will explain in detail the concept of fear, its evolutionary origin and how we can channel it effectively on our path to trading success.

The Nature Of Fear

Fear is an instinctive response to situations perceived as threatening or dangerous. It is an emotion that has evolved in humans as a way of survival. Rooted from the first humans who faced dangers in their environment, this emotion allowed them to react quickly to avoid threats and stay safe. This fight or flight reaction is a basic characteristic of fear that still persists in our brains today.

Fear As Impulse And Paralysis

In human history, fear has been a driver of action and also a paralyzer. Some people have used fear as a motivator to overcome obstacles and face challenges, while others have become trapped in the paralysis it sometimes causes, avoiding situations that could be beneficial.

Fear In Trading: Two Divergent Approaches

When it comes to trading, fear can have a profound impact on our decisions and results. Some traders allow themselves to be dominated by the fear of losing money, which can lead to impulsive decisions and unnecessary losses. Others use fear as a signal of caution and manage risk more prudently.

Use Fear As Positive Energy

The key to harnessing fear in trading is to turn it into a source of energy and focus. Instead of allowing fear to paralyze us, we can recognize it as a warning sign that encourages us to be more cautious and make informed decisions. By identifying what causes us fear and addressing those aspects, we can transform it into a driving force to research, plan and execute our operations with greater confidence.

Managing Fear In Trading

To manage it, it is essential to build a resilient and strategy-focused mindset. Establishing clear rules and a solid trading plan can help us stay calm even in times of volatility. Additionally, practicing emotional control techniques such as meditation, conscious breathing, and visualization can help us stay focused and prevent fear from overwhelming us.

Embracing fear: Transforming it into your greatest strength in trading

Have you stopped to consider the powerful influence that fear has on our lives? Since the dawn of humanity, fear has been our faithful companion, an instinct rooted in our being that has been both our protector and our obstacle. By paying attention to fear and understanding how it affects your behavior, you are already a person with an advantage and will embark on a profound journey to unravel its mysteries and discover how to make it your greatest ally.

The Dance Of Fear Through History

Imagine the ancient times, when the first humans wandered through an unknown world full of dangers. Fear, that ancestral instinct, allowed them to survive, prompting them to act quickly in the face of imminent threats. As society evolved, fear continued to shape our decisions, whether to avoid a predator or face a new challenge. But here's the fascinating twist: some people harnessed this fear, tamed it, and used it as a propellant, while others were swept away by its paralyzing power.

You can read 1,001 books and you can go to all the seminars related to the domain of fear. The solution is for you to decide. Since you have reached this chapter, it is time for you to stop and say it out loud: "I, NAME AND LAST NAME, FROM THIS MOMENT ON I HAVE DECIDED TO TURN MY FEARS INTO MY BEST ALLIES." The paradoxical thing about fear is that it is not from fighting against it. He is not someone different from you, he is you, you must understand him, know him and use him to your advantage. I assure you something: the people you most admire, those who have achieved incredible feats, are also afraid, it is something natural for human beings, something beautiful and worthy of admiration for how useful it has been for humanity to develop. But it will only be good if you manage to disarm it, understand it, decipher it and use it as your best ally. To give you a clearer idea, you can decide to use fear to fear failure, so much fear of failure that it makes you try harder than anyone else to succeed. And do you know what will happen? You will succeed. It is better to be afraid of failure than to be afraid of success, simple as that, my dear friend.

The Enigma Of Fear In Trading

As we enter the exciting realm of trading, we once again encounter the duality of fear. Is it an obstacle that weakens us or a force that propels us forward? Imagine being in front of your screen, your palms sweaty and your heart racing as you face a crucial decision. Fear can be an ally if you interpret it correctly, a signal that tells you "Caution, evaluate, plan!" But be careful, it can also be an adversary that leads you to make hasty and emotional decisions or to remain paralyzed.

The Transformative Power Of Channeling Fear

Have you ever wondered how some traders manage to

manage fear so effectively, while others get caught in its grip? The answer is in the channeling of fear. Imagine fear as a torrent of raw, powerful energy. Instead of letting this energy dominate you, what if you made it your secret weapon? The key is to use that jolt of adrenaline to investigate, analyze and execute with determination and discipline.

Mathematics And Fear: A Formula For Success

Dare to immerse yourself in the field of mathematics. Imagine that fear is a complex equation. Every decision, every risk, every moment of uncertainty is a variable in this equation. A successful trader not only knows the variables, but also knows how to balance them to obtain the desired result: profitability and consistency. As? Setting risk limits applying profit to risk ratios and staying true to a solid trading plan.

The Transformation Of Fear Into Your Greatest Strength

How to embrace fear and transform it into your greatest strength? Learn to recognize the emotional patterns that arise from it and channel them into informed and strategic action. You will discover how to establish risk limits and clear rules that will allow you to operate with confidence and emotional resilience.

Your Journey To Emotional Mastery

Get ready to peel back the layers of fear and unravel its deepest secrets. By understanding the influence of fear on your decisions and emotions, you will be equipped to approach each trade with informed confidence and a clear mind. Embrace fear, make it your ally and transcend self-imposed limitations. On your journey towards emotional mastery in trading, fear will cease to be an obstacle and will become a driving force that will lead you to achieve consistent and lasting results.

Controlling Fear In Trading: Practical Strategies

It is time to equip yourself with concrete strategies to control it in your career as a trader. Remember that fear can be a useful emotion if you know how to use it to your advantage.

And I'll tell you a very curious fact: if you read this entire book or 1,000 more and you don't put what you read into practice and you don't delve into the ideas, it's the same as nothing. So be afraid of being a failure and strive to go beyond what I propose, strive to develop your own tools that eliminate all thoughts of failure from your mind. It is in your hands to turn your mind into that of a winner.

1. Education as an antidote

One of the most effective ways to deal with fear is to face it with knowledge. Education gives you the power to understand the factors that influence market movements and how to react to them. Constantly research, study patterns and analyze historical trends. The more you know, the less mysterious and threatening the market will seem.

2. Planning and preparation

Fear often arises from uncertainty. A solid plan is your best defense against this. Before each trade, set your objectives, entry and exit points, and loss limits. Not only will this give you a clear structure, but it will also reduce the anxiety of making impulsive decisions.

3. Practice the "WORST CASE SCENARIO" technique

This is one of my favorite techniques , I have already applied in everything, when I have developed business, when I am going to carry out any risky activity, when I am going to ask for meal in a restaurant, when I am going to have sex, when I am going to invest, when I am going to spend great quantities of money, in everything you can imagine, I use this calculating mentality and I feel that I have developed it very well, sometimes it takes me secondos to do a calculation how much I can lose and if that risk is worth the effort or resources

I was fortunate to have an economist father and since I was little I developed a love for economics, which is nothing more than the science that studies the distribution of resources. When I was at university they gave me some concepts that stayed in my mind forever; were the salvage value and the economic feasibility of a project, just as large studies are done to see how profitable a project is and, if wrong, what its salvage value will be. All this is nothing more than the evaluation of the worst case scenario and it is really very powerful to develop an analytical mind. It will help you live without fear. I invite you to investigate these concepts: "Rescue value of a project" and "economic feasibility of a project." They will make you a more skilled person in the use of your resources, starting with the most valuable resource you have: Your time.

Visualize the worst possible scenario. What would happen if your trade goes against you? How would you feel? By facing your fears realistically, you can prepare yourself emotionally to deal with losses. This will lessen the intensity of the emotional reaction should it occur.

4. Keep a trading journal

Recording your trades and your emotions associated with them can provide valuable introspection. When you feel fear, write down what triggered it and how you reacted. Over time, you will begin to identify patterns and develop specific strategies for dealing with it in similar situations.

5. Develop a resilient mind

Mental resilience is essential to control fear. Practice meditation and mindfulness to stay calm in times of uncertainty. Learn to recognize and change your negative thinking patterns into a more positive and realistic one.

6. Set clear boundaries

Setting limits on your trades and trading time will help you avoid falling into the trap of overtrading. When the fear of losing becomes overwhelming, remember that you have a plan and that it protects you.

7. Keep perspective

Always remember that trading is a marathon, not a sprint. Fear tends to cloud our long-term vision. Keep your focus on your long-term goals and consistency rather than immediate gains.

A New Approach: Embracing Fear

At the end of the day, fear is a powerful tool at your disposal. Acknowledge its presence, respect it, but do not let yourself be dominated by it. Learn to turn that tickling in your stomach into a compass that guides you toward trading mastery. Fear doesn't have to be your enemy; can be your teacher. Dare to embrace it and transform it into your greatest strength on the path to financial and personal success.

Fear As A Catalyst For Human Evolution

Imagine an ancient scene: a group of prehistoric hunters venture out in search of food. They know they must face dangerous creatures and unknown territories. Fear pulses in the air as they advance, but instead of paralyzing them, this fear becomes their ally. By sharpening their senses to be more attentive and react faster to possible dangers, fear becomes their guardian angel, even helping them to have much greater strength, resistance and speed. Fear is designed by nature to be your ally in survival. Hating, fighting, hiding and ignoring your fear is putting out your inner fire.

Fear, in this case, is transformed into an energy that increases their senses, sharpens their concentration and prepares them to act in the event of an encounter with a predator. Every movement is synchronized and every decision is guided by the impulse of survival. This fear does not weaken them, but rather drives them to face danger with courage and strategy.

Now, let's transfer this idea to the world of trading. Like the ancient hunters, the trader finds himself in an environment full of uncertainty and potential dangers. However, the approach is different. Instead of facing a physical predator, the trader faces market fluctuations and crucial financial decisions.

♦ ♦ ♦

Hate, fight and hide your fear, is to put out your internal fire.

♦ ♦ ♦

In both cases, fear is a natural response that has evolved to maximize the chances of survival. But here's the key: fear is not an enemy to defeat, but rather an emotion that can be channeled and controlled. Just as prehistoric hunters did not allow themselves to be paralyzed by fear, the successful trader does not allow fear to dominate him.

Taming Fear Through Knowledge

Historically, fear has been a mechanism that has driven human beings to learn and adapt. Prehistoric hunters, for example, learned to recognize signs of danger in their environment and develop more efficient hunting strategies. This knowledge not only made them survive, but helped them thrive.

In the world of trading, knowledge is also a powerful tool to control fear. As you educate yourself about financial markets, price patterns, technical and fundamental analysis, you will develop a deeper understanding. This knowledge will not only allow you to make more informed decisions, but will also give you the confidence to face fear bravely.

The Evolution Of Brave Adaptation

Let's look again at our prehistoric hunters. Over time, their understanding of animal movement patterns, hunting seasons, and improved tactics made them more efficient hunters. They have learned to channel fear productively and to adapt to their changing environment.

In trading, adaptation is also key. As you face various market conditions, you will learn to adjust your strategies and make decisions based on the information available. Fear can be your cue to stop, analyze, and adapt your approach depending on the situation. This is where fear stops being an obstacle and becomes a driver of constant improvement.

A Brave Future In Trading

Fear is an intrinsic emotion that has guided human evolution and it can be an essential factor for trading success. Learning to recognize, control and channel fear will allow you to face the market with a brave and adaptable mindset. Just as our ancestors used it as an ally in the search for food and security, you can transform it into a tool for profit and financial growth. Remember: fear is not your enemy, but a reminder of your inherent bravery and your ability to evolve in the world of trading.

The Physiology Of Fear: Understanding Your Own Body

To better understand how fear works in your mind and body,

it is essential to explore the physiology behind this powerful emotion. Fear is not just an abstract concept; It has tangible effects on your body that can influence your decisions and behaviors. This is where the connection between evolution, biology and trading become fascinatingly intertwined.

When faced with a threatening situation, your brain activates a "fight or flight" response to prepare you for action. This response involves the autonomic nervous system; a part of your nervous system that works automatically and involuntarily. It is divided into two branches: the sympathetic nervous system and the parasympathetic nervous system.

The sympathetic nervous system is the one that comes into action when you feel fear. Your heart rate accelerates, your pupils dilate, your lungs expand to take in more oxygen, and your muscles tense. In short, your body prepares to fight or flee.

This physiological response, which developed in our ancestors as a way to deal with physical threats, can influence your behavior as a trader. When you feel fear during an operation, your body is experiencing the same changes that we experience when faced with real danger. Your heart beats faster, your breathing quickens, and your muscles tense.

This is a crucial moment in trading. Will you let fear paralyze you or use it as a stimulus to make informed decisions? The difference between the successful trader and the one who falls into the trap of fear lies in how they interpret and channel this biological response.

A Brave Future In Trading

Fear is an intrinsic emotion that has guided human evolution and can be an essential factor for trading success. Learning to recognize, control and channel fear will allow you to face the market with a brave and adaptable mindset. Just as our ancestors used it as an ally in the search for food and security, you can transform it into a tool for profit and financial growth. Remember: fear is not your enemy, but a reminder of your inherent bravery and your ability to evolve in the world of trading.

The Physiology Of Fear: Understanding Your Own Body

To better understand how fear works in your mind and body, it is essential to explore the physiology behind this powerful emotion. Fear is not just an abstract concept. It has tangible effects on your body that can influence your decisions and behaviors. This is where the connection between evolution, biology and trading become fascinatingly intertwined.

When you feel afraid. Your heart rate accelerates, your pupils dilate, your lungs expand to take in more oxygen, and your muscles tense. In short, your body prepares to fight or flee.

This physiological response, which developed in our ancestors as a way to deal with physical threats, can influence your behavior as a trader. When you feel fear during an operation, your body is experiencing the same changes that we experience when faced with real danger. Your heart beats faster, your breathing quickens, and your muscles tense.

This is a crucial moment in trading. Will you let fear paralyze you or use it as a stimulus to make informed decisions? The difference between the successful trader and the one who falls into the trap of fear lies in how they interpret and channel this biological response.

Transforming Fear Into An Asset

The amount of fear your body generates is directly proportional to the amount of success you can achieve in any activity. In other words: The more afraid you are, the more successful you will be.

This is where your knowledge comes into play. Knowing that this physiological response is a natural reaction to uncertainty can help you take control. Recognizing that your body is reacting to a situation perceived as threatening allows you to remain calm and objectively evaluate the situation. This will give you enough energy and drive to act accordingly. The positive thing is that if you manage to channel it into action it will bring you benefits.

Imagine you are looking at a price chart and you see a sharp drop. Your heart begins to beat faster and you feel a wave of fear. Instead of giving in to this instinctive response, you can remind yourself that this reaction is normal. You can pause, take a deep breath, and analyze the situation clearly.

This awareness and control is what separates the emotionally intelligent trader from the one who acts impulsively. Instead of allowing fear to dictate your actions, you can use it as a reminder and fuel of the importance of caution and making decisions based on analysis. It is important to clarify: being afraid does not mean remaining paralyzed, on the contrary, it means using all that energy to analyze the best option.

The Power Of The Mind-Body Connection

Understanding how fear operates in your body gives you an invaluable advantage in trading. You can separate the physiological response from your conscious decisions; You can transform it into a signal to reflect instead of acting impulsively.

As you develop your emotional intelligence and master the connection between your mind and body, you will become more resistant to emotional fluctuations that can sabotage your operations. Remember: fear is not an enemy, but a natural part of the human experience. By understanding and working with it, you can use it as a tool to make informed and courageous decisions in the world of trading.

The Force Of Fear Channeled

Ultimately, fear is a powerful tool that can influence our actions and decisions. By approaching fear from an informed and balanced perspective, we can use it to propel us forward rather than hold us back. By understanding the evolutionary origin of fear and how it manifests in our lives, we can take control and leverage it as a source of motivation and focus in the world of trading and beyond.

By understanding how fear can be an ally or an enemy, we are in a better position to use it effectively and achieve success in our operations. Through managing fear, building a resilient mindset, and channeling its energy, we can make informed and prudent decisions in the world of trading and in all areas of our lives.

◆ ◆ ◆

It may be the fear of failure what drives you to get up early every day and focus on your goals.

◆ ◆ ◆

Your Journey To Emotional Mastery

Get ready to peel back the layers of fear and unravel its deepest secrets. By understanding its influence on your decisions and emotions, you will be equipped to approach each trade with informed confidence and a clear mind. Embrace fear, make it your ally and transcend self-imposed limitations. On your journey towards emotional mastery in trading, fear will cease to be an obstacle and will become a driving force that will lead you to achieve consistent and lasting results.

CHAPTER 12: THE ETERNAL SEARCH FOR KNOWLEDGE IN TRADING

In a world where change is the only constant, education is like the lighthouse that guides us to the shore of success. As we dive into the changing waters of trading, we realize that only those willing to continually learn can masterfully navigate these choppy waters.

The Silent Evolution Of The Markets

Financial markets are not static entities. They are living organisms that breathe and pulse to the rhythm of global events, emerging technology and economic fluctuations. Those who believe they can apply an outdated strategy indefinitely will soon find themselves stranded on the shore of irrelevance. Artificial intelligence is already entering with great force, have you thought about that? There are many countries that they will eliminate their coins, have you thought about that? And many other changes are happening in the world. How will all these changes affect the markets that are currently operating in the near future? You have to adapt to the changes and to do so you must be attentive but above all, you must force your mind to learn new skills.

Today's Trader Is The Eternal Learner

Imagine a lone sailor on a vast ocean. What keeps you moving? It is the compass that guides your course, your knowledge of the stars and winds or your ability to adapt to changing currents. Similarly, the modern trader is an eternal learner, a seeker of truth in numbers and charts.

From Average to Exceptional: The Power of Education

Continuous learning can be the divider between average and exceptional. Imagine two athletes competing in a race. One has trained diligently, studied the most effective techniques, and kept his or her body in tip-top shape. The other trusts in his natural talent but does not strive to improve. Who will reach the finish line first? The first, without a doubt.

The Infinite Cycle Of Improvement

Education is an endless dance between curiosity and action. When you embrace learning, you enter a virtuous cycle of constant improvement. Each new knowledge is a brick in the construction of your success. Each new strategy is an additional tool in your box. Every new trend you catch puts you one step ahead.

Building Your Arsenal Of Knowledge

Education is not just about knowing the latest indicator or

the hottest strategy. It's about building an arsenal of knowledge that allows you to face any challenge. It's about understanding the fundamentals, unraveling the secrets of charts and studying the psychology of the markets. Each piece of knowledge is a precious stone in your crown of skills.

Learning As A Path To Mastery

Continuing education in trading is the path to mastery. But remember, education is not just the accumulation of facts and figures; it is deep understanding, skillful application and constant adaptation. It is about cultivating an open mind, willing to unlearn and relearn in search of truth.

So, are you ready to take on the role of the eternal learner? Are you willing to immerse yourself in the changing currents of knowledge and emerge as an exceptional trader? Education is the lighthouse that will guide your journey. Embrace the eternal pursuit of knowledge and watch your sails swell with the breeze of success.

Awakening the sleeping brain: Exploring the horizon of knowledge.

Imagine your brain as a vast unexplored territory, filled with mountains of information, valleys of wisdom, and rivers of creativity. Each new knowledge you acquire is like a stepping stone that takes you higher on the path of understanding. But don't limit this journey to trading alone; Venture beyond, through meadows of diverse abilities and forests of unknown disciplines.

The Brain As An Infinite Tool

Your brain is your most valuable resource, and its potential is practically unlimited. He has always been willing to work for you, you just need to give him the right direction. He focuses his energy not only on understanding the market, but also on learning new languages, communication skills, leadership techniques or musical instruments. By doing so, you feed your mind with intellectual nutrients, allowing it to develop and flourish into a garden of multifaceted abilities.

◆ ◆ ◆

Knowledge does not take up space.

◆ ◆ ◆

Curiosity As Fuel

Do you remember childhood, when every day was an adventure and every raised stone hid exciting secrets? That innate curiosity should not be lost on the path to adulthood. Keep curiosity as a beacon in your life. Allow yourself to explore, investigate and question. Curiosity is the driving force of continuing education, driving you to seek answers to questions you didn't even know you had.

The Mosaic Of Skills: A Multifaceted Brain

Don't lock yourself into a narrow niche of knowledge. The brain thrives when presented with a diverse mosaic of skills. Learning to play an instrument, paint a picture, develop culinary skills, or learn to program will not only bring you joy and satisfaction, but will also nourish the flexibility of your brain. The synergy between seemingly disparate skills often results in creative and original thinking.

Exploring The Unknown: Expanding Your Horizons

Would you dare to enter a field that you had never explored? Learn something completely new and challenging? Continuing education is not just about accumulating familiar knowledge, but about venturing into uncharted territory. Learn to program even if you've never touched a computer, study psychology even if you're a trader, or delve into philosophy even if you're an engineer. Each new discipline is an additional set of musical notes in the symphony of your life.

◆ ◆ ◆

Each new discipline is an additional set of musical notes in the symphony of your life

◆ ◆ ◆

The Evolving Brain: Your Golden Egg

Remember that the brain, as in trading, constantly evolves. Don't limit yourself to just one way of thinking or learning. Embrace the metamorphosis of knowledge. Keep your mind open, willing to change, rethink and grow. You are not just a trader; you are a human being capable of learning and thriving in countless areas.

So why limit yourself? Embrace the adventure of continuing education. Let your brain dance with new ideas, explore new lands and embrace the diversity of knowledge. Feed your mind, cultivate your skills and witness the vast horizon of knowledge unfold before you, ready to be conquered.

The Expanding Brain: The Power Of Continuing Education

Increasingly, science is revealing that continuous learning is not only beneficial, but essential for the optimal functioning of our brain and our mental health. Here I present data that supports the idea that keeping your brain constantly active is a gift for life:

Neuroplasticity: The Constant Change Of The Brain

Neuroplasticity is the amazing phenomenon by which the brain can adapt and change throughout life. This means that as you learn new skills and gain knowledge, you are literally reshaping your brain. Connections between neurons are strengthened, new pathways are formed, and more efficient networks are created. This process allows the brain to remain agile and flexible, which is essential for problem solving and decision making in trading and in life.

Cognitive Aging Delay

Continuing education is like exercise for the brain. Just as staying physically active can prevent muscle deterioration, keeping your brain moving can slow cognitive aging. Studies have shown that people who dedicate themselves to learning new skills and acquiring new knowledge are less likely to experience age-related memory loss and other cognitive functions.

Greater Mental Resilience

Continuing education can improve mental resilience, meaning you are better able to face stress and adversity calmly and clearly. By learning new ways of thinking and approaching problems, you train your brain to find solutions instead of feeling overwhelmed. This is crucial in trading, where quick and informed decisions are essential for success.

Dopamine Stimulation: The Pleasure Of Learning

When you learn something new and challenging, your brain releases dopamine, a chemical associated with pleasure and reward. This not only makes you feel good, but also reinforces motivation to continue learning. Imagine if you could apply this process to your trading routine. Every time you acquire new skills and knowledge, your brain receives an internal reward that reinforces your commitment to continuous learning.

Breaking the routine: Greater creativity and critical thinking

Learning new skills challenges mental routine and opens new avenues of thinking. This not only makes you a more versatile trader, but it can also increase your creativity and critical thinking skills. By approaching problems from different angles, you become better able to find innovative solutions and develop unique trading strategies and improving throughout your life. Don't limit yourself; Open the doors of knowledge and allow the light to illuminate every corner of your mind. Keep learning as a constant companion on your journey, not only in trading, but in all areas of your life. Your brain, your future and your possibilities will thank you.

Continuing Education: A Journey Of Mental Empowerment

As we explore the importance of continuing education in trading and in life, it is essential to understand that this journey goes beyond simply accumulating knowledge. It's about empowering your mind, expanding your horizons and challenging the limits you have imposed on yourself. Here are some practices and approaches that will help you make the most of this learning journey:

1. Cultivate infinite curiosity

Embrace your innate curiosity and never stop asking yourself questions. Every day is an opportunity to discover something new and exciting. In trading, this curious mindset can push you to explore new strategies, analyze different approaches, and study market movements from unexplored angles. By staying curious, you will never stop learning and growing.

A Gift For Your Future

Imagine your brain as a treasure chest, full of infinite potential. Continuing education is the key that unlocks that treasure and allows your brain to continue evolving and adapting

2. Learn from diverse sources

Don't limit yourself to a single approach or source of learning. Explore a variety of resources, from books and online courses to seminars and conferences. Learning from diverse sources allows you to gain a broader and richer perspective. Additionally, it challenges you to consider different points of view and develop a more well-rounded approach to your trading.

3. Develop the habit of daily learning

Just as daily practice improves your trading skills, daily learning improves your ability to understand and adapt. Take time each day to learn something new, whether it's about trading, finance, psychology or any other topic that interests you. Even a few minutes a day can add up and make a big difference over time.

4. Learn from your mistakes

Continuing education is not only about acquiring new knowledge, but also about learning from your mistakes. Analyze your past trades, identify what worked and what didn't, and use those lessons to adjust and improve your strategy. Every mistake is an opportunity for growth and refinement.

5. Share your knowledge

Sharing what you have learned not only benefits others, but also reinforces your own learning. Explain concepts to others, blog or participate in forums and online trading groups. Teaching is a powerful way to consolidate your own knowledge and see it from different perspectives.

6. Embrace change and adaptation

Financial markets are constantly evolving, and the same applies to the world around us. Embracing continuing education allows you to adapt to changes and be prepared for any situation. The ability to learn and adjust quickly is an invaluable skill in trading and in life.

7. Keep an open mind

Continuing education is a lifelong journey, and that means there will always be more to discover and learn. Keep an open mind to new ideas, approaches and concepts. Allow yourself to question your own beliefs and be willing to reconsider them as you gain new knowledge.

Continuing education is not only a tool for trading success, but it is also a path to a richer mind and a more fulfilled life. Take advantage of every opportunity to learn, grow and strengthen your mind. Knowledge is a treasure that is never devalued, and the more you acquire it, the more valuable it becomes on your journey to success and personal fulfillment.

The Brevity Of Life And The Greatness Of Knowledge

Life is ephemeral; a sigh in the vastness of time. We find ourselves in a tiny corner of the universe and our existences are fleeting sparks in the immensity of eternity. Faced with this reality, a crucial question arises: how do we decide to live our lives? What will we do with the time we have been given?

Every day that passes is a unique and unrepeatable gift. However, it is common to fall into routine, into the monotony of daily activities, leaving aside opportunities to learn, explore and grow. Imagine all the wonders the world has to offer: from natural wonders to the diversity of cultures and flavors. Every corner of the Planet contains a story, knowledge, and a unique experience.

Try as many different foods as possible, get to know different countries, learn new languages; All of these actions not only enrich us intellectually, but also connect us with the essence of humanity. They are windows that allow us to look at the world through different perspectives, understand the vastness of the human experience and explore the wonders that the universe offers us.

It is true that not all of us can visit every corner of the planet or master all the existing languages, but the essence of this search goes beyond quantity. It's about having an open mind, about being willing to venture into the unknown, about embracing the opportunity to learn in every moment. Learning does not take up space; In fact, the more we learn, the more mental space we create for new experiences and knowledge.

Knowledge is a treasure that we carry with us wherever we go. Through it, we transcend the physical and temporal limitations of our lives. Every fact learned, every skill acquired, every language mastered becomes a legacy we leave behind for generations to come.

So, as we walk this short path of existence, let us remember that our lives are like a blank canvas waiting to be filled with vibrant colors and enriching experiences. Let's take advantage of the time we have been given to learn, explore, love and live intensely. May the greatness of knowledge be our beacon, guiding us through the darkness of ignorance and into the luminosity of personal fulfillment. Life is short, but knowledge allows us to live it fully and with a heart full of gratitude and wonder.

The Treasure Of Learning: Filling Your Life With Meaning

Often, the idea of studying or learning something new can generate some resistance. Full schedules, daily responsibilities, and the comfort of routine can conspire to keep us in our comfort zone. However, the act of learning should not be perceived as a daunting task; rather, it is an opportunity to expand horizons and give deep meaning to our lives.

Imagine this scenario: you are at the cusp of your golden years, a stage in which retirement or retirement presents itself as an option. You find yourself surrounded by memories, some of which fill you with joy and pride, while others bring with them a veil of regret. What would you like to see when you look back? A life full of opportunities taken or a series of opportunities wasted?

The key here is to understand that learning should not be seen as a burden, but as an investment in yourself. Learn to dive, to pilot a plane, to play an instrument, to cook an exotic dish; These are activities that add flavor to life. Every time you venture out to learn something new, you are drawing lines on the canvas of your memories. You are creating moments that will accompany you throughout the years, they will weave a story of adventures and learning.

Why is it so important to embrace this constant learning mindset? Because every time you challenge your limits, explore new terrain, and expand your repertoire, you are giving your life unmatched depth. You are replacing monotony with a palette of vibrant and rich experiences. You are awakening the passion, curiosity and enthusiasm that often atrophies in the midst of routine.

It's true, life is short. Time is a priceless and non-renewable resource. Imagine that day in the future when you reflect on your life. Would you like that day to be filled with regrets for untapped opportunities or would you like it to be illuminated by the satisfaction of having lived fully?

So, embrace learning. Do it not as an obligation, but as a celebration. Every new knowledge acquired, every new skill mastered, is a treasure that you carry with you forever. The sense of accomplishment, awakened passion, and personal enrichment that come from learning are the ingredients that will allow you to look back and smile with pride. Life is a journey and learning is the fuel that gives life to that journey. Don't let time pass in vain; Instead, fill your days with experiences that make you feel alive and proud of the legacy you are creating. And when I talk about a legacy I don't mean something you leave to others, I mean legacy as those memories that make you proud.

We don't know how much time we have left until we know how much time we have left, don't wait for that day to come to do the things that make you happy; Remember that a winning mentality is made up of many factors, but the main one is the vision you have of yourself. When you look in the mirror you should be proud of yourself and you will only be so if you live your life with intensity, with courage, without leaving time behind. Taking control of your life.

We don't know how much time we have left until we know how much time we have left.

◆ ◆ ◆

CHAPTER 13: THE PSYCHOLOGY OF SUCCESS: MINDSET OF ABUNDANCE AND GRATITUDE

The Power Of The Abundance And Gratitude Mentality: Transforming Your Reality

In the journey of life, our mind plays a crucial role in how we experience the world around us. The mindset we choose to adopt can shape our outcomes and perspectives in profound and surprising ways.

The abundance mentality is not only about material wealth, but also about a mental approach that sees opportunities around every corner and is grateful for what you have in the present. When you cultivate this mindset, your perspective changes; You begin to see life as an ocean of opportunity instead of a desert of lack. You begin to make decisions based on the belief that there is always more to gain and less to lose.

Gratitude is a crucial ingredient in this process. Practice

Gratitude not only helps you recognize the blessings you already have, but it also opens the door to more good things in your life. Imagine a trading approach where you are grateful for every opportunity, regardless of whether it results in profit or loss. This not only reduces stress but also frees you from the trap of despair and worry.

Abundance and gratitude extend beyond trading and infiltrate all areas of your life. In your personal relationships, the abundance mindset allows you to be generous with your time, energy, and affection. You are willing to share your knowledge and successes, knowing that your success does not diminish if others also succeed.

Why is the mindset of abundance and gratitude so powerful? Because the way we think and perceive the world becomes our reality. If you choose to see the glass half full, you will begin to attract more positive things into your life. If you focus on what you have instead of what you lack, your satisfaction will increase and anxiety will decrease.

Ultimately, the choice between a scarcity mindset and an abundance mindset is in your hands. It is not simply a naive and optimistic perspective; It is a conscious decision of how you want to experience your life. Practicing gratitude, believing in the generosity of the universe, and embracing abundance in all its forms will allow you to transcend the limits your mind has set. By adopting this mindset, you will discover that the opportunities are countless and that success becomes a natural consequence of your beliefs and actions.

The Transformation Of The Abundance Mentality: Giving Without Waiting

Imagine living in a world where you wake up everyday knowing that you have enough and that there are endless opportunities waiting to be discovered. An abundance mindset allows you to experience life in this way, freeing you from the fear and anxiety that comes with the scarcity mindset.

When you think about abundance, you are not only considering material wealth, but also the abundance of love, time, positive relationships, and meaningful experiences. This mindset allows you to appreciate what you have instead of lamenting what is missing. You begin to understand that you don't need to accumulate to feel complete. Instead, you realize that you are already complete and that everything else is a complement.

A powerful aspect of the abundance mindset is the ability to give without expecting anything in return. This practice is based on the belief that by giving, you do not diminish your own abundance, but rather you expand it. By giving love, time, support and resources to others, you create a positive cycle that attracts more good things into your life.

When you give without expecting anything in return, you free yourself from the weight of expectations and conditions. You become an agent of change in the lives of others, and that positive energy inevitably returns to you in ways it could never have anticipated. The law of give and take operates constantly in the universe and when you adopt a mindset of giving, you are participating in this natural flow of energy.

Imagine sharing your trading knowledge and experiences with other traders, not with the expectation of receiving something specific but simply because you want to help and contribute. This act of generosity creates a network of support and camaraderie in the trading community. Although you may think you are giving "for free," you are actually sowing seeds that can eventually grow and manifest in the form of new opportunities, connections, and learnings.

The key is to abandon any idea that you should receive something immediate in return. Gratitude from others, respect, and admiration are gifts you can reap, but they are not the primary goal of giving. When you give sincerely, you are enriching your own life in ways that are not always tangible or quantifiable.

Cultivating an abundance mindset and learning to give without expectations can be a paradigm shift that transforms your life and your relationships. Start by recognizing and appreciating what you already have and then look for ways to give to others. It is not about sacrificing your own needs, but understanding that by giving, you are contributing to the creation of a more abundant and generous world for all. By doing so, you are on the path to a richer life in every way.

Abundance Mentality: Beyond Philanthropy

It is important to clarify that adopting an abundance mentality does not mean being a naive philanthropist or an extreme social Darwinist. It's not about giving away everything you have without considering the consequences. Instead, it's about understanding that living with a scarcity mindset can limit and restrict your opportunities, while an abundance mindset can expand your horizons and create a positive effect on all aspects of your life.

When you have a scarcity mindset, you are constantly

worried about losing what you have and how to protect it. This can lead to fear-based decisions, such as withholding information, resources, or helping others. Ultimately, this mindset can lead to isolation and feeling like the world is against you.

In contrast, an abundance mindset allows you to see the world as a place full of opportunities and resources. You see possibilities where others see obstacles. By sharing your knowledge, time and resources with others, you are not losing, but sowing seeds of growth and prosperity.

Think of the metaphor of the glass half full and the glass half empty. When you have a scarcity mindset, you tend to see the glass as half empty and focus on how to prevent it from becoming even more empty. This keeps you in a state of constant tension and fear of loss. On the other hand, an abundance mentality leads you to see the glass as half full and ask how you can fill even more. You're looking for opportunities to add, expand and grow.

An abundance mentality is not about ignoring reality or denying challenges. Instead, it's about changing your focus and perspective. When you face problems, instead of thinking about how to minimize losses, you ask how you can learn from the experience, grow from it, and find creative solutions.

Ultimately, living with an abundance mindset allows you to experience life more fully and richly. It frees you from fear and anxiety and allows you to embrace opportunities with confidence and joy. As you practice gratitude and adopt a mentality of giving without expectations, you will not only be benefiting your own life, but also creating a positive impact on the world around you.

◆ ◆ ◆

When you have a scarcity mindset, you tend to see the glass as half empty and focus on how to prevent it from becoming even more empty. This keeps you in a state of constant tension and fear of loss. On the other hand, an abundance mentality leads you to see the glass as half full and wonder how you can fill it even more.

◆ ◆ ◆

CHAPTER 14: OVERCOMING PROCRASTINATION: TAKING ACTION IN THE MOMENT

One of the biggest obstacles to success: procrastination. Why do we tend to postpone important tasks? How to overcome this tendency to achieve a higher level of productivity and success in trading and life in general?

The Procrastination Trap

Procrastination is the tendency to postpone tasks despite being aware of their importance and urgency. Often, we find ourselves falling into this trap without even realizing it, letting tasks pile up and create stress and anxiety. But why do we procrastinate?

One of the main reasons behind procrastination is the avoidance of pain or effort associated with a task. Our brain tends to seek instant rewards and avoid uncomfortable situations. This can lead us to opt for more pleasant and less challenging activities instead of tackling tasks that require more effort.

Analysis Paralysis

Another common reason for procrastination is what is known as "analysis paralysis." Instead of taking action, we spend excessive time analyzing and planning, looking for the perfect way to approach a task. This pursuit of perfection can paralyze us and prevent us from acting at all.

The Five Minute Rule

An effective technique for overcoming procrastination is the "Five Minute Rule." The idea is that if a task can be completed in five minutes or less, you should do it immediately instead of putting it off. This can apply to small tasks like answering emails, organizing your workspace, or making a quick call.

Visualize The Future

A powerful technique to overcome procrastination is to visualize the future if you don't take action. Imagine the consequences of postponing an important task: stress, anxiety, and the possibility of missed opportunities. Also visualize how you would feel once you have completed the task. This vision can provide the motivation needed to act in the moment.

Divide And Conquer

Procrastination often occurs when a task is perceived as overwhelming. Instead of seeing it as one giant task, break it down into small chunks and focus on completing one chunk at a time. This makes the task seem more manageable and allows you to see steady progress, which in turn increases your motivation.

Celebrate Small Achievements

When you manage to overcome procrastination and complete an important task, don't hesitate to celebrate the achievement, no matter how small. Celebration reinforces the connection between effort and reward, which can further motivate you to take action in the future.

The Time Is Now

Procrastination only delays your goals and dreams. Time is a valuable and limited resource, and every moment you spend procrastinating is a moment you can't get back. Take advantage of each day to move towards your goals and dreams. Action in the moment is the key to overcoming procrastination and achieving the success you want.

Remember that every time you overcome procrastination, you are training your mind to take action instead of falling into patterns of avoidance. With determination and consistent practice, you can break the cycle of procrastination and begin to achieve your goals more effectively and more effectively and satisfactorily.

Tools To Overcome Procrastination

Set clear goals: Define specific and achievable goals. Having a clear goal will give you purpose and motivation to avoid procrastinating.

Create an action plan: Break your goals into smaller steps and create a detailed plan for each one. This makes tasks seem less overwhelming.

Use the Pomodoro technique: Work for 25 minutes on a task, then rest for 5 minutes. This technique encourages concentration and prevents the feeling of exhaustion.

Eliminate cognitive distortions: Identify and question the negative thoughts that lead you to procrastinate. Change your mindset to view tasks more positively.

Visualize success: Close your eyes and imagine how you would feel once you have completed the task. Visualizing the positive outcome can increase your motivation.

Set a deadline: Set a realistic time limit to complete a task. The sense of urgency can prompt you to act. No matter how simple the task may seem, it is essential that you set a deadline, because having many small tasks accumulated is even worse than having a single large task pending. Do not allow them to accumulate and for this it is important to act as soon as possible and if it warrants setting a deadline, do so.

Eliminate distractions: Turn off notifications, close unnecessary tabs, and create a distraction-free environment to increase your focus.

Use a to-do list: Write down the tasks you need to complete and cross them off as you go. Seeing your progress can be rewarding and motivating.

Rewards and self-compassion: Set rewards for yourself after completing tasks. And remember to be compassionate with yourself if you are having a less productive day.

Practice emotional self-regulation: Learn to manage your emotions and avoid using procrastination as a way to avoid stress or anxiety.

The Choice Is Yours

Ultimately, overcoming procrastination is a personal choice. Recognize that postponing only takes you away from your goals and prevents you from growing. The path to success requires effort and commitment. Don't let procrastination steal your time and opportunities; It is better to be terrified of being a failure and use that energy to act.

Remember that every small step you take brings you closer to your dreams. Harness the power of the present and start taking action today. Every time you face and overcome procrastination, you will be building a path to a more satisfying and successful life. What are you waiting for? The time to act is now!

CHAPTER 15: THE TRAP OF SELF-DECEPTION: FOCUSING ON QUALITY, NOT QUANTITY

A common trap we fall into: the self-deception of believing we are being productive when, in reality, we are dispersing our energy on half-finished tasks. Remember to strain your mind and ask yourself deep questions about your behavior, for example; discuss how a lack of focus can sabotage your progress and how you can overcome this habit to achieve truly effective and satisfying performance.

The False Sense Of Productivity

It is easy to fall into the trap of self-deception when we are surrounded by constant distractions. Spending hours on a task while constantly checking our phone, social media, or email makes us believe we are being productive. However, this scattered multitasking actually takes us away from the concentration and depth necessary to do meaningful work.

Quality Over Quantity

It is essential to recognize that spending time on a task does not guarantee a valuable result. Instead of measuring your productivity in terms of how much time you spend on a task, focus on the quality of the work you are producing. It is better to invest limited but focused time on a task and deliver a high-quality result than to spend hours doing a half-assed task.

Eliminate Distractions

To overcome this trap of self-deception, it is crucial to eliminate distractions that take us away from our main task. Turn off notifications, set specific times to check email or social media, and create a workspace free of distracting items.

The Importance Of Deep Focus

The "deep focus" technique involves dedicating a specific period of time (such as 90 minutes) to a task without interruptions. During this time, you completely immerse yourself in the task and avoid any distractions. This approach allows for more effective work and greater achievement in a short period.

The Power Of Total Concentration

When you dedicate yourself completely to a task, you immerse yourself in a state of flow, where concentration is maximum and performance is optimal. By eliminating distractions and focusing on the task at hand, you increase your efficiency and ability to achieve significant results in less time.

◆ ◆ ◆

Spending time concentrating on an activity and not being focused is the same as nothing

◆ ◆ ◆

The Reward Of Authentic Productivity

By overcoming the trap of self-deception and adopting a quality-focused mindset, you will experience a sense of genuine achievement. Instead of filling your time with superficial tasks, you'll commit to creating impactful and valuable work. This change in your focus will not only improve your productivity, but will also increase your confidence and satisfaction in what you do.

The Decision To Focus On What Is Important

The choice to focus on quality and focus is yours. Don't let self-deception trick you into thinking that being busy equals being productive. Choose to invest your time and energy in meaningful tasks and achieving results that really matter. By doing so, you will be building a solid foundation for success and personal fulfillment.

Practical Tools To Overcome The Trap Of Self-Deception

Set clear goals: Define clear and specific objectives for your tasks. Knowing what you want to achieve will help you stay focused and avoid distractions.

Create a conducive work environment: Designate a workspace free of distractions. Keep your environment tidy and eliminate elements that distract you.

Prioritize tasks: Identify the most important and urgent tasks and focus on them first. Avoid falling into the trap of trivial tasks that make you feel busy but provide no real value.

Turn off notifications: Turn off notifications on your devices while you work on a task. This will help you avoid the temptation to constantly check your phone or social media.

Set review times: Designate specific times of the day to check emails and social media. Avoid interrupting your work to respond to each notification.

Practice mindfulness: Practicing it will help you be present in the task at hand instead of wandering into scattered thoughts. This will improve your focus and productivity.

Eliminate parallel tasks: Avoid performing multiple tasks at the same time. Instead, focus on one task at a time to achieve higher quality results.

Set rest time: Schedule moments of rest rest and disconnection between your work blocks. This will help you recharge and stay focused.

The Power Of Quality And Focus

Overcoming the trap of self-deception requires a change in mindset and constant practice. By choosing quality over quantity and focus over distraction, you are taking control of your time and effort. Remember that time is a valuable and limited resource. Instead of fooling yourself with half-assed tasks, choose to invest it in activities that bring you closer to your goals and give you a genuine sense of achievement. By doing so, you will be on your way to a more productive, satisfying, and meaningful life.

Real Life Examples

Imagine an Olympic athlete who is preparing for an important competition. When it's time to train, there's no room for self-deception. He knows that his performance in the competition depends on the quality of his training. If you decide to train half-heartedly, just because you want to feel good about yourself, you will be sacrificing your performance and your chances of success.

This athlete understands the importance of every repetition, every movement and every effort. He knows that every day of training counts and that there is no time to waste on distractions or poorly performed tasks. When he is on the training ground, he is fully committed, focused and 100% dedicated.He doesn't let self-deception get in the way of excellence.

Another example is a musician who is rehearsing for a concert. He knows that if he doesn't fully focus on his practice and strive for perfection in every note, his performance on stage could suffer. Therefore, when you sit at your instrument, you completely immerse yourself in the music, blocking out distractions and striving to constantly improve.

These examples illustrate, as in any area of life, that focus and dedication are essential to achieving success. When it comes to achieving your financial, personal or professional goals, there is no room for self-deception. If you are committed to improving, growing, and overcoming your limitations, you must adopt a mindset of excellence and let go of half-hearted activities that only give you a false sense of achievement.

Life is too short to waste it on incomplete tasks and distractions. Choose to face your responsibilities and challenges with an attitude of 100% commitment and focus. Only through total dedication will you be able to achieve your goals and experience a true sense of achievement and satisfaction.

Remember that overcoming self-deception and procrastination is a gradual process. It requires patience, practice and commitment to yourself. By adopting tools like those mentioned and cultivating a mindset of focus and dedication, you will be on the path to a higher level of productivity, achievement and satisfaction in all areas of your life.

Live Without Regrets: Give Your Best

Living without regrets is a deep aspiration that many people have. However, few understand that the key to achieving this is giving one's best in every task and challenge we face. If you decide to give yourself with total concentration and effort, regardless of the end result, you will ensure that you will have no regrets. If you achieve it, it will be a triumph. If you don't make it, at least you'll know that you gave it your all.

Imagine that you are in a stadium full of expectations, facing a challenge that you can only overcome if you give your best. It could be a sports game, a presentation at work or a trading operation. If you decide to put all your concentration, passion, and effort into that task, you have already won an internal victory, regardless of the external result.

In contrast, if you deceive yourself, if you settle for doing things half-heartedly, if you allow procrastination and lack of concentration to dominate your focus, you will be in constant internal conflict. You will know that you could have done better and that your performance was below your potential. In this case, regret will be inevitable.

Living without regrets means that every day, every task, every challenge is an opportunity to prove to yourself your ability to do your best. If you manage to internalize this mentality and apply it to all areas of your life, including trading, you will be on a constant path of improvement and growth. You will be your own judge and your own motivator, and you will be able to face any challenge with confidence and pride.

Remember: the battlefield is your mind and only you have the power to direct your thoughts, your actions and your efforts. Don't let self-deception and mediocrity keep you from your goals. Live each day with the satisfaction of knowing that you did your best, regardless of the outcome, and build a life full of achievement, satisfaction, and true pride.

These tools led me to finish this book. I spent years putting it off precisely because I was deceiving myself and procrastinating until I decided to put an end to that and managed to finish it. This does not mean that I no longer procrastinate on some things, nor does it mean that I do everything well, but thanks to these tools I began to control my life.

Keep in mind that all famous people, elite athletes, great fund managers, investors, millionaires, absolutely everyone, have a daily battle with themselves and they are all human even if some do not seem like it. Losers are not those who have weaknesses, losers are those who give up. The biggest fight is with yourself, start little by little by conquering the cerebral territory and turning it into a winning territory, put the winner's flag in every corner of your brain and only then will you conquer your dreams.

CHAPTER 16: FORGING A WINNING MINDSET: A GUIDE TO SUCCESS IN TRADING AND LIFE

We come to the end of our journey through the complexities of trading and the human mind. You have walked the path of self-discipline, responsibility, emotional management and positive mindset. In each chapter, you've explored the secrets and tools to build a winning mindset that propels you toward success in trading and in life. Now, in this last chapter, I will try to unify everything you have learned into a practical guide so that you can implement it and transform yourself into the trader and person you want to be.

Step 1: Put your lazy mind to work

The parable of the lemon. Do you remember how something as simple as a lemon taught us to see beyond the obvious? To question our assumptions and think outside the box? This story contains a valuable reminder that our mind is a powerful tool, capable of transforming our perception and reality if we dare to look beyond the superficial.

Step 2: Self-knowledge and acceptance

Before you can build a winning mindset, you must know yourself. Recognize your strengths and weaknesses, your emotional patterns and your reactions to stress. Accept that you are human and that making mistakes is part of growing up. Destructive self-criticism will only hold you back. Instead, use your mistakes as opportunities to learn and improve.

Step 3: Define your objectives and action plan

Set clear and achievable goals for your trading career and your life in general. What do you want to achieve? How do you plan to get there? Break down your goals into specific, realistic actions. Remember, a plan without action is just a wish.

Step 4: Abundance and Gratitude Mindset

Cultivate an abundance mentality in all aspects of your life. Abandon the mentality of scarcity and envy. Practice gratitude daily, focusing on what you have instead of what you lack. Positive thinking will strengthen you in the face of challenges and allow you to see opportunities instead of obstacles.

Step 5: Emotional control and risk management

Learn to manage your emotions. Identify your emotional triggers and develop techniques to stay calm in stressful situations. Establish clear risk management rules and follow them rigorously. Your capital is your most valuable tool; Protect it at all costs.

Step 6: The mathematics in trading

Who would have thought that numbers and calculations could be such powerful allies in financial decision making? We have discovered how sound capital management, based on data and probability, can make the difference between success and failure in trading. Put the numbers in your favor.

Step 7: Continuing Education

Learning is an investment in yourself. Stay up to date with changes in the markets, acquire new knowledge and skills. Consider education as a constant process, similar to tuning a musical instrument. As you learn, you become more fine-tuned and precise in your decisions.

Step 8: Discipline and Eliminate Procrastination

Discipline is the backbone of a winning mentality. Eliminate procrastination by adopting solid work habits. Break your tasks into manageable steps and set realistic schedules and deadlines. Do it even when you don't feel like it; Constant action will lead you to success.

Step 9: Face challenges objectively

Face challenges objectively. Put aside hope blind and illusion. Analyze situations with concrete information and real data. Make decisions based on facts, not wishes. Learn to deal with uncertainty by staying calm and focusing on the big picture.

Step 10: Persistence and continuous improvement

The path to success is not linear. There will be ups and downs, failures and moments of doubt. However, persistence is key. Use every failure as an opportunity to learn and grow. Continuous improvement is a path that never ends. Keep your standards high and work to constantly improve yourself.

Step 11: Visualization and focus on the present

Visualization connects you to your goals and gives you the right mindset to achieve them. But don't be left alone in the future. Practice mindfulness and focusing on the present. Take advantage of every moment to make informed and conscious decisions.

Step 12: Stay proud of your career

Finally, celebrate your progress. No matter how small the steps you have taken, each one is an achievement in itself. Look back and admire the path you have traveled. There will always be challenges, but with a winning mentality you have all the tools to overcome them.

This book has been your guide to developing a winning mindset in trading and in life. It is not an easy path nor a quick fix, but it's a worthwhile trip. Now it's your turn to take the reins and apply these teachings in your daily life. No matter what stage you are at, you can take steps toward a stronger, more confident, and successful version of yourself.

Remember, success is not measured only in monetary gains, but in the personal growth you experience along the way. Every time you make an informed decision instead of an impulsive one, every time you approach a challenge calmly and determinedly, every time you strive to improve, you are building your winning mindset.

So go ahead, dare to forget a winning mentality that transcends trading and becomes the foundation of your life. Become the leader of your thoughts and actions. At the end of the day, remember that you have the power to write your own success story. Get started today!

I want to take a moment to express my gratitude for accompanying me on this journey throughout these pages full of reflections, tips and tools to develop a winning mindset. I know that at times it may have seemed like I have repeated certain concepts and I apologize if that has been the case. My intention has been clear: I want these ideas to penetrate deeply into your mind and heart.

Understand that the biggest enemy of your success is

yourself. But we also know that you are capable of overcoming your own barriers, which is why I have tried to provide you with a variety of perspectives and techniques to address each aspect of the winning mindset. I value your time and effort, and I have worked hard so that every word has a purpose; a reason to be here.

I know that in this age of distractions and multitasking, it can be challenging to stop and reflect on these issues. But remember that life is short and time is an invaluable resource. Just as you have taken the time to read this book, I encourage you to take the time to apply these lessons to your life. Not only in your trading, but in all areas of your existence.

The time you spend improving your mindset, cultivating self-discipline, practicing gratitude, and facing your challenges with courage will not only benefit your financial results, but will also enrich your life overall. It's not just about making more money, but about being a better version of yourself, being happy and making the people around you happy.

So, once again, thank you for being part of this journey. I urge you to not only read these words, but internalize them and put them into action. Success does not come by accident; It is built through conscious choices and coherent actions. You have the power to transform your mindset and, ultimately, your destiny. Go ahead, forge your path to a full and successful life!

If you have questions, concerns, or simply want to share your thoughts on the content you have read, I want you to know that I am here for you. You can follow me on my social networks, where I share additional content, reflections and practical tips for trading and personal development. Don't hesitate to contact me, although sometimes it may take a little time to respond due to my commitments and responsibilities. I always respond.

I also invite you to share your comments and experiences regarding this book. Your opinion is valuable and can help other readers discover and benefit from these ideas. If you have found value in these pages, I would greatly appreciate it if you would share your testimony online, on social media or on review platforms. Together, we can bring these teachings to more people and help build a community of traders and people seeking success and fulfillment in their lives.

Remember, the path to success is not just a matter of technical analysis or complicated strategies. The real difference lies in the way you face challenges, how you manage your emotions, and the mindset with which you approach each situation. I am convinced that you have acquired the necessary tools to forge a winning mentality, a mentality that will lead you to conquer your goals and achieve your dreams.

Thank you again for joining me on this journey. I wish you all the success and happiness you deserve. Let's continue growing together and building a bright future!

CHAPTER 17: MY COMMITMENT. MY GIFT

We're almost done, but first I'll give you three gifts.

A contract that you must print, read and sign if you agree. The important thing is that when you sign it you are 100% in agreement and committed to complying with it to the letter, it is valid whether you want to add or remove it. The only one you are going to defraud or deceive if you don't comply is you.

I'm also going to give you an idea of an Excel template that you can use to keep track of your trading operations daily, weekly and monthly. Very simple, of course it is just an idea, you can add or remove information as you see fit to make it more comfortable for you, but it is essential that it is that or another that you use, that way you get used to keeping track of your operations , with as much detail as possible. And remember that if you control it, you manage it.

And last but not least; I will give you an idea of a diary for your operations, this diary is focused on your thoughts, sensations, emotions, especially in creating habits that help you meet your goals and maintain a winning mind. Remember that your goals should be clear, broken down into steps and, if possible, printed in plain sight. This template can help you identify patterns in your emotions and thoughts before and after trading. It will allow you to keep an objective record of your mental and emotional state, which in turn can help you make more informed decisions in the future and improve your trading performance.

Commitment Letter For Success In Trading And In Life

Place, _____

I, _____, take the pen and this paper to commit to myself to live a life full of success, meaning and passion. I understand that the key to achieving my dreams and goals lies in my mind and my attitude towards life. I have learned valuable lessons on how to master my mind and develop a winning mindset. Now, I am committed to applying these lessons in my daily life.

Abundance mentality: I accept that the abundance mentality is my ally in trading and in life. I will let go of the scarcity mentality and instead adopt an attitude of gratitude and generosity. I am determined to see opportunities where others see obstacles.

Eliminating procrastination: I recognize that procrastination is an enemy of success. I promise to eliminate the distractions and focus on my goals with determination and discipline. Each day, I will dedicate significant time to my goals.

Maintain passion and motivation: I understand that living without passion is like being dead in life. I promise to keep my passion alive, remembering my goals and actively working towards them. I will strive to maintain my motivation and determination, even in difficult times.

Constantly learn and grow: I take responsibility for my own growth. I am committed to constantly learning new skills and gaining knowledge. I understand that continuing education is essential for success in trading and in life.

Mastery of mind and emotions: I assume control of my thoughts and emotions. I will practice self-awareness and emotional management. I will not let fear, doubt or negativity stop me. From now on fear will be my best ally.

Accept Responsibility: I accept full responsibility for my actions and decisions. I will stop blaming others or circumstances. I will learn from my mistakes and use them as a springboard to success.

Commitment to Excellence: I will seek excellence in everything I do. I will not settle for mediocrity. I will look for opportunities to improve and grow in every aspect of my life.

Money management and risk: I understand the importance of money management in trading. I commit to following a sound risk management plan and not to get carried away by hope or the illusion.

Money: I commit to love money, to understand that it is a very powerful energy that moves the world and that by working with it and not for it, I will achieve my goals and help my loved ones achieve theirs.

Practice gratitude: Each day, I will reflect on the things I am grateful for. I will practice gratitude as a way to maintain a positive mindset.

Contribute to others: I understand that true wealth comes from giving and contributing to others. I am committed to helping and supporting those around me whenever I can.

Be happy: I commit to value every minute of my life, to be happy and make my loved ones happy, happiness multiplies, it is contagious like laughter. I will always prefer to spread laughter than tears.

Zero regrets: I commit to preferring to run the risk of being wrong than to run the risk of not doing it and live with regrets.

I sign this commitment with determination and conviction. I know that by doing so, I am taking responsibility for my own life and success. I am determined to live a life full of purpose, achievement and happiness.

Signature:_____

Name:_____

Date: _____

Template Idea To Keep Track Of Your Operations

			Mes _____				
Análisis de operaciones manuales, 1era semana: ____ al _____ . Riesgo por operación 0,3%.							
Número	Fecha	Activo	Long	Short	Resultado	Riesgo/Beneficio	Resultado en %
1	03-XX-20XX	USDCAD		1	TP	1/3	0,90%
2	03-XX-20XX	AUDUSD	1		SL		-0,30%
3	03-XX-20XX	GBPUSD	1		SL		-0,30%
4	03-XX-20XX	AUDUSD		1	N/A		0,00%
5							0,00%
							0,30%
				Resultados:	0,30%		

Month

Analysis of monthly transactions, from 1st week....... up to .... Risk for transaction 0,3%

Number Date Asset Long Short Result Risk/benefit Result in %

Results.

Análisis de operaciones manuales. 2da semana: ____ al _____ . Riesgo por operación 0,3%.

Número	Fecha	Activo	Long	Short	Resultado	R/B	Resultado en %
1	07-0X-20XX	AUDUSD	1		SL	3	-0,30%
2	07-0X-20XX	AUDUSD	1		TP	3	0,90%
3	08-0X-20XX	AUDUSD	1		SL	3	-0,30%
4	08-0X-20XX	AUDUSD		1	SL	3	-0,30%
5	08-0X-20XX	AUDUSD		1	BE	3	0,00%
6	09-0X-20XX	AUDUSD		1	SL	3	-0,30%
7	09-0X-20XX	AUDUSD		1	TP	3	0,90%
8	10-0X-20XX	AUDUSD	1		SL	3	-0,30%
9						3	0,00%
							0,30%
					Resultados:	0,30%	

Month

Analysis of monthly transactions, from 2nd week....... up to .... Risk for transaction 0,3 %

Number Date   Asset   Long Short Result   Risk/benefit Result in %

Results.

Número	Fecha	Activo	Long	Short	Resultado	R/B	Resultado en %
	Análisis de operaciones manuales. 3ra semana: ____ al _____ . Riesgo por operación 0,3%.						
1	14-0X-20XX	AUDUSD		1	TP	3	1,20%
2	17-0X-20XX	AUDUSD		1	SL	3	-0,30%
3	17-0X-20XX	AUDUSD		1	TP	3	0,90%
4	18-0X-20XX	AUDUSD		1	N/A	3	0,00%
5						3	0,00%
							1,80%
				Resultados:	1,80%		

Month

Analysis of monthly transactions, from 3rd week....... up to .... Risk for transaction 0,3 %

Number   Date   Asset   Long   Short   Result   Risk/benefit   Result in %

Results

Analysis of the month

Month_____
1st week
2nd week
3rd week
4th week
Results

Results in %
0,30%
0,30%
1,80%
0,00%
2,40%

Análisis de operaciones manuales. 4ta semana: ____ al _____ . Riesgo por operación 0,3%.

Número	Fecha	Activo	Long	Short	Resultado	R/B	Resultado en %
1	21-0X-20XX	GBPJPY		1	BE	3	0,00%
2	25-0X-20XX	AUDUSD	1		N/A	3	0,00%
3						3	0,00%
							0,00%
				Resultados:		0,00%	

Month

Analysis of monthly transactions, from 4th week....... up to .... Risk for transaction 0,3 %

Number Date   Asset   Long Short Result Risk/benefit Result in %

Results
TP: Take profit
SL: Stop loss
BE: Break even
N/A: No asset

Recording Sheet For Emotions And Thoughts In Trading

Date: _____

Before Operating:

Mood: Rate your mood on a scale of 1 to 10, where 1 is very negative and 10 is very positive.

No.: _____

Brief detail of your state of mind: _____

_____

_____

_____

Dominant emotions: Write down the emotions you feel most intensely (example: anxiety, confidence, fear, euphoria).

What is the name of your emotion?: _____

Predominant thoughts: Record the thoughts that are occupying your mind before trading (example: "I think this trade will be successful", "I am afraid of losing money").

What thoughts are going through your mind? Detail them: _____

_____

_____

Stress level: Rate your stress level on a scale of 1 to 10, where 1 is very relaxed and 10 is very stressed.

No. _____

How many habits have I made before operating. (example: I meditated, exercised, did conscious breathing, read for 15 minutes, among others).

Describe your rituals that you do before trading that make

you feel in control: _____
_____
_____

After Operation:

Did I stick to my trading plan? There are no grays here, it is "YES or NO".

Yeah:___

No:___   Why   not?_____
_____

Did I fulfill my operational plan? There are no grays here, it is "YES or NO".

Yeah:___

No:___ Why not?_____
_____
_____

Trade result: Write down whether the trade was successful, losing or neutral.

Positive: _____

Negative: _____

Break even: _____

Mood after surgery: Rate your mood after surgery on a scale of 1 to 10.

No.:_____

Brief detail of your state of mind: _____
_____
_____

Emotions experienced: Record the emotions you felt after the operation (example: relief, frustration, joy).

What is the name of your emotion?:_____

Afterthoughts: Write down the thoughts that come to your

mind after closing the trade (example: "I am proud of my decision", "I should have waited longer").

What thoughts are going through your mind? Detail them:
_____
_____
_____

Learnings: Reflect on what you learned from this day of trading, regardless of whether it was successful or not.

What have I learned? _____
_____
_____

Additional Notes (Optional): _____
_____
_____

Brainstorm to be better tomorrow, talk freely to yourself. You have all the answers you need in your hands and in your mind. You are the only hero, winner and champion you need. You are the owner and in control of your life:
_____
_____
_____
_____
_____

ACKNOWLEDGMENTS

I want to express a deep gratitude to all the people who have been a fundamental part of the creation of this book. Your support, your words of encouragement and your trust have been a fundamental pillar in this journey of self-discovery and personal growth.

First of all, I want to dedicate a special thank you to my parents, who have always been by my side, giving me their unconditional love and constant support. Their dedication and sacrifice have been an inspiring example to me, and this book is a testament to their positive influence on my life.

To my beloved wife Laura, I want to express my gratitude for being my life partner, my unwavering support, and my constant source of inspiration. Her discipline, which I have always admired, has encouraged me to be better and more disciplined with my goals. Her love and understanding have been fundamental pillars on my path.

To Ludoberto Bravo, for helping me with his comments. To my friends and fellow traders, who have shared experiences, knowledge and moments of reflection with me, I sincerely thank them. Their unique perspectives and exchanges have enriched this book and pushed me to grow as an individual and as a trader.

To my editor and proofreader Mariam Ramírez, who has helped me with her professionalism and patience so that this book could be completed. I would like to thank and make a special mention to Viviana Rousseaux for helping me with the translation of this book.

I cannot fail to mention all the people who in one way or another have contributed to this process, from providing valuable advice to offering words of encouragement in moments of doubt. Each of them has left a mark on this book and on my heart.

This book is the result of a collective effort and I am grateful for every person who has been a part of it. Every word written, every reflection shared, and every idea expressed has been guided by the positive influence of those around me.

To you, I want to thank you for taking the time to explore these pages and for opening yourself to the ideas and reflections presented here. My wish is that you find inspiration, guidance and valuable tools to cultivate a winning mentality, both in trading and in all areas of your life.

Thank you for being part of this journey. Let's continue growing together and building a future full of success, happiness and fulfillment!

www.ingramcontent.com/pod-product-compliance
Lightning Source LLC
Chambersburg PA
CBHW071158240526
45470CB00017B/294

Sommaire :

1. LES LEVIERS POUR CRÉER UNE MARQUE FORTE
2. L'IDENTITÉ DE LA MARQUE
3. LES ARCHITECTURES DE MARQUE
4. LE STATUT DE LA MARQUE ET SON ÉVOLUTION
5. LES DIFFÉRENTS DISCOURS DE LA MARQUE : LE MAPING SÉMIOTIQUE
6. LES STRATÉGIES D'UN DÉVELOPPEMENT EFFICACE
7. L'IMPORTANCE DE LA MARQUE DANS LA COMMUNICATION DE L'ENTREPRISE
8. L'AUDIT DE LA MARQUE

1. LES LEVIERS POUR CRÉER UNE MARQUE FORTE

LE RÔLE DE LA MARQUE DANS LES MARCHÉS SATURÉS

L'OFFRE PLÉTHORIQUE

TABLEAU DE PHILIP KOTLER

Le tableau de Philip Kotler

Années	Demande # Offre	Type de Marketing
50 - 60	D > O	MKT de Prod.
60 - 70	D ≥ O	MKT Cial.
70 - 80	D = O	MKT de l'Offre
80 – 90	D ≤ O	MKT de Distri.
90 - 2000	D < O	One to One MKT
2000 ...	D < O	Permission MKT

Les axes de positionnement du Permission Marketing

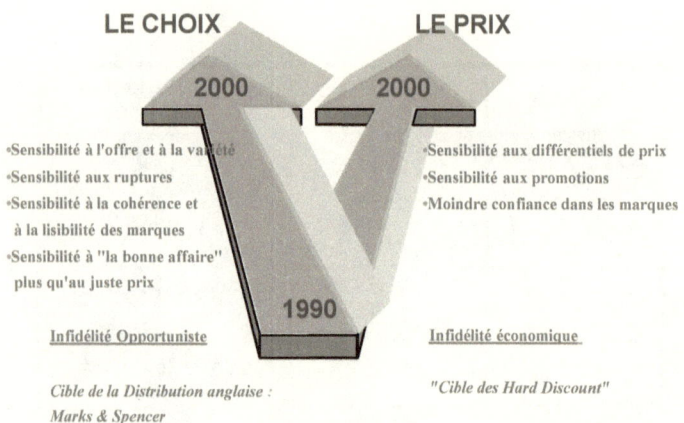

LE CHOIX **LE PRIX**

2000 2000

- Sensibilité à l'offre et à la variété
- Sensibilité aux ruptures
- Sensibilité à la cohérence et à la lisibilité des marques
- Sensibilité à "la bonne affaire" plus qu'au juste prix

- Sensibilité aux différentiels de prix
- Sensibilité aux promotions
- Moindre confiance dans les marques

1990

<u>Infidélité Opportuniste</u> <u>Infidélité économique</u>

Cible de la Distribution anglaise : Marks & Spencer *"Cible des Hard Discount"*

Une situation différente selon la maturation des économies

- En analysant le tableau de Kotler, il va de soi qu'on ne pratiquera pas le même marketing selon que l'on se trouve en haut du tableau ou en bas.
- Les pays émergents comme la Chine ou l'Inde se trouvent en haut du tableau :
    - On y pratiquera un marketing de production.
- Les ex-pays de l'Est comme la Pologne au milieu :
    - On y pratiquera un marketing de l'offre comme on devait le faire dans nos pays dans les années 70/80.
- Et nos pays à économies avancées en bas :
    - On y pratiquera du Permission Marketing avec ses deux axes.

LES VALEURS
POUR LE CONSOMMATEUR

Relations entre l'analyse macro économique du tableau de Kotler et l'analyse micro comportementale issue de la Pyramide de Maslow

- Pour les marketeurs désormais, il y a une relation entre l'analyse de l'offre effectuée à partie du tableau de Kotler et l'analyse des comportements faite à partir de la Pyramide de Maslow.

La Pyramide de Maslow

La Pyramide de Maslow

- Selon la théorie des "motivationistes ", les besoins et les motivations expliquent le comportement d'un individu. L'analyse des valeurs, plus récente, renforce ce cadre théorique.
    - Le **besoin** correspond à une situation inconfortable, provoquée par un état de manque physiologique (faim, soif ...) ou psychologique (affection, reconnaissance ...).
    - La **motivation** est une force qui pousse à l'action, déclenchée par un besoin impérieux. Le contraire d'une motivation est un **frein**.
    - Les **valeurs** sont de grands principes ou des croyances fondamentales permettant d'évaluer une situation (voire une personne) ou de justifier une action. Elles sont innées ou forgées par l'entourage ou l'éducation, mais sont indépendantes de la situation.

La Pyramide de Maslow

- Un besoin peut être conscient ou inconscient.
- Dans le premier cas, le consommateur est capable de l'exprimer spontanément.
- Dans le second cas, le besoin est latent. Sa verbalisation est délicate.
- Tous les besoins ne se transforment pas en motivation : ils doivent atteindre un niveau critique pour que l'individu agisse. En effet, le consommateur, confronté à un nombre illimité de besoins, ne peut à chaque fois satisfaire ses besoins par un achat. Il arbitre selon ses propres priorités que le marketing doit identifier.

Le fonctionnement du cerveau

Les scientifiques nous donnent des clefs pour comprendre et adapter nos comportements.

Le quotient émotionnel
par David Servan-Schreiber,
neuro-psychiâtre, chercheur, écrivain…
Des découvertes surprenantes et utiles !

Sources et mécanismes émotionnels

Le quotient émotionnel (David Servan-Schreiber)

- On a tendance à penser que les gens intelligents, ceux dont le Q.I. est élevé nous sont supérieurs et qu'ils réussissent mieux que nous. On peut en fait se demander si le Q.I. est vraiment déterminant.
- Il semble que le Q.I. n'ait finalement pas autant d'importance. Ce qui semble déterminer le succès des gens en société, ce n'est pas tant la puissance de leur intellect que leur capacité à :
  - Communiquer avec les autres ;
  - À évaluer les situations sociales et émotionnelles ;
  - À contrôler leurs émotions, à ne pas céder à la colère, à inhiber leur agressivité ;
  - À émettre les signaux émotionnels appropriés ;
  - À rester en phase avec les autres et à naviguer harmonieusement sur les flots des relations humaines autour d'eux. "

Sources et mécanismes émotionnels

Le quotient émotionnel (David Servan-Schreiber)

"Bien sûr, c'est ce que nous essayons d'apprendre à nos enfants à l'école : "l'esprit d'équipe" et le reste... Mais il n'y a effectivement que ceux qui le comprennent et qui apprennent à capitaliser là-dessus qui gagnent et qui font gagner leur équipe.

C'est tout cela que l'on désigne par quotient émotionnel par opposition au quotient intellectuel, le Q.E. au lieu du Q.I.

Il se trouve que c'est le Q.E. qui détermine la réussite sociale, beaucoup plus que le Q.I. qui ne permet de prédire que la performance scolaire et qui se limite à cela."

Sources et mécanismes émotionnels

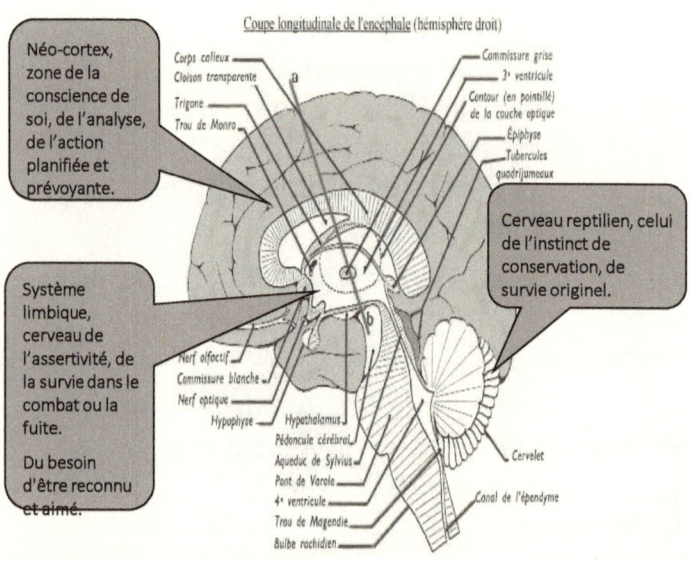

Suivant le chercheur
Paul Mac Lean,
spécialiste du cerveau

Les pulsions

- Les pulsions sont à l'origine de tout acte. On peut les définir comme une poussée énergétique et motrice qui met en marche l'individu vers un but.
- Le plus souvent, elles sont liées à notre cerveau limbique.

Les besoins

- On trouve leurs fondements dans le domaine corporel, lorsque l'individu ressent un décalage entre un état actuel et un état souhaité.
- Ils se traduisent par un état de manque d'une nature et d'une intensité variable.
- Pour activer la pulsion, le déséquilibre doit générer une intensité forte.

Les besoins humains

LA PYRAMIDE DES BESOINS HUMAINS (MASLOW) 5 GRANDES CATÉGORIES

- **Physiologiques** :
    - Liés à la survie de l'individu,
    - Faim / soif / se réchauffer…
- **Sécurité** :
    - Sécurité d'un abri (logement, maison),
    - Sécurité des revenus et des ressources,
    - Sécurité physique contre la violence, délinquance, agressions…
    - Sécurité morale et psychologique,
    - Sécurité affective,
    - Sécurité médicale,
    - Sociale et de santé.
- **Appartenance / affection** :
    - L'homme, animal social
    - Se sentir accepté/aimé par sa famille/son groupe →club /association/parti …

Les besoins humains

- **Estime/reconnaissance** :
  - Être estimé par soi-même/par les autres,
  - Respect de soi, respect que semblent vous porter les autres,
  - Rôle social,
- **S'accomplir/Spiritualité** :
  - Sommet des aspirations humaines.
- **Besoins hiérarchisés**
  - Passer de N-1 à N quand le besoin est satisfait.

Les désirs

- Les désirs correspondent à l'image mentale interne qui répond à la pulsion.
- En réalité, c'est une modalité particulière de satisfaction d'un besoin parmi toutes celles qui auraient pu répondre à la satisfaction du désir.
- L'inverse du désir est la répulsion.

Les motivations

La notion de "besoin" n'est pas assez élaborée pour permettre de construire un modèle de comportement d'achat.

D'où le concept de motivation :

"État de tension mettant l'organisme en mouvement jusqu'à ce qu'il ait réduit la tension". (Guy SERRAF)

"Buts que l'on s'assigne pour réduire un état de tension". (Howard)

Les motivations

CLASSEMENT DES MOTIVATIONS SELON LEUR CARACTÈRE PLUS OU MOINS INNÉ (PRIMAIRES VS SECONDAIRES OU "ACQUISES")

➡ **Association des motivations avec des " stimuli " :**

    transformer en besoin actif

    symbole ou signe : Pavlov/réflexe conditionné

➡ **Conflits entre différentes motivations :**

    assurance sur la vie → affection famille

    envisager sa propre disparition → son besoin sécurité : assurance

➡ **Détection et mesure des motivations :**

    choix ou non → indique indice des motivations

Les attitudes

Tendance ou prédisposition de l'individu à évaluer d'une certaine manière un objet et à réagir face à lui :

⇨ VARIABLE INTERMÉDIAIRE, CAR LA RELATION DIRECTE ENTRE MOTIVATION ET COMPORTEMENT N'EST PAS SUFFISAMMENT EXPLICATIVE.

2 . L'IDENTITÉ DE LA MARQUE

Le consommateur face au Mur du Choix
La matrice d'explication des valeurs de la marque
Les facettes de l'identité de la marque

COMMENT CRÉER UNE MARQUE FORTE ?

Le rôle de la marque dans la transaction d'achat

- Pour comprendre comment fonctionne classiquement une marque dans le processus de choix, prenons la place du consommateur dans l'épreuve du supermarché.
- Ce processus comporte six étapes :
    - LE BESOIN
    - LA CONFRONTATION AU MUR DU CHOIX
    - L'ÉVALUATION DES PROPOSITIONS
    - LE CHOIX DU PRODUIT
    - L'EXPÉRIMENTATION DU PRODUIT
    - LA POSTÉVALUATION

Le rôle de la marque dans la transaction d'achat

- Étape 1 : le besoin
    - Il peut être conscient ou latent, l'offre produit pouvant aussi le créer ou le révéler.
    - *Imaginons par exemple que sur notre liste de courses figure l'article* **dentifrice.**
- Étape 2 : la confrontation au mur du choix
    - Face à la profusion, le consommateur se retrouve confronté à une difficulté majeure : identifier la proposition susceptible de satisfaire au mieux son besoin.
    - *Nous nous trouvons maintenant dans notre magasin, or le rayon* **dentifrice** *ne compte pas moins* **de 50 références.**
- Étape 3 : l'évaluation des propositions
    - Devant ce mur, le consommateur est contraint d'effectuer un travail d'analyse important en tentant **d'évaluer les propositions a priori** selon l'ensemble des paramètres observables (d'où l'importance des packagings) ou bien de faire appel à son expérience passée ou encore aux conseils de son entourage.
    - *Nous disposons de moins de 5 minutes pour faire notre choix de dentifrice et nous réalisons que les marques proposent toutes quelque chose de différent : anti-caries, antitartre, dents sensibles, antitaches, blancheur, haleine, goût menthol, fraise, tube avec bouchon, doseur pression, flacon souple... et tout ça plus ou moins cher. Que choisir ?*

Le rôle de la marque dans la transaction d'achat

- **Étape 4 : le choix du produit**
  - Nous arrivons à l'arbitrage : la décision finale qui va conduire le consommateur à s'approprier un produit et sa marque.
  - *Vademecum, Colgate, Aquafresh, Fluoryl, Signal Plus, Sanogyl, Sensodyne, Ultrabrite, Denivit, Teraxyl, Tonygencil... devant l'embarras du choix et sur la base de son analyse préliminaire, le consommateur se lance et achète.*
- **Étape 5 : l'expérimentation du produit**
  - C'est le verdict : une plus ou moins grande satisfaction (éventuellement comparativement au prix payé).
  - *" Le goût n'est pas terrible", "très pratique, ce doseur", "au moins çà fait tout", "j'adore la fraîcheur", "j'aime bien, c'est comme dans la pub".*
- **Étape 6: la postévaluation**
  - Le consommateur associe directement son jugement à la marque et au produit et requalifie éventuellement leur classement initial dans son répertoire mental d'achat.
  - *"Je le garde", "il faudra que j'en essaye un autre" "tous les mêmes, la prochaine fois je prends le moins cher".*

Le rôle de la marque dans la transaction d'achat

- En cas de postévaluation positive du produit, lorsqu'il sera à nouveau confronté au mur du choix le consommateur pourra utiliser la marque pour éviter l'étape 3, la plus difficile. Il pourra alors grâce à elle repérer directement le produit ayant précédemment optimisé son besoin.

- Cette recherche d'économie est caractéristique des boucles d'apprentissage de l'intelligence humaine. Imaginons qu'à chaque fois que nous devons faire les courses nous ayons à réévaluer méthodiquement l'ensemble de l'offre?

Le rôle de la marque dans la transaction d'achat

- LE **RACCOURCI DE LA MARQUE** A DONC POUR EFFET DE DÉVELOPPER RAPIDEMENT LES DIMENSIONS DE CONFIANCE ET DE FIDÉLITÉ QUI SOUS-TENDENT LE RACHAT.

- C'EST ALORS L'HABITUDE QUI PREND LE RELAIS, PERMETTANT À NOTRE CONSOMMATEUR DE RÉSERVER SES RESSOURCES INTELLECTUELLES À D'AUTRES ARBITRAGES PLUS ESSENTIELS POUR LUI.

- AINSI POUR CONVAINCRE UN CONSOMMATEUR DE BIEN VOULOIR MODIFIER LES LIENS QU'IL A ÉTABLIS AVEC UNE MARQUE, IL FAUT NON SEULEMENT ÊTRE VU, PLAIRE, AVOIR DES ARGUMENTS PERSUASIFS, MAIS AUSSI ARRIVER À CONTRER L'HABITUDE, CE QUI N'EST PAS TOUJOURS LE PLUS FACILE.

Le rôle de la marque dans la transaction d'achat

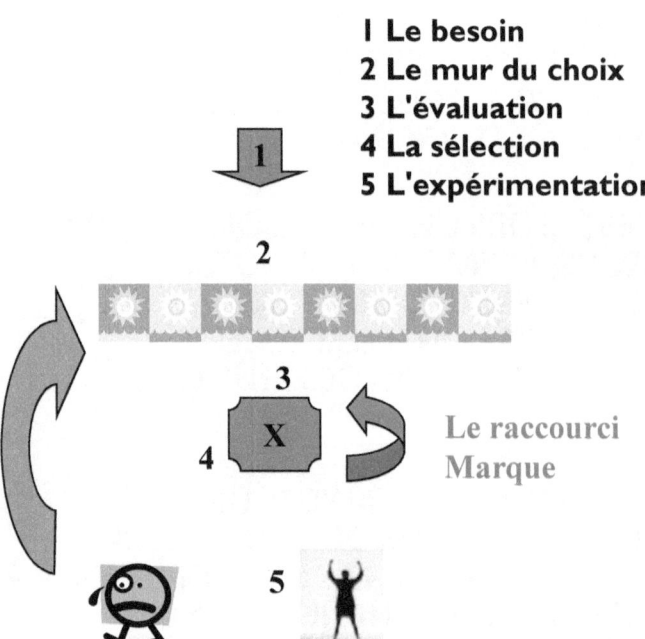

1 Le besoin
2 Le mur du choix
3 L'évaluation
4 La sélection
5 L'expérimentation

Le raccourci Marque

Quelles raisons pour une marque forte ?

- Le processus de choix du consommateur nous donne les raisons qui permettent de construire une marque forte.
    - EN PREMIER LIEU, IL Y A LE PRODUIT, SES CARACTÉRISTIQUES, SES VALEURS D'INNOVATION.
        - Nous trouvons là dans l'ordre du **matériel** des **valeurs tangibles** du produit, lesquelles bien évidemment ont une influence sur l'image que je me fais de la marque. Les bénéfices dégagés par les valeurs tangibles doivent être perçus par les consommateurs.
    - EN SECOND LIEU, IL Y A LE POUVOIR D'ATTRACTION DE LA MARQUE DEVANT LE MUR DU CHOIX VÉHICULÉ PAR LE PACKAGING AVEC UNE RESSOUVENANCE DE LA COMMUNICATION SUR LA MARQUE QUAND ELLE EXISTE ET QUAND ELLE MODIFIE L'ATTITUDE DU CONSOMMATEUR.
        - Nous trouvons là dans l'ordre de **l'immatériel,** de **l'imaginaire né de** L'IDENTITÉ DE LA MARQUE que nous allons expliquer. Il conforte les processus de rachat, s'il y a appréciation des valeurs tangibles apportées par le/les produits appartenant à la marque.
    - EN TROISIÈME LIEU, IL Y A LA SATISFACTION D'USAGE QUI N'EST PAS NÉCESSAIREMENT LIÉ À TOUTES LES CARACTÉRISTIQUES PRODUITS.
        - Nous nous trouvons là dans les **valeurs d'usage** apportées par le/ les produits de la marque et qui combinent valeurs d'usage et immatériel. (cf. Pyramide de Maslow dans l'usage produits).

Quelles raisons pour une marque forte ?

- Il y a, nous le verrons de multiples raisons qui aident à construire une marque forte.

- Si l'on résume, face au mur du choix, les trois premières que l'on peut retenir sont :

  - **Le/ les Produit** (s). N'oublions pas ce qu'on a toujours dit, à savoir que c'est d'abord par les produits et leurs **valeurs tangibles** que la marque prend la parole.
  - **Le pouvoir d'attraction** de la marque qui se fonde sur les **évocations imaginaires** qu'elle me renvoie (d'abord par le packaging qui doit à son tour renvoyer vers la communication).
  - **L'usage des produits** ou les **valeurs d'usage** qui me renforcent ou non dans mon attachement à la marque.

Quelles raisons pour une marque forte ?

- Pour construire ou faire perdurer une marque forte, on doit continuellement innover au niveau des produits.

- Il faut constamment pouvoir annoncer au consommateur des bénéfices produits nouveaux. Ce sont eux qui font l'actualité de la marque.

- C'est l'innovation qui assure la pérennité de la marque.
    - Exemple de succès : le repositionnement de CITROËN.
    - Exemple contraire de perte de vitesse : l'attentisme de NOKIA.

Quelles raisons pour une marque forte ?

- Pour qu'une marque devienne forte, nécessairement à un moment ou à un autre il faut qu'elle soit **en mesure de générer un imaginaire fort.**
- Cela est lié aux **RACINES DE LA MARQUE**, à son code génétique, à **SON IDENTITÉ** que nous allons évoquer dans le chapitre qui suit.
- Ainsi, lorsqu'on veut optimiser son capital marque, outre les réalités produit (plus produit, innovation, rapport qualité/prix), on doit travailler sur son identité afin d'exprimer toutes les positivités imaginaires que cette dernière promet.
    - Exemple MARLBORO, le travail de communication fait pour enrichir le cœur identitaire de la marque, l'enrichissement du portefeuille produits.

Quelles raisons pour une marque forte ?

- Enfin le capital d'une marque se construit avec ses valeurs d'usage.
- L'usage répété de la marque ne doit pas décevoir. Valeurs tangibles/bénéfices produit ou valeurs d'usage.
- **LES BÉNÉFICES PRODUITS ET LES VALEURS D'USAGE** sont immédiatement verbalisables par le consommateur. Un simple questionnaire permet de s'assurer qu'elles sont bien perçues par lui.
- L'usage de la marque doit générer aussi des bénéfices immatériels qui sont de l'ordre de la satisfaction fantasmatique que m'apporte l'usage d'une marque.
- Ces valeurs d'imaginaire ne sont pas totalement conscientes. Seules des études qualitatives en profondeur (cf. Focus group) permettent de savoir si oui ou non elles existent dans l'esprit des consommateurs.
    - Exemple: «EVIAN, *l'eau de l'éternelle jeunesse*».

Quelles raisons pour une marque forte ?

- Pour optimiser la gestion d'une marque, on doit donc actionner trois leviers :
    - Le/les produits avec les **bénéfices tangibles** qui lui sont reconnus dont le résultat est de générer les valeurs d'usage.
    - **L'imaginaire de la marque** et les bénéfices immatériels qu'elle génère dans l'esprit du consommateur en travaillant à partir de l'identité de façon à ce que les supports de communication (notamment les packagings) les suggèrent.
    - Ses **valeurs d'usage**, c'est-à-dire les bénéfices tangibles perçus ou valeurs de satisfaction en vérifiant au moyen d'études que de plus le couple bénéfices tangibles + bénéfices immatériels fonctionne parfaitement ou s'harmonisent dans l'esprit du consommateur.

GÉRER L'IMMATÉRIEL À PARTIR DES RACINES DE LA MARQUE

PRÉAMBULE

La marque n'est surtout pas un nom mais des phonèmes

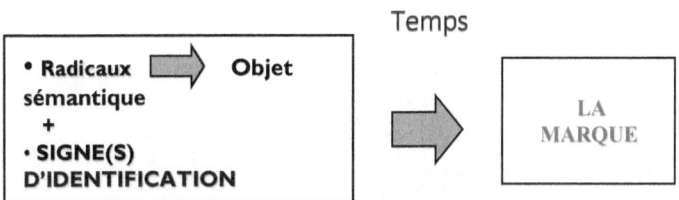

Les radicaux

- Avant d'être un nom, la marque est constituée de radicaux.
- On pourrait dire qu'ils constituent le souffle vital de la marque, comme ce qui permet à l'artiste d'être créatif, ou encore ce qui se cache derrière l'habit de lumière que porte le clown, soit ce supplément d'âme qui est à la source de son inspiration.

Les radicaux

DÉFINITION :

- Les radicaux, c'est quoi ?
- Ce sont les racines des mots de nos langues actuelles. Un peu comme les atomes pour la matière. Ils nous viennent des langues préhistoriques. Sur un arbre destiné à retracer l'évolution des langues, ils se situent dans celles du tronc ou sur les premières branches alors que nos langues actuelles prennent place sur les plus jeunes.
- En ce qui concerne la marque, dans notre inconscient – qui les retrouve – ils jouent le rôle de déclencheur de l'imaginaire.
- Il faut donc bien connaître les radicaux d'une marque pour être en mesure d'appréhender les images et les sens inconscients qu'elle véhicule.
- Pour trouver les radicaux d'une marque, on utilisera un dictionnaire étymologique (par ex. Le Larousse), après avoir cherché dans la marque quels sont les composants qui peuvent s'en rapprocher.

Les radicaux

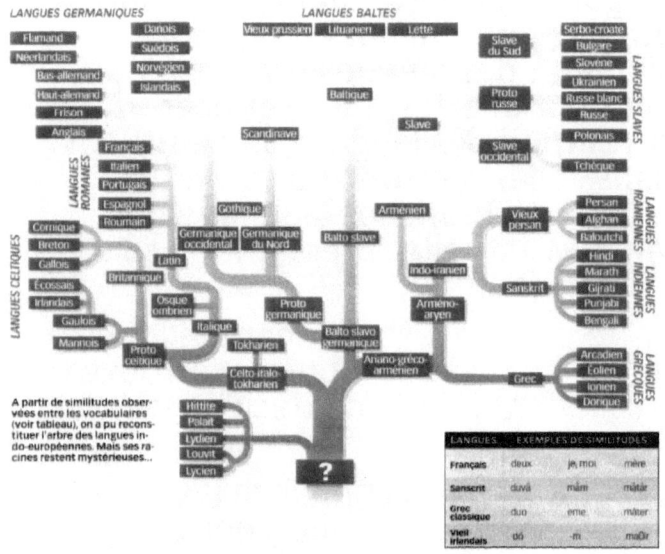

L' Étoile ou les facettes de l'identité de la marque*

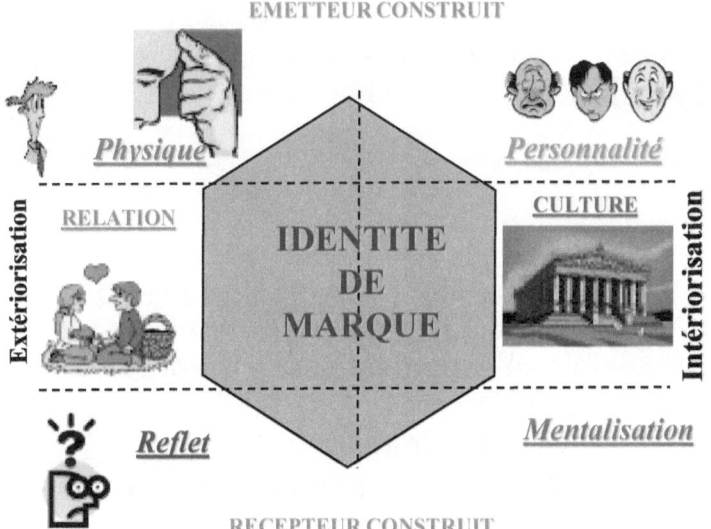

·Source : Kapferer, Les marques,
Le Capital de l'Entreprise

- **LES 6 FACETTES DE LA MARQUE DOIVENT CONSTITUER UN ENSEMBLE COHÉRENT ET HARMONIEUX POUR QUE LA MARQUE PUISSE FAIRE AUTORITÉ SUR UN TERRITOIRE STRATÉGIQUEMENT SÉLECTIONNÉ PAR L'ENTREPRISE.**

- **EXAMINONS-LES L'UNE APRÈS L'AUTRE :**

1/ *Le physique*

- C'est la dimension **concrète** et **tangible** de la marque. Cette dimension doit être immédiatement perceptible par la cible sélectionnée par l'entreprise pour constituer :
    - Une valeur ajoutée
    - Une différence concurrentielle

- Ex. :
    - L'Écureuil pour la CAISSE D'ÉPARGNE
    - La bouteille ronde pour ORANGINA
    - Le Cow-boy pour MARLBORO
    - Le cassoulet pour WILLIAM SAURIN
    - Le fromage en portion enveloppé dans de l'aluminium pour la VACHE QUI RIT

2/ La personnalité

- C'est à travers sa communication (publicité, sponsoring, relations publiques) ce que la marque a acquis et qui lui donne un véritable caractère.

- Ex. :
    - VEDETTE : c'est du solide, c'est la tradition de la mère Denis
    - LACOSTE : c'est la classe discrète et le bon goût
    - MARLBORO : c'est la virilité dans les grands espaces
    - HOLLYWOOD Chewing-gum : c'est la jeunesse " branchée "
    - LA VACHE QUI RIT : c'est la bienveillance et la générosité
    - CITROËN : c'est l'idéalisme et la technicité
    - PEUGEOT : ce sont les valeurs sûres, le conservatisme.

3/ L'univers culturel

- **Ce sont les principes fondamentaux** qui gouvernent la marque dans ses manifestations et dans lesquels se retrouve la cible visée. Il doit y avoir adéquation entre le système de valeurs de la marque et celui de sa cible.
- Les sociostyles du CCA constituent un moyen pour comprendre le mode de vie des Français et leurs modes de choix des marques.

- Ex. :
  - APPLE : est la manifestation symbolique d'une culture californienne. (Cf. convivialité)
  - COMPAQ : à la différence, c'est l'avance technologique "C'est à suivre"
  - BENETTON : c'est "united colors , le monde de la couleur et du métissage
  - CITROËN : c'est l'innovation « dont on veut être fier »
  - RENAULT : ce sont " les voitures à vivre "
  - FINDUS : c'est la libération de la femme.

4/ Le mental (ou mentalisation)

- C'est le **miroir interne**. Celui à l'intérieur duquel son utilisateur se complaît.

- Ex. :
    - FACOM : intérieurement, en moi-même, je suis heureux d'utiliser du matériel de professionnel.
    - SONY : Je suis à la pointe de l'innovation (" j'en ai rêvé, Sony l'a fait ")
    - CRÉDIT AGRICOLE : c'est la banque de ma région (bien que la plus grande banque française)
    - LACOSTE : même si je ne fais pas de sport, je m'auto-analyse comme membre d'un club à base sportive et élitiste.

5/ *Le reflet*

- C'est le **miroir externe**. Celui qu'attribue la majorité des gens à tel utilisateur d'une marque.
- Ex. :
    - PORSCHE : est qualifiée de marque des " frimeurs ".
    - HERMÈS : est vue comme la marque des égéries distantes, passant le plus clair de leur temps sur la Riviera. C'est le reflet qui fait vendre, car beaucoup de femmes aimeraient être aussi cela.
    - HOLLYWOOD Chewing gum : c'est la liberté, la sportivité, la convivialité. Le signe que l'on s'est émancipé de la tutelle parentale.

6/ *La relation (c'est presque une conversation)*

- En effet, la marque doit instaurer une " relation " avec ses utilisateurs. Au même titre qu'il existe une **relation entre deux personnes**.
- Cette facette prend une dimension particulière dans le domaine des marques de services

- Ex. :
    - DHL : " nous tenons vos promesses "
    - DARTY : " Le contrat de confiance ».

- Néanmoins, cette facette "relation" existe dans tous les autres secteurs et jouer un rôle important.

- Ex. :
    - TWINGO : " A vous d'inventer la vie qui va avec "
    - YVES ST LAURENT : même si aucun homme ne figure dans ses communications implicitement suggère une relation sensuelle homme/femme.
    - KERASTASE : " Demandez-le à votre coiffeur-conseil ".

La culture et la mentalisation

- Nous venons de voir comment l'Étoile de la marque se construit à partir des radicaux.
- Il est évident, cependant, que la communication et le packaging, qui en est une composante privilégiée, contribuent fortement à façonner certains pôles de l'Étoile.
  - C'EST EN PARTICULIER LE CAS DE LA CULTURE ET DE LA MENTALISATION.
  - C'EST LE CAS AUSSI DE LA RELATION.

La propagation de la valeur

- Dans le modèle classique du marketing, l'énergisation venait de l'amont par la puissance des médias, l'investissement publicitaire et l'impact des créations faites par les agences.
- Kotler en faisait d'ailleurs la base d'un marketing réussi en préconisant l'usage des marques produit.

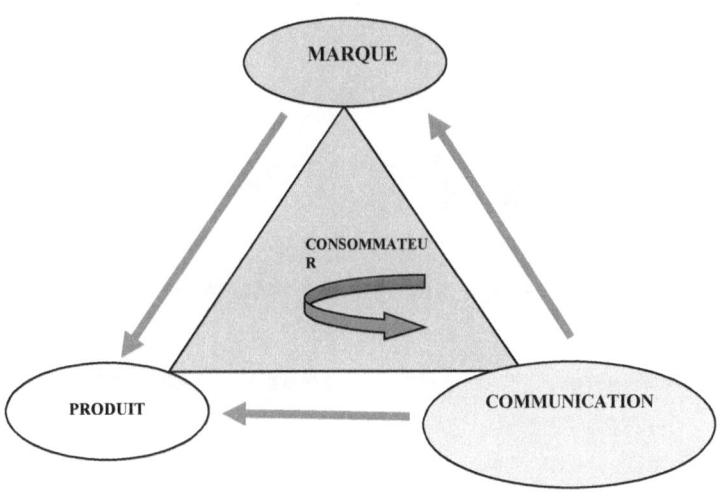

La propagation de la valeur

- On constate que l'émiettement des médias et supports, la prolifération des produits, la dispersion de l'attention des consommateurs mettent à mal ce modèle à moins d'investir toujours davantage en budgets médias et en GRP.

- AUJOURD'HUI, L'ESSENTIEL C'EST D'AGIR **EN AVAL, LÀ OÙ LA MARQUE SE CONSTRUIT**, AU NIVEAU DE **L'IDENTITÉ DE LA MARQUE,** C'EST-À-DIRE AU NIVEAU DE L'ÉTOILE EN METTANT EN SCÈNE LES POTENTIELS D'IMPLICATION QUI CRÉENT LES FIDÉLITÉS ET ATTACHEMENTS DURABLES.

- **QUELQUES CHIFFRES :**

  - Selon Seth Godin un consommateur américain recevait en l'an 2000 en moyenne 1 million de messages par an, soit 3000 tous les jours.
  - Cela n'a fait qu'empirer depuis.
  - Aux États unis, ce sont 17 000 nouveaux produits alimentaires, qui sont lancés chaque année. Ceci sans compter les produits d'autre nature.

 LA PUBLICITÉ SOUFFRE D'HYPERTROPHIE TOUT COMME L'OFFRE FAITE ACTUELLEMENT AUX CONSOMMATEURS.

 IL FAUT ACTIONNER D'AUTRES FAÇONS DE COMMUNIQUER (LE SPONSORING EN EST UNE D'OÙ LE DÉVELOPPEMENT DES MÉGA-MARQUES) LE MÉDIA MAGASIN EN EST UNE AUTRE (AVEC LE RÔLE PRÉPONDÉRANT DANS CE CADRE DU PACKAGING ET DES PROMOTIONS).

LA BRAND EQUITY

La brand equity

- Nous venons de voir quelles étaient les stratégies gagnantes pour disposer sur le marché de marques fortes qui entraînent l'adhésion du consommateur et génèrent sa fidélisation.
    - LES PRODUITS, ET LES VALEURS D'USAGE QUI RAMÈNENT À LA SATISFACTION À LAQUELLE LEUR UTILISATION CONDUIT.
    - L'ÉTOILE QUI RÉSUME L'IDENTITÉ DE LA MARQUE ET DONC L'IMAGINAIRE QU'ELLE SUSCITE DANS L'ESPRIT DES CONSOMMATEURS.
    - LES POSSIBILITÉS D'EXTENSION GÉOGRAPHIQUE.
- Alors selon vous, ce serait quoi la brand equity ?

La brand equity

- C'est la valeur ou les valeurs qui crée(nt) la valorisation de la marque.
- Il y a deux façons d'aborder la question :
    - **L'approche financière** et la valorisation de la marque comme actif de l'entreprise.
    - **L'approche consommateur** et la valorisation de la marque comme déclencheur d'achat.
        - Qu'est-ce qu'une marque et donc sa *brand equity* ? C'est fondamentalement des *radicaux* (par conséquent un nom) et ses signes associés qui influencent l'achat (notamment son *Top of Mind*). Qu'est-ce qu'une grande marque ? C'est l'ensemble de ces éléments auquel est liée une **émotion** auprès d'un très grand nombre d'acheteurs potentiels.
        - C'est cet attachement qui engendre ce désir de **poursuivre la relation, du point de vue de l'acheteur**, ce qui se traduit par la fidélité à la marque.
        - La valeur d'une marque ou sa *brand equity* se mesure donc à sa **capacité à créer un lien de fidélité pérenne avec le consommateur, à un certain niveau de prix.**

La Brand equity

- La brand equity est donc un véritable capital pour l'entreprise, quelle que soit la façon dont on l'envisage :

    - FINANCIÈREMENT
    - OU COMME MOYEN DE CRÉER DE LA FIDÉLISATION.

- Aujourd'hui, certains vont même jusqu'à considérer que dans les actifs de l'entreprise la brand equity est quelque chose de plus important que les actifs matériels.

3. LES ARCHITECTURES DE MARQUE

Les différentes solutions

RAPPEL DES DIFFÉRENTES ARCHITECTURES DE MARQUE

LES STRATÉGIES d'architectures POSSIBLES

- **La Marque PRODUIT :**
  un produit + un nom + un positionnement

- **La Marque GAMME :**
  un nom + un positionnement + des produits

- **La Marque OMBRELLE :**
  un nom + des produits dans des univers différents

- **La Marque SOURCE :**
  un nom + un prénom + des produits dans des univers différents

- **La Marque CAUTION :**
  une signature + un ensemble de qualités et d'attributs garantis à l'acheteur.

LA MARQUE PRODUIT

- **Un produit + un nom + un positionnement**

- Quelques exemples :
  - LUX : le savon des stars
  - PERSIL : le blanc plus blanc
  - CORAL : les couleurs
  - OMO : « Maousse Kosto »
  - SOFITEL
  - NOVOTEL
  - IBIS
  - MERCURE.

Les marques produits

- Ce sont des marques qui se confondent avec le produit qu'elle supporte.
- Ce fut une règle en marketing jusque dans les années 80 :

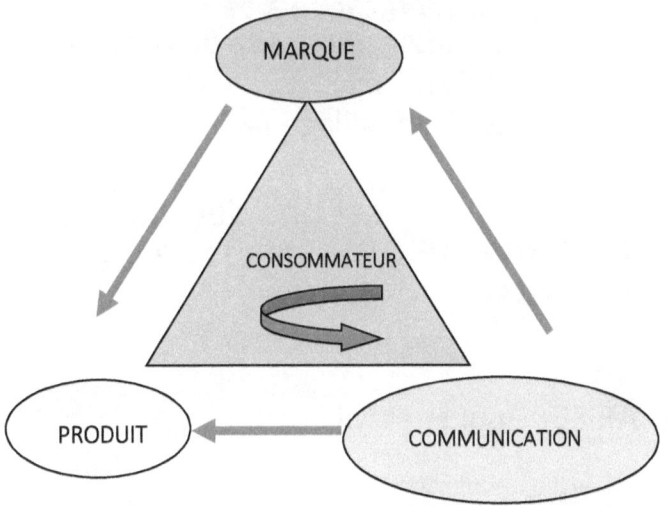

NOUS AVONS DE NOMBREUX EXEMPLES DE CETTE STRATÉGIE DE MARQUE : COCA-COLA, ARIEL, NOVOTEL.

- Dans cette configuration, la marque se nourrit des relancements successifs du produit à partir des innovations techniques touchant le produit ou son emballage, tout en ayant soin de s'appuyer sur les courants porteurs :

- Exemple :
    - ARIEL : Élimination des tâches
        Puis, efficacité à basse température (crise de l'énergie)
        Puis micro.
        Puis emballage recyclable.

- La Marque LIGNE est une déclinaison de la Marque PRODUIT dans un univers restreint.

- Exemple :
    - ARIEL : Liquide et Micro.

- Elle facilite les extensions rapides de gamme sans investissements publicitaires ou presque.

AVANTAGES	INCONVENIENTS

- Une stratégie de prise de pouvoir ! L'entreprise définit l'organisation du marché et sa segmentation
- Elle impose sa supériorité d'innovateur sur les marques qui suivront.
- Une clarification de l'offre par des positionnements uniques.
- Un référence ment plus aisé.
	- Pas de capitalisation inter-produits (synergie, effet de source)
	- Coûts élevés des investissements :
	  - Création de notoriété
	  - Faire comprendre le concept produit
	  - Créer un contenu d'image
	- Risque de vieillissement de la marque avec celui du produit (ex : Monsavon : savon familial)
	- Limite des possibilités de redéploiement de la marque (Ex : Société des Vins de France). Bienvenue.

La marque produit

- Compte tenu du renchérissement des coûts médias et de la situation d'offre pléthorique produits que connaissent les marchés, ce type d'architecture n'est plus à privilégier, sauf dans des cas très précis (ACCOR par ex.).
- Comme *Trop d'impôts tuent l'impôt, Trop de marques tuent la marque.*

Statut des marques produit

- Sans vouloir faire de lapalissade, ce sont des marques qui sont également un produit ou des marques extension de ligne.

Position de la marque sur le packaging

Le nom de marque étant également le nom du produit, il se situe en plein milieu du packaging

LA MARQUE GAMME

- **Un nom + un positionnement + des produits**

- **Quelques exemples :**

    - FINDUS :
      Heureusement il y a Findus !
      (plus de 100 produits surgelés)
    - PHILIPS : Philips, c'est déjà demain !
    - AUDI : A3, A4, A6, A8

- Dans cette configuration, la marque se nourrit d'innovations multiples de produits appartenant à un même univers. La communication est générique même si le thème change selon le produit. Les produits portent le plus souvent leur nom descriptif (Bâtonnets de FINDUS. Plats cuisines Findus : " Poisson à la bordelaise " " Poisson sauce oseille ").

- À partir d'un principe fédérateur, elle définit un territoire de marque précis.

- Elle est caractéristique des marchés sur lesquels les extensions de gamme sont multiples et les durées de vie des produits courtes.

AVANTAGES	INCONVENIENTS
Permet de capitaliser sur l'acquis et : - d'entretenir l'image en permanence - de protéger et renforcer son territoire - d'introduire des nouveautés ⬇ Une stratégie qui garantit la cohérence et la pérennité de la marque.	Des risques de banalisation de la marque devenue générique (ex Bic) Une limite à l'innovation : on reste dans le cœur de la marque Ex : FINDUS (le surgelé : voire le poisson).

La marque gamme

- C'est une structure à privilégier dans le cadre des marques concept.
  - Quelles sont alors les règles à suivre ? :
    - Dénomination produits
    - Packaging
    - Emplacement des produits en linéaire.

Statut des marques gamme

- Ce peuvent être soit des marques savoir faire, soit des marques intérêt.

Position de la marque sur le packaging

Le nom de marque doit toujours précéder
le nom des produits et se trouver en haut.

LA MARQUE OMBRELLE

- Un nom + des produits dans des univers différents

- Quelques exemples :

    - YAMAHA : (motos, ski, pianos)
    - SONY : (TV, Hi Fi, Informatique)
    - PALMOLIVE : (les bienfaits de l'huile d'olive : liquide vaisselle, savons, shampooings, mousse à raser).

- Dans cette configuration cohabitent plusieurs produits, appartenant à des territoires différents, nécessitant des communications devant être en adéquation avec les marchés sur lesquels les produits se trouvent et avec les cibles qu'ils entendent toucher.

- La stratégie de la MARQUE OMBRELLE permet de la faire évoluer en l'associant à des marchés (cas de la distribution) ou à des produits qu'elle ne couvrait pas jusqu'alors.

- Dans tous les cas, il importe de s'interroger sur la contribution de chacun des produits à la personnalité de la marque.

AVANTAGES	INCONVENIENTS
- Capitalisation sur l'image de marque - Transfert de notoriété - Synergie (marchés/activité) - Facilité de notoriété internationale.	Exige une marque très forte sous peine de *rubber effect*. ➢ ombrelle et non ombrage - Des limites à l'extension ➢ compétences perçues - Risque de patchwork.

Position de la marque sur le packaging

Le nom de marque doit toujours précéder le nom des produits et se trouver en haut.

LA MARQUE SOURCE

- **Un nom + un prénom + des produits dans des univers différents**

- Quelques exemples :
    - DANONE : (marque mère)
    - Produits (yaourts, crèmes desserts, en-cas)
    - *Prénoms, DAN'UP, DANINO, DANETTE* (cf. radical ramenant à la marque mère)
    - <u>HEUDEBERT</u> :
    - Produits (biscottes, pains grillés, pains suédois)
    - *Prénoms, CROQUINE, BRAISOR, GRANY, PTIT GRILLE*
    - NESTLÉ : (marque mère)
    - Produits (à base de chocolat, lait, café)
    - *Prénoms, NESCAFE, NESQUIK, CRUNCH, GALAK, Barres SUNDY.*

La marque source

- RAPPEL :

  - Lorsque l'on affaire à des marques source, nous nous trouvons confrontés à deux (ou plusieurs) Étoiles :
  - Ces Étoiles doivent s'enrichir les unes les autres :
    - Celle de la marque mère
    - Celles des marques filles.

Marques Intermarché sources

- Paturages
- Chabrior
- Labell.

La marque source

- Dans cette configuration, pour que la MARQUE SOURCE fonctionne, il est nécessaire que les territoires produits soient limitrophes.

- Car la marque se détermine en cohérence avec les produits

- La contribution de chacun de ceux-ci à la personnalité de la marque est déterminante.

Position de la marque sur le packaging

Le nom de marque doit toujours précéder
le prénom des produits et se trouver en haut.

Exemple d'outil pour élaborer une architecture de marque source

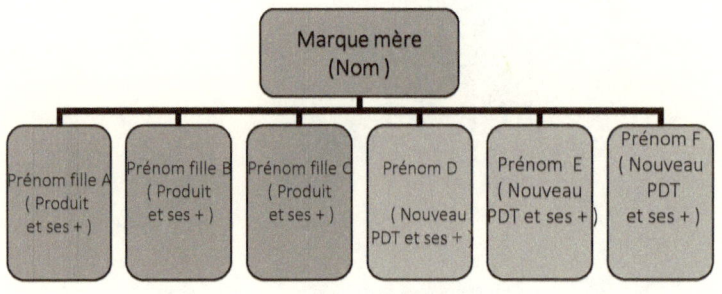

LA MARQUE CAUTION

- Une marque pivot + des marques produits + des produits dans des univers identiques ou semi identiques.

- Quelques exemples :

    - GENERAL MOTORS : (marque pivot)
      > *Marques Produits (PONTIAC, BUICK, CHEVROLET, OPEL)*

    - JOHNSON : (marque pivot)
      > *Marques Produits (PLIZ, FÉE du LOGIS, WIZARD, CANARD WC).*

AVANTAGES	INCONVENIENTS
▪ 2 niveaux de sens : ➢ la marque pivot qui fonctionne comme une marque label « powered by General Motors » GM signe sur toutes les voitures du groupe ➢ la marque produit qui apporte son image particulière ▪ Enrichissement sémantique ▪ Liberté de manœuvre dans les positionnement.	▪ 2 niveaux de communication : ➢ la marque pivot ➢ la marque produit ▪ Plus difficile à gérer ▪ Équilibre à maintenir entre 2 marques.

Position de la marque sur le packaging

De préférence on doit entrer par la caution. Mais elle se trouve souvent en signature (en bas du packaging) également.

4. LES DIFFÉRENTS STATUTS DE LA MARQUE

Les marques Extension de ligne

- Ce sont des **marques produits qui s'étendent au-delà du simple produit**, pour avec un même usage proposer des produits différents non pas dans leur finalité, mais dans la forme ou le support.

- Exemple ARIEL
- Pour lequel on trouve ARIEL poudre, **marque produit.**
- ARIEL Tablets,
- Ariel Micro
- ARIEL Liquide.

Les marques savoir faire

- Ce sont les marques auxquelles le consommateur reconnaît un savoir-faire, une expertise dans un domaine ou un univers de produits donnés.
- Par exemple : WILLIAM SAURIN et les plats cuisinés, le monde du textile et la mode, le monde de l'automobile et l'innovation en la matière.
- Ce sont des marques auxquelles le consommateur attribue un statut soit lié à l'avance technologique, soit lié à un savoir-faire difficile à acquérir.
- Par exemple : les marques du luxe CARTIER, l'horlogerie BREITLING, la technologie IBM, une tradition culinaire POILANE, AUDI et les voitures de luxe performantes.

Les marques intérêt

- Ce sont les marques qui véhiculent un concept d'usage produit ou d'imaginaire qui **dépasse les produits** et auquel se rallient des franges importantes de segment de consommateurs.
- Ce concept peut être lié au mode de vie, à des valeurs de consommation, à des prises de position idéologique.
- Par exemple : La France des produits authentiques du terroir REFLET DE FRANCE, GERBLÉ et la santé, L'Amérique authentique et le textile country avec MARLBORO CLASSIC, etc.
- C'est dans cette catégorie que l'on trouvera les marques de distributeurs que l'on appelle concept ou positionnantes.

Les marques philosophie

- Ce sont des marques qui véhiculent outre des produits **une philosophie de l'existence.**

- "*Just do it*" et NIKE et le dépassement de soi, la sorte d'ascèse qu'elle préconise,"*l'excellence*" et YAMAHA, et là encore la volonté d'être le meilleur auquel la marque incite. DANONE et la santé, l'équilibre entre gourmandise et prendre soin de soi.

- C'est dans cette catégorie que l'on trouvera aussi les marques d'enseigne (en ce qui concerne les points de vente essentiellement), car ce sont des marques qui véhiculent une "idéologie" et qui sont donc des marques citoyennes.

- Peu de marques arrivent à ce stade, il faut en convenir.

Statut et extension

- Plus le statut de la marque est riche plus l'extension de celle-ci sur un nombre important de produits est possible.
- Plus on s'éloigne de la marque produit plus la marque peut recouvrir d'univers de consommation et plus son domaine de légitimité est étendu.

Les Différents statuts de marque avec TENSION / EXTENSION DE LA MARQUE*

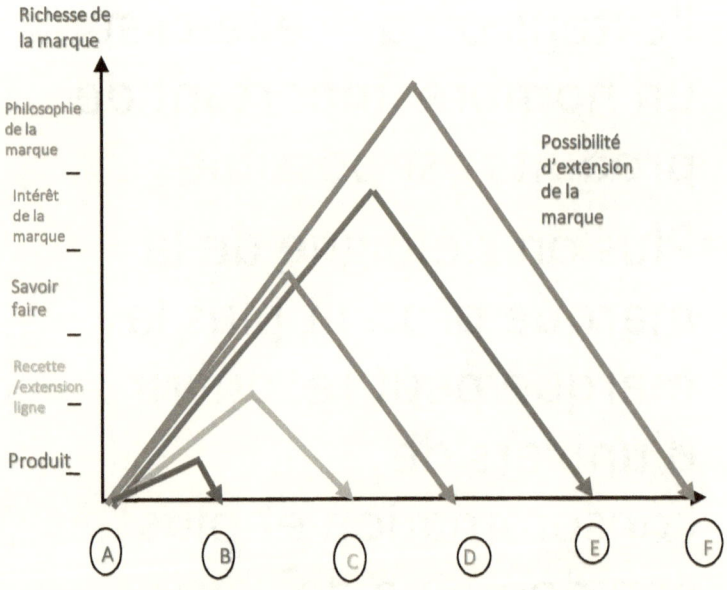

* Source : Jean-Noël KAPFERER : Les marques, Capital de l'entreprise

Statuts et EXIGENCES NECESSAIRES A L'EXTENSION DE MARQUE*

NATURE DES MARQUES	EX. DE POSSIBILITES D'EXTENSION
Produit	Extension de ligne (Ex : Ariel : poudre, liquide, tablets)
Recette/ extension de ligne	Extension par voisinage : Lesieur peut signer le colza, l'olive, le tournesol en plus de l'arachide. On ne voit pas en quoi la graine imposerait sur le plan imaginaire des valeurs différentes.
Savoir-faire	Extension à tout ce qui s'y rapporte : Palmolive, la marque adoucit tout ce qu'elle touche. Bic, la marque simplifié à l'extrême et rend jetable et bon marché aussi bien les stylos à bille que les briquets.
Centre d'intérêt	Extension à tout ce qui y participe : Sony. Au départ la marque était exclusivement haute fidélité. En quelques années, elle a acquis une légitimité sur d'autres marchés : télévision, vidéo, informatique et ainsi évolué dans sa signification. Mais ses valeurs centrales restent toujours : technologies, innovations, sensibilité.
Philosophie	Extension très large. Lorsque le cœur de la marque véhicule une philosophie, presque toutes les extensions sont possibles. Ainsi Général Electric, dont la philosophie était les bienfaits de l'électricité a pu s'étendre des centrales nucléaires aux grille-pains pour le petit déjeuner.

* Source : Jean-Noël KAPFERER : Les marques, Capital de l'entreprise

LES EXTENSIONS SOUS-EXPLOITEES

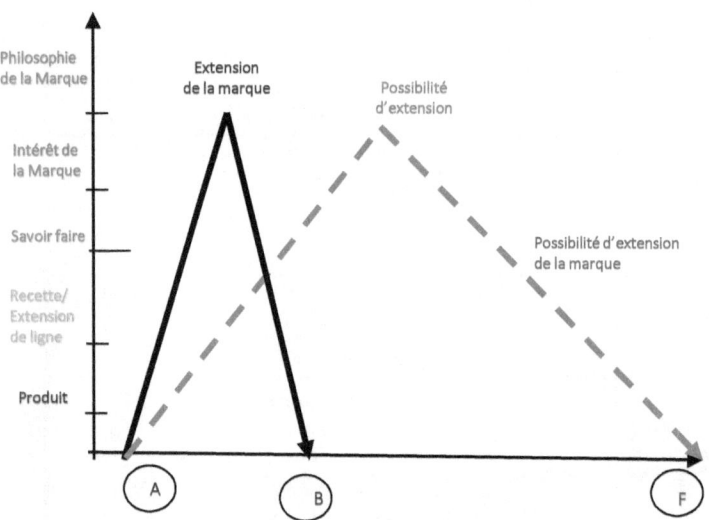

- Par exemple : la marque, la Roche aux Fées, marque de produits frais supprimée par NESTLÉ, aurait pu sans aucun problème, outre les produits laitiers signer :

  - Une ligne de vêtements pour enfants
  - Une collection de livres ou une maison d'édition
  - Des jouets, etc.

CAR SON POTENTIEL IMAGINAIRE LUI PERMETTAIT DE RETOMBER SUR MAINTES CATÉGORIES DE PRODUITS POUR ENFANTS.

À partir du statut : L'EXTENSION DE MARQUE COMMENT ?

- Le préalable à toute extension, on ne saurait trop le répéter, est de connaître sa marque :

  - Quelle est sa personnalité ?
  - Quelle est sa culture (Étoile)
  - Quelle est sa vocation ? Son âme ?
  - De quels contrats est-elle porteuse vis-à-vis de ses consommateurs ?
  - Quels sont ses attributs ?
  - Quelles sont ses potentialités latentes ?

LA RÉPONSE A CES QUESTIONS SUPPOSE DES FOCUS GROUPS (POUR CONNAÎTRE L'ÉTOILE DE LA MARQUE ET SON CONTENU D'IMAGE.

- Les Anglo-saxons, dont Davidson, distinguent plusieurs zones d'extensions possibles de la marque.

- Ils ont coutume de parler :

    - D'inner core (le noyau interne)
    - D'outer core (ou noyau externe)
    - Puis des zones d'extensions larges
    - Et enfin de *no go areas*.

- Ceci nous conduit à synthétiser les différentes sortes d'extension de la marque, selon le schéma en anneaux ci-après :

La matrice de Dadvidson

- Son rôle est de permettre au marketer de ne jamais **surétendre la marque**.
- Cela est fondamental, car si la marque est pour les consommateurs un repère, elle se doit donc de proposer des produits qui sont crédibles soit :
    - Par ce que suggère en tant qu'imaginaire son savoir-faire,
    - Par ce que son Histoire et les produits qui l'ont illustrée laissent attendre.

Une autre façon de concevoir l'extension à partir de l'Étoile et du statut

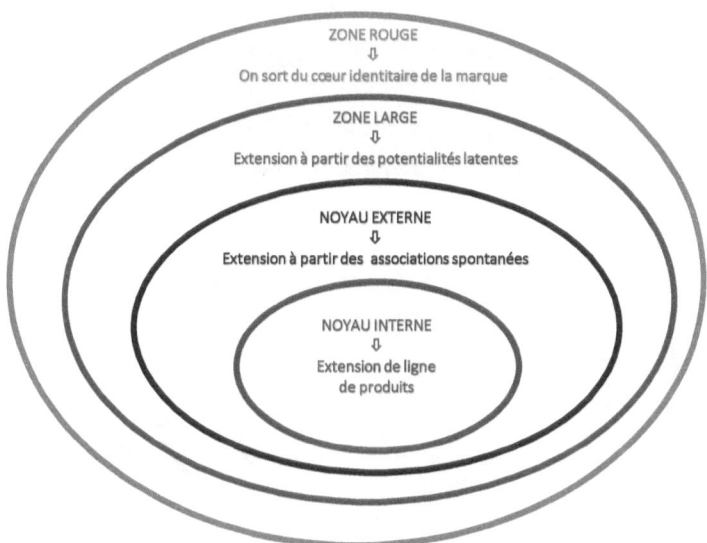

Sortir du cœur identitaire de la marque

- **Exemple LIPTON :**

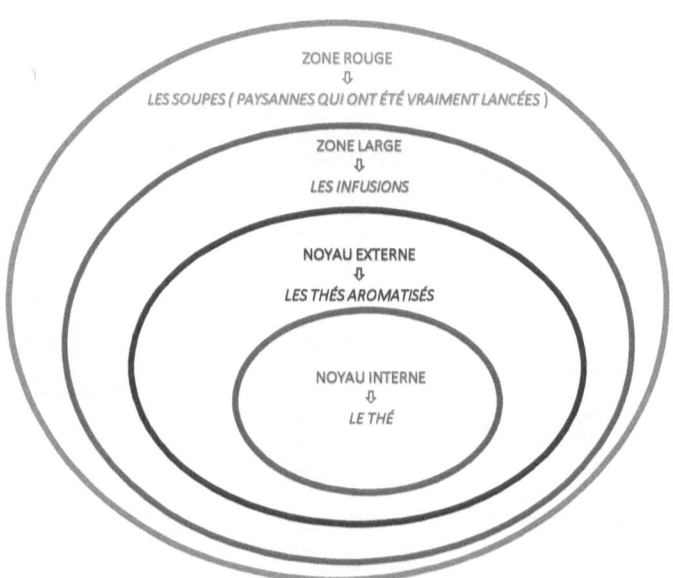

LES DIFFÉRENTS TYPES DE MARQUE

Les différents types de marques fabricants

- Nous avons trois types de marques fabricants:

    - LES MARQUES RÉGIONALES OU TERRITORIALES
    - LES MARQUES LOCALES (NATIONALES QUI NE SONT PAS À L'INTERNATIONAL).
    - LES MÉGA BRANDS QUI SE DÉVELOPPENT (nous l'avons vu à cause du renchérissement des médias et de la volonté des fabricants de sponsoriser des événements de portée mondiale comme Coupe du Monde, Jeux olympiques, etc.) .

Les marques régionales

- Elles sont moins nombreuses qu'il y a une vingtaine d'années.
- Elles sont l'apanage des PME.
- Elles ont une notoriété forte dans leur région.
- Elles reposent sur une tradition ou un savoir-faire régional.
- Le cas GEYER. J-P Barjon rachète une micro entreprise provinciale. Son CA 1M€. Elle opérait sur une niche, la limonade artisanale (bouteille en verre vieille de cent ans, bouchon traditionnel) avec la promesse de retrouver "le goût de son enfance". J-P Barjon relança le produit sous la marque LORINA. Actuellement LORINA dans 700 Pdts de Vente en France, soit 90 % de DV. Seule LORINA peut prétendre à la mention légale "fabrication artisanale", ce qui conduit à ce que les copies qui en ont été faites n'ont pas été des succès.

    - RÉFLÉCHISSONS :
        - QUEL PEUT ÊTRE LE RÔLE DES MARQUES RÉGIONALES POUR LES CONSOMMATEURS ?
        - QUEL PEUT ÊTRE LE RÔLE DES MARQUES NATIONALES POUR LES CONSOMMATEURS ?

Les marques locales

- Ce sont des marques nationales qui n'opèrent que dans un ou plusieurs pays (limitées dans leur diffusion à l'international).
- Le cas BONUX par exemple (revenu aux sources qui fit son succès en France). En avril 2001, une nouvelle campagne de publicité télévisée fut décidée, visant à relancer BONUX dans le respect de son capital de marque (la blancheur et les cadeaux). La marque est passée à la suite de cette campagne en quelques mois de 1,5% de part de marché à 2,3% avec une seule référence.
- Elles ont une forte notoriété dans les pays où elles opèrent.
- Elles ont une identité et des valeurs fortes dans ces mêmes pays.

  - RÉFLÉCHISSONS
    - POUR QUELLES RAISONS LES FABRICANTS REMETTEN-ILS À L'HONNEUR DES MARQUES LOCALES ?
    - CES MARQUES APPORTENT-ELLES QUELQUE CHOSE AUX DISTRIBUTEURS ?

Les méga marques

- Ce sont des marques qui se veulent "universelles".
- Elles entendent proposer les mêmes catégories de produits quels que soient les pays dans lesquels elles opèrent.
- C'est une stratégie qui est en train de se généraliser.
- Cependant, on le sait, la marque est un système vivant qu'on tente d'expliquer et de faire comprendre à travers l'outil de l'Étoile :
    - Qui couvrira à un(ou des) produit(s) service(s)
    - Auquel sera attaché une promesse globale de qualité (plus produit), sécurité et d'appartenance dans un univers donné et un imaginaire dont on a vu qu'il dépendait également des segmentations.
- La globalisation dans son sens strict, soit une homogénéisation marketing peut donc concerner soit la totalité de ces éléments, soit un ou plusieurs d'entre eux seulement.
- Car, si l'on prend l'exemple des radicaux qui influent fortement sur l'imaginaire de la marque, de toute évidence ils ne sauraient être les mêmes en France et en Chine (cf. influence des groupes de langues).

Quelques exemples de méga-marques

- **COCA-COLA**
- **EVIAN**
- **L'ORÉAL**
- **DANONE**

- RÉFLÉCHISSONS :

    - POUR QUELLES RAISONS ONT-ELLES PU DEVENIR DES MÉGA-MARQUES (RADICAUX, l'ÉTOILE, AUTRES) ?
    - QU'EST-CE QUE LES MÉGA-MARQUES APPORTENT AUX CONSOMMATEURS ?
    - QU'EST-CE QUE LES MÉGA-MARQUES APPORTENT AUX DISTRIBUTEURS ?

Exercice

- Pourquoi de plus en plus de marques ont-elles tendance à privilégier la mondialisation ?
- Pourquoi assiste-t-on également à un recentrage sur les marques locales ?
- N'y a-t-il pas donc un intérêt à jouer la complémentarité et à utiliser la force que pourrait constituer un portefeuille de marque ?
- En vous appuyant sur l'exemple de DANONE avec CHARLES GERVAIS et de la LAITIERE avec NESTLÉ, essayer de démontrer et de justifier quelle est la stratégie gagnante ?

5. LES DIFFÉRENTS DISCOURS DE LA MARQUE

Le maping sémiotique
Les territoires de marque
Le co-branding

Le maping sémiotique

TRANSCENDANTAL

On trouvera en général dans ce cadran
les marques philosophie

On trouvera en général
Dans ce cadran
Les marques intérêt.

ANALYTIQUE **LUDIQUE**

On trouvera en général dans ce cadran
les marques produits
ou extension de ligne

On trouvera en général
Dans ce cadran
Les marques savoir faire,
Voire intérêt.

INSTRUMENTAL

L'intérêt du maping

- Prenons l'exemple d'EMAP, il est clair que chaque titre aura un contenu rédactionnel élaboré en fonction de sa place sur le maping.
- L'Étoile, les valeurs de la marque, l'Histoire de la marque définissent une identité qui à son tour appel ou non des catégories de consommateurs.
- En fonction de leur propre identité, ces derniers ne sont pas sensibles au même type de discours.
- Il doit y avoir une adéquation entre discours de la marque (le maping sémiotique nous aide à en définir les valeurs) et l'identité de la marque.
- EMAP le joue ainsi.

Le cas Emap

- EMAP est l'un des 5 grands groupes de presse européens.
- Le groupe possède de nombreux titres en France comme **AUTO PLUS, Sport Auto, L'auto Journal, Pleine Vie, Modes & Travaux, Télé Poche, Télé Sar.**
- Chaque titre est à la fois une marque et un parti pris éditorial.
- EMAP s'est posé la question de savoir comment optimiser ses portefeuilles de marques.

Le cas Emap

- Prenons le cas des publications auto :
- Il y a plusieurs titres dans le groupe :
    - L'auto Journal
    - Auto Plus
    - Sport Auto
- Comment ne pas produire de concurrence entre eux, mais rendre ces titres complémentaires ?
- **ACTION N° 1: La segmentation et l'adéquation marque/segment**
- EMAP a procédé à des études de marque :
- Elle en a défini des segmentations consommateurs et à partir de là à réorienté les contenus éditoriaux de chaque titre en fonction des segments concernés.
- Chaque titre ne s'adresse pas aux mêmes segments de clientèle.
- Mais il ne s'agit pas de segment reposant sur les CESP, il s'agit de segments comportementaux. En effet, les CESP sont transversaux aux segmentations comportementales.

Le cas Emap

- **Action N° 2 : L'extension et la création de nouveaux produits.**
- Action en cours.
- Ainsi AUTO PLUS pourrait devenir une marque mère avec des filles :
  - MOTO PLUS
  - BATEAUX PLUS
  - AÉRO PLUS.
- C'est exactement la stratégie qui fut adoptée POUR LES NULS :
- On est parti de **Windows pour LES NULS, Words pour LES NULS** pour arriver à **La cuisine pour les NULS, L'histoire pour LES NULS.**

Exemple de positionnement des magazines véhicules

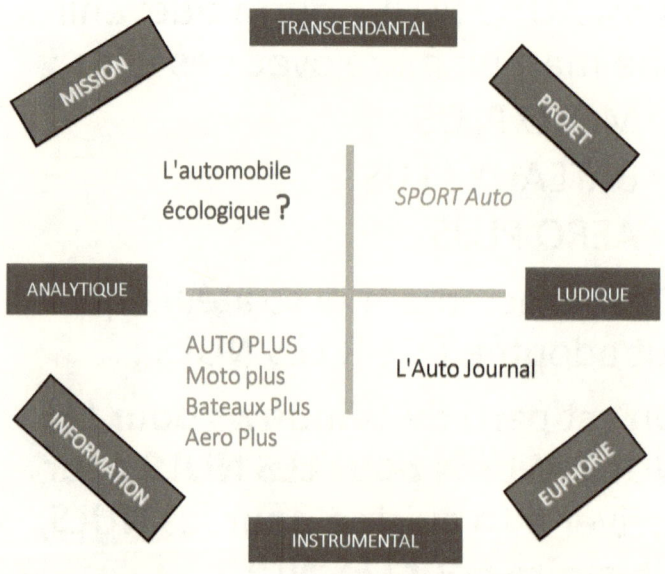

Le packaging : dernier message avant l'acte d'achat

- Lorsque le consommateur entre dans un supermarché, on peut penser que son acte d'achat va être conditionné par tout ce qu'il aura perçu au travers de la publicité, prospectus ou le bouche-à-oreille...

- Pourtant, au moment même où la main se tend, presque téléguidée vers le produit médiatisé, le regard, lui, peut être accroché par un emballage concurrent plus séduisant qui fera appel à d'autres signifiants, stimuli.

- N'oublions pas que le consommateur se trouve confronté au **mur du choix** et que c'est à ce moment décisif que sa décision d'achat intervient.

- Au moment de l'acte d'achat, le packaging est donc déterminant.

Le packaging : la théorie de l'attractivité visuelle

- L'attractivité visuelle d'un emballage est la capacité que ce dernier possède pour déclencher notre regard le temps nécessaire à une mémorisation et susciter l'impulsion d'achat.
- Rappelons le mécanisme de la vision :
    - Ce qui entre dans le champ visuel est traité par les deux rétines du fond de l'œil.
    - La première, dite *périphérique* détecte.
    - La seconde, dite *centrale* identifie.
- La rétine périphérique enregistre toutes les informations visuelles en passant d'un centre d'intérêt à l'autre et soudain sélectionne à notre insu une information qui nous intéresse.
- Elle mobilise alors la rétine centrale qui par sauts successifs va puiser des informations suffisamment précises pour que certaines cellules de notre cerveau les mémorisent.
- Notre rétine périphérique zappe tous azimuts sur les linéaires de gauche à droite sur les étagères en haut et en bas, puis soudain notre rétine centrale s'attarde sur un emballage, mémorise à notre insu l'information, *le message* qui justement répond à notre attente consciente ou non.
    - **CE DERNIER MESSAGE PERÇU EN SITUATION D'ACHAT VA ORIENTER NOTRE CHOIX DÉFINITIF.**

Le packaging : un potentiel d'attraction visuelle

- On distingue deux types de critères :
    - Les *critères objectifs*
    - Les *critères suggestifs*
- Les critères *objectifs* d'attractivité visuelle sont :
    - L'esthétique
    - La couleur
    - Le graphisme
    - Soit tout ce qui facilite la compréhension du/ des message(s) véhiculé(s) par le packaging.
- Les critères *suggestifs* d'attractivité visuelle sont tous ceux qui emportent l'esprit vers l'imaginaire et les mondes immatériels que suscite la marque. Plus fortes sont ces évocations plus le packaging va retenir l'attention, car il va faire remonter à l'esprit tout un vécu du consommateur en relation avec ses valeurs et sa force d'être.

Le packaging

- Le packaging est le premier vecteur de communication de la marque et des produits qui ont rejoint son portefeuille.
- Il doit véhiculer le **statut de la marque** (Nous n'aurons pas les mêmes packagings lorsque nous aurons des marques produits ou des marques intérêt par exemple).
- Il doit véhiculer le **type de marque** auquel on a affaire(Mission, Information etc.).
- Il doit rendre évident le **monde imaginaire** auquel la marque renvoie à partir de son Étoile identitaire.
- Il doit enfin mettre en exergue le ou les **avantage(s) concurrentiel(s) du produit** qu'il communique.

Packaging et maping sémiotique

TRANSCENDANTAL

MISSION
- Les packagings ouvriront vers le monde. Ils quitteront le produit pour véhiculer un message.
- Économie durable, écologie, éthique, entreprise citoyenne;, etc.
- ILS SERONT "OPEN MINDED".

PROJET
- Les packagings insisteront sur Les bénéfices hédoniques que m'apportent les produits.
- Ils mettront en avant la valorisation de moi que grâce à eux je peux obtenir.
- ILS SERONT TRÈS ESTHÉTIQUES

ANALYTIQUE
- Les packagings mettront en avant les bénéfices produits.
- Ils développeront une information consommateurs poussées:
  - Bénéfices nutritionnels
  - Composition produits, etc.
- ILS SERONT TRÈS SOBRES ET INFORMATIFS.

LUDIQUE
- Les packagings insisteront sur l'utilisation des produits.
- Sur le fait qu'ils sont destinés à toute la famille.
- Sur les plaisirs que leur utilisation apporte.
- ILS SERONT TRÈS LUDIQUES.

INFORMATION

EUPHORIE

INSTRUMENTAL

De l'identité au maping sémiotique*

- Le maping sémiotique est un outil qui permet d'analyser et de mettre en évidence l'identité de la marque.
- C'est une autre façon que celle de l'Étoile de l'approcher.
- Il comprend 4 pôles :

  - INSTRUMENTAL
  - TRANSCENDANTAL
  - ANALYTIQUE
  - LUDIQUE

* Source des principales slides du maping sémiotique: Andréa Semprini

LE MAPING SÉMIOTIQUE: LES VALORISATIONS

Le maping sémiotique

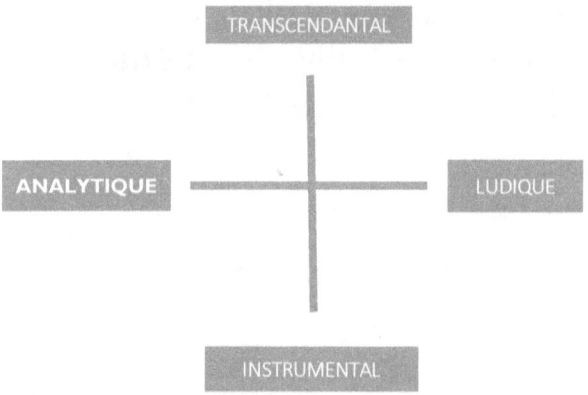

Le maping sémiotique

- La valorisation **INSTRUMENTALE** est liée à la valorisation des valeurs d'usage.
- Valeurs qui s'opposent aux valeurs de base par leur finalité éminemment concrète et utilitariste.
- Appliquée aux produits par ex. la valorisation instrumentale aura tendance à souligner les caractéristiques objectivement certifiables de ces derniers.
- L'objet par ex. sera apprécié et recherché pour sa solidité.
- Un des aspects de la valeur instrumentale c'est d'être *product-oriented.*
- D'un point de vue sémiotique on ne saurait cependant opposer l'instrumentalité réelle d'un produit à sa "beauté", sa "sympathie" ou son caractère "à la mode". Il s'agit toujours de stratégies sémiotiques qui conduisent les récepteurs à privilégier certains parcours de lecture.

Le maping sémiotique

- La valorisation TRANSCENTDANTALE se définit par une association aux valeurs de base de la marque.

- Derrière ces valeurs se retrouve toujours un *projet,* c'est-à-dire une tension vers quelque chose qui n'est pas encore là au moment où la tension débute. C'est à ce projet que la valorisation transcendantale ramène.

- La valorisation transcendantale est donc plutôt *future-oriented.* La valorisation transcendantale est donc peu préoccupée des caractéristiques immanentes ou objectivables des produits. Ce sont les variables subjectives et contextuelles qui retiennent l'attention des consommateurs et prennent le pas sur les valeurs objectivables.

Le maping sémiotique

- La valorisation **ANALYTIQUE** se définit essentiellement par une volonté de questionnement et de prise de distance.
- Dans le terme même d'analytique se trouvent les notions de comparaison, d'évaluation et de jugement.
- Alors que dans la valorisation instrumentale l'objet se suffit à lui-même, dans la valorisation analytique l'objet est toujours soumis à des critères d'évaluation inspirés de principes externes.
- Une autre dimension de la valorisation analytique est sa préoccupation d'attribution de sens. On se demande :
  - Utile pour quoi faire ?
  - Robuste par rapport à quelle utilisation ?
  - Cher pour quelle durée d'usage ?

Le maping sémiotique

- La valorisation **LUDIQUE** se caractérise, quant à elle, à l'opposé de la valorisation analytique, par son manque de distance, par l'adhésion, par la complicité, la participation, l'appropriation de l'objet.
- Les valeurs de ludicité sont des valeurs en soi, qui ne peuvent pas prétendre à quelque forme de transcendance.
- La ludicité est un projet plus individuel que collectif, un projet limité, qui marque un relatif désintérêt pour les éléments objectivables du produit.
- Ce qui est visé c'est une recherche de dépassement de soi par la recherche des plaisirs, du bonheur individuel, du besoin de distraction et de divertissement.
- Le type de public concerné par cette valorisation s'attache plus à la situation contextuelle et au climat psychologique générés par les produits qu'à leur réalité objectivable.

Le maping sémiotique

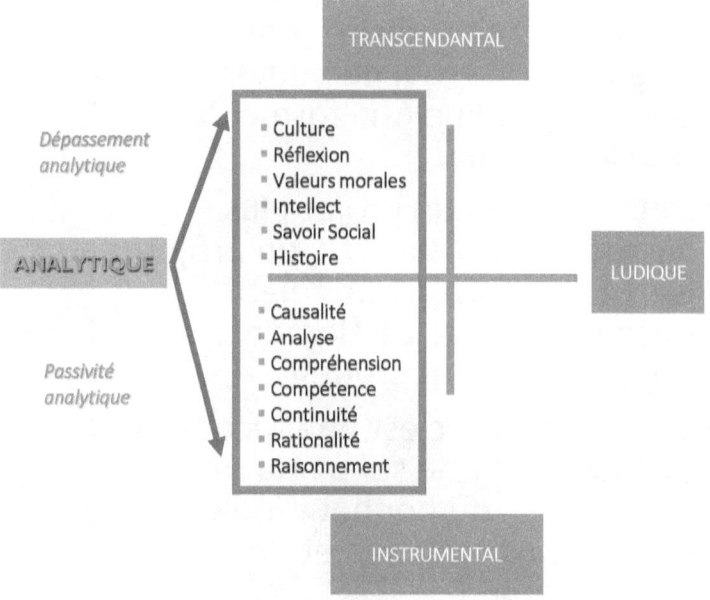

Le maping sémiotique

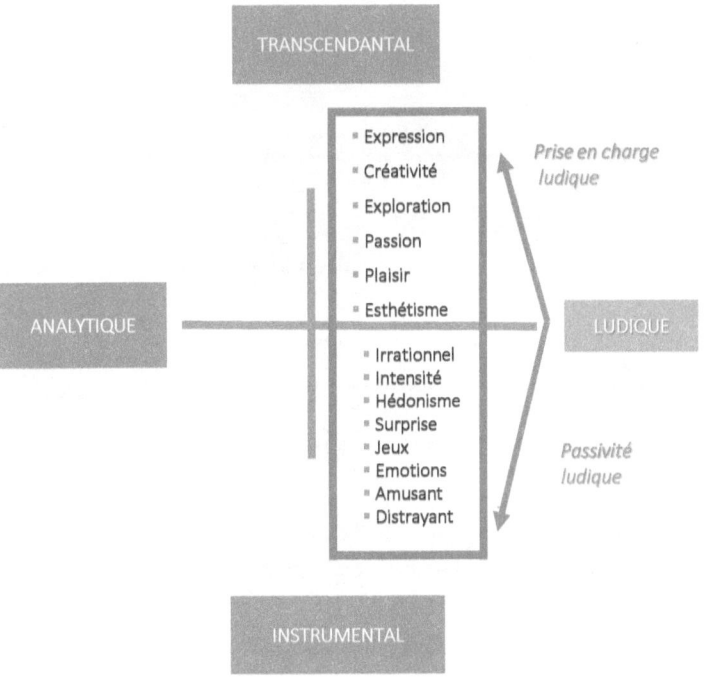

Le maping sémiotique

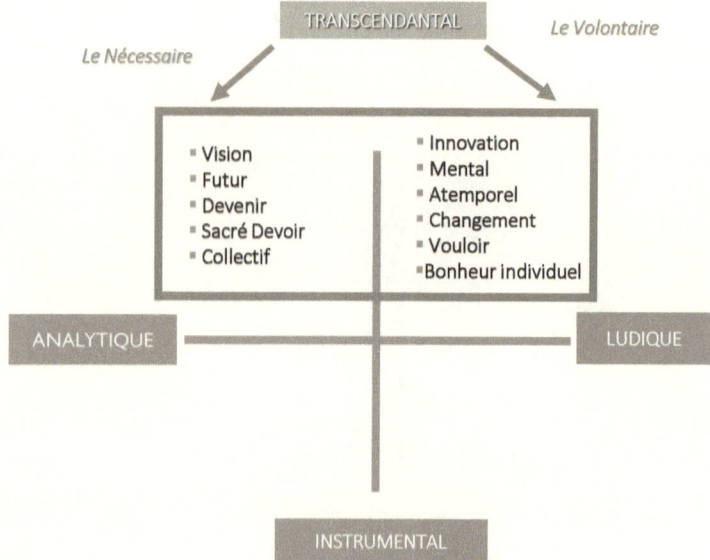

Le maping sémiotique

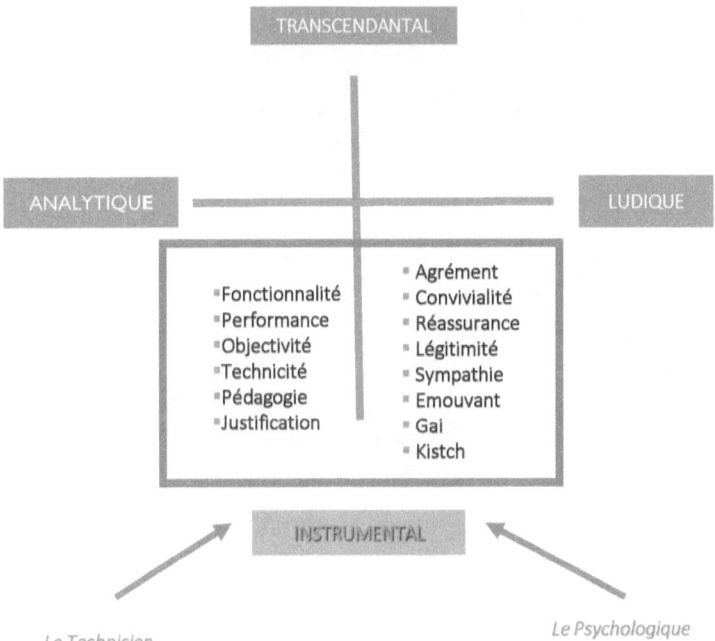

LE MAPING SÉMIOTIQUE : LES QUADRANTS

Les quadrants

- Le maping sémiotique se compose de 4 quadrants:

  - Le NORD-OUEST qui correspond aux marques *Missions*,
  - Le SUD-OUEST qui correspond aux marques *Information*,
  - Le NORD-EST qui correspond aux marques *Projet*,
  - Le SUD-EST qui correspond aux marques *Euphorie*.

Le maping sémiotique

- Le quadrant NORD-OUEST se situe à la convergence de la valorisation transcendantale et de la valorisation analytique.
- Son identité est de l'ordre de l'ouverture vers le monde et les hommes. la mission.
- Ce qui caractérise les valeurs de cette identité ce sont les notions de :

  - DÉFRICHAGE
  - REMISE EN DISCUSSION
  - QUESTIONNEMENT
  - LABORATOIRE
  - NOUVELLE SOCIÉTÉ
  - ENGAGEMENT
  - L'IMPOSSIBLE
  - VISIONNAIRE
  - MYTHE COLLECTIF

Les marques-m*issions*

- Il s'agit de marques qui proposent une nouvelle vision de la société.
- Des marques qui suggèrent des voies nouvelles pour atteindre de nouveaux objectifs ou plus simplement des manières originelles de penser l'être ensemble et la vie sociale.

Les marques-m*issions*

- Le quadrant des marques-m*issions* se caractérise donc par :

  - UNE RECHERCHE DU DÉPASSEMENT
  - UN QUESTIONNEMENT
  - UNE PROJECTION EN AVANT
  - DES PRISES DE POSITION
  - UNE ATTITUDE CRITIQUE ET PROSPECTIVE EN MÊME TEMPS.

Maping sémiotique : Les quadrants

- Le quadrant NORD-EST se situe à la convergence de la valorisation ludique et de la valorisation transcendantale. C'est le quadrant qualifiant les identités de l'ordre du projet, avec des notions comme :

  - EXLORATION
  - ÉVASION
  - AVENTURE
  - RÊVE
  - NOUVELLES RELATIONS
  - CONSCIENCE
  - PRISE EN CHARGE
  - MÉTAMORPHOSE
  - RENOUVELLEMENT
  - TRANSGRESSION

Les marques-p*rojets*

- Les marques-p*rojets* gardent une préoccupation pour la transcendance et le dépassement propres aux marques-*missions,* mais sans en conserver les valeurs sociales et collectives.
- Elles se concentrent exclusivement sur l'individu.
- La forte valorisation des dimensions de l'expression du corps est typique de la culture de ce quadrant et peut être déclinée par ces marques de façon différente :

    - L'INDIVIDU PEUT ÊTRE DÉFINI COMME UN PUR POTENTIEL COMMUNICATIF ET DANS CE CAS SA PHYSICITÉ AURA TENDANCE À ÊTRE RELATIVISÉE.
    - OU BIEN C'EST L'ASPECT NARCISSIQUE ET ESTHÉTIQUE DE L'INDIVIDU QUI SERA PRIVILÉGIÉ ET ALORS LE CORPS AURA UNE PLACE BEAUCOUP PLUS IMPORTANTE.

Maping sémiotique : Les quadrants

- Le quadrant SUD-EST se situe à la convergence de la valorisation ludique et de la valorisation instrumentale. C'est un quadrant où se développent les dimensions psychologiques et émotionnelles des récepteurs. Donc un quadrant dont l'identité de Marque est caractérisée par l'euphorie. Avec des notions comme :

  - SUBJECTIF
  - ÉMOTIONNEL
  - AMUSANT
  - DISTRAYANT
  - DÉCORATIF
  - GADGET GRATUIT
  - SURPRENANT
  - EXCESSIF
  - PROVOCANT

Les marques-e*uphorie*

- Dans cette catégorie, on trouvera toutes les Marques qui proposent comme valeurs fondatrices :

    - L'ÉVASION
    - LA POSITIVATION DES RELATIONS
    - LA RÉGRESSION DANS UN UNIVERS PROTÉGÉ ET CHAUD
    - LE PARTAGE ET L'ÉCHANGE D'AFFECTS ET DE SENTIMENTS.

- Dans ce quadrant, les publicitaires développeront un discours de communication fondé sur la réassurance et la protection face à la dureté d'un monde perçu comme hostile.

- Ce n'est pas un hasard si de nombreuses marques alimentaires se trouvent dans ce quadrant.

Maping sémiotique : Les quadrants

- La quadrant SUD-OUEST se situe à la convergence de la valorisation instrumentale et de la valorisation analytique. C'est un quadrant qui présente une forte homogénéité et une relative objectivité. La nature identitaire des Marques s'y positionnant est de l'ordre de l'information, avec des notions comme :

    - UTILE
    - ESSENTIEL
    - FAIRE
    - SOBRE
    - BASIQUE
    - AVANTAGEUX
    - ÉCONOMIQUE
    - APPROPRIÉ
    - NÉCESSAIRE
    - FONCTIONNEL
    - TECHNIQUE

Les marques-i*nformation*

- Les marques-i*nformation* ne visent aucunement la transformation de l'homme ou de la société. Elles ne veulent pas non plus tranquilliser ou dorloter les consommateurs dans un romantisme à l'eau de rose.
- Les marques-*Information* se veulent rationnelles et utilitaires. Elles professent un attachement scrupuleux à la réalité et aux produits dont elles énumèrent la plupart du temps la liste des qualités et des performances. Donc le discours de ces marques est argumenté et référentiel.
- Les acteurs sont souvent des personnes dont le témoignage ne saurait être remis en question :

    - L'EXPERT
    - LE SCIENTIFIQUE
    - LE CONSOMMATEUR LUI-MÊME PRIS COMME TÉMOIN DE LA "VÉRITÉ" DU PRODUIT.

Exemple de marques : Les produits de soins

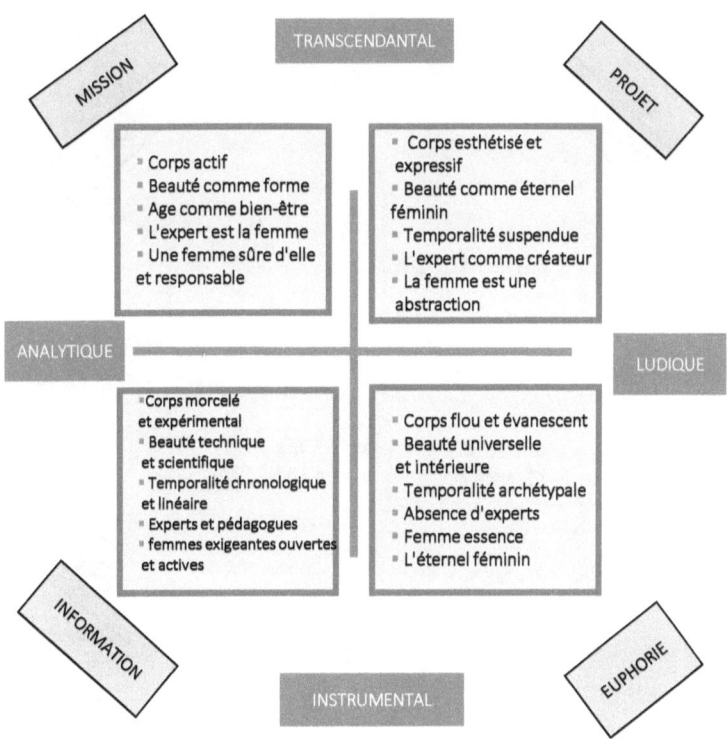

Exemple de marques :
Les produits de soins

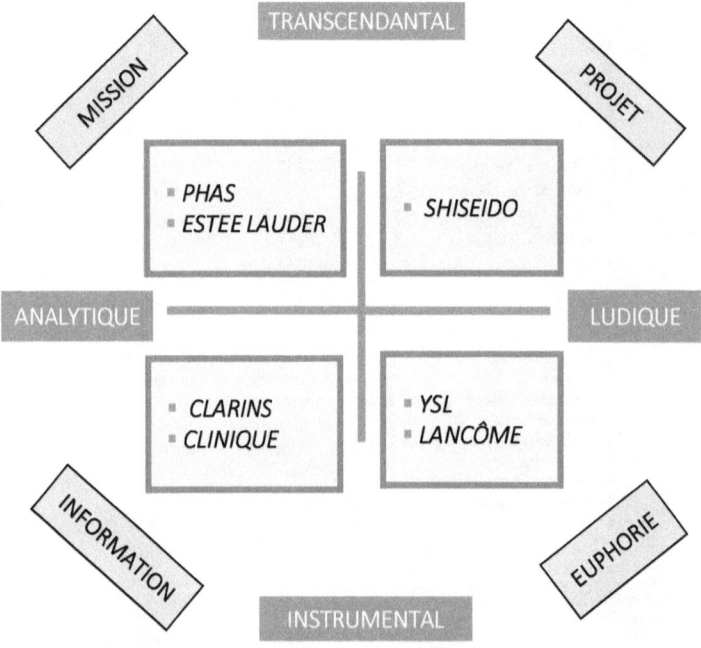

Exemple de marques : Les dentifrices

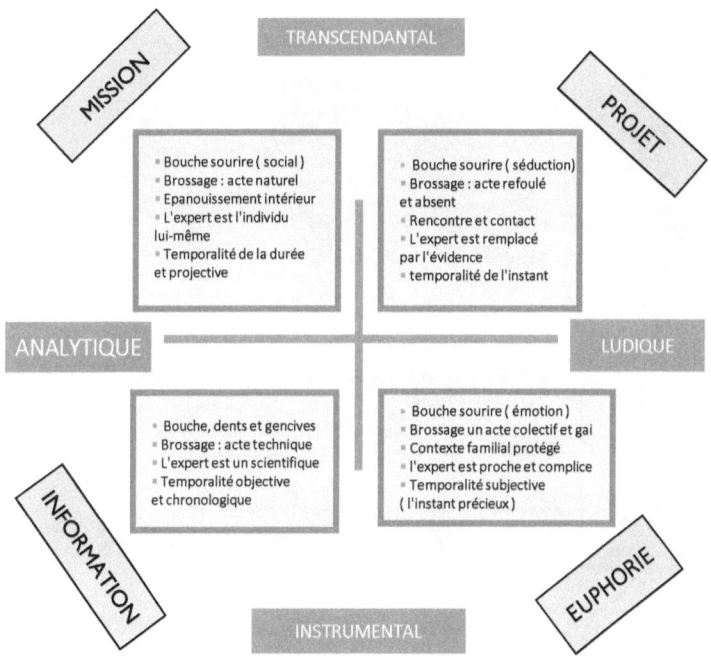

Exemple de marques : Les dentifrices

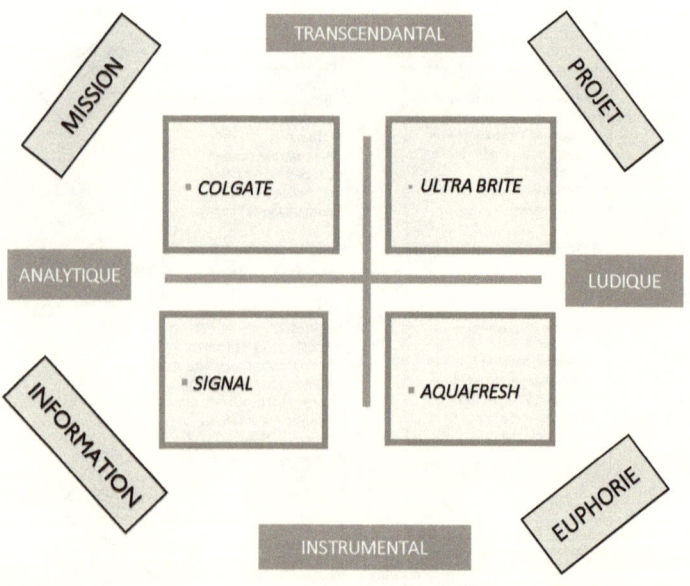

Exemple de marques : Les eaux minérales

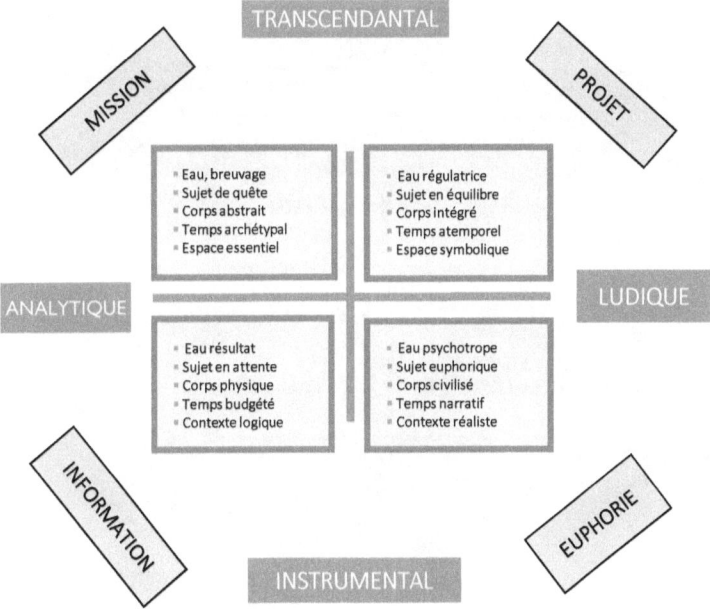

Exemple de marques :
Les eaux minérales

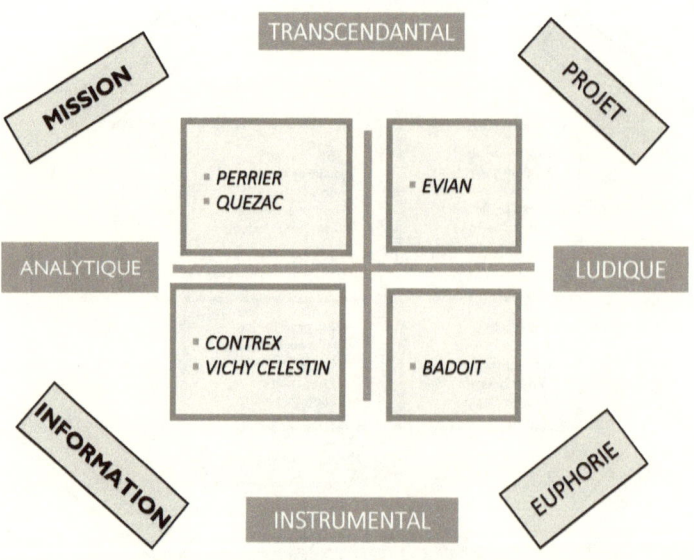

Le cas Benetton

OU COMMENT PERTURBER
LE CONSOMMATEUR
EN OCCUPANT SUCCESSIVEMENT
LES 4 QUADRANTS DU MAPING
SÉMIOTIQUE DE LA MARQUE.

Le cas Benetton

- Si l'on observe une sélection des principales affiches des campagnes de communication de la marque Benetton ces dernières années, on est frappé par l'évolution du discours de la marque.

Le cas Benetton

- La phase qui correspond à la valorisation du quadrant de *l'information* n'a pas beaucoup d'importance en soi, mais elle permet de comprendre l'évolution de la marque et d'en repérer les origines qui sont d'ailleurs tout à fait classiques.

- En effet, jusqu'en 1982 la communication de Benetton est standardisée sur les codes du segment du casual wear pour jeunes. Des groupes de jeunes sont ainsi montrés habillés bien sûr avec les pulls et autres vêtements de la marque.

- La représentation est réaliste, les photos sont vraies et montrent des individus réels. Les décors aussi sont banaux, objectifs. Les sujets représentés sont des mannequins professionnels, avec tout ce que cela implique en termes de posture de corps, de positions de tête, de type de sourire.

Le cas Benetton

- Alors le discours de la marque est clair et explicite :
    - Il est question avant tout de présenter des produits et ensuite de les valoriser par des voies connotatives en les associant à une jeunesse belle et dorée.

Le cas Benetton

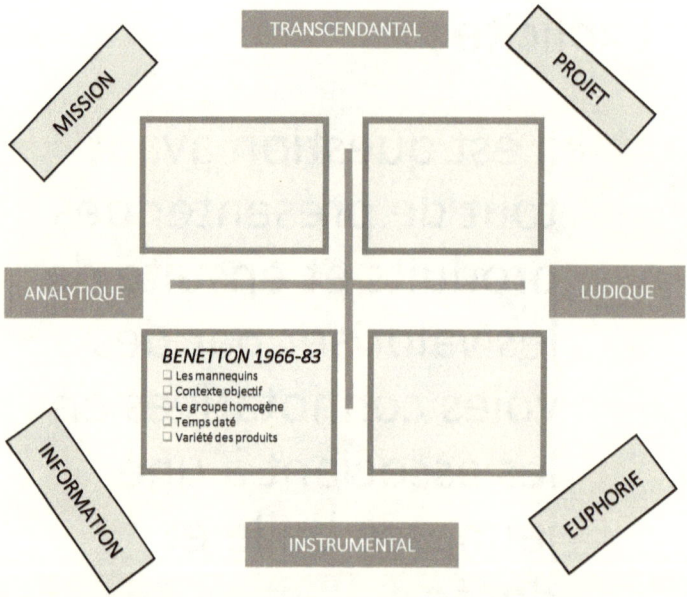

Le cas Benetton

- La deuxième phase de la communication Benetton peut être positionnée dans le quadrant de *l'euphorie*.
- Elle correspond aux années 1983-84.
- C'est une phase importante parce que le style et la conception de l'identité visuelle s'élaborent et se structurent à ce moment-là.
- Lors de cette deuxième phase, le système expressif évolue du photographique vers le graphisme.
- Durant cette période, les jeunes restent les jeunes, mais ils ne connotent rien d'autre. Les personnages sont dépourvus de la charge symbolique que l'on verra apparaître dans la phase Projet.

Le cas Benetton

Le cas Benetton

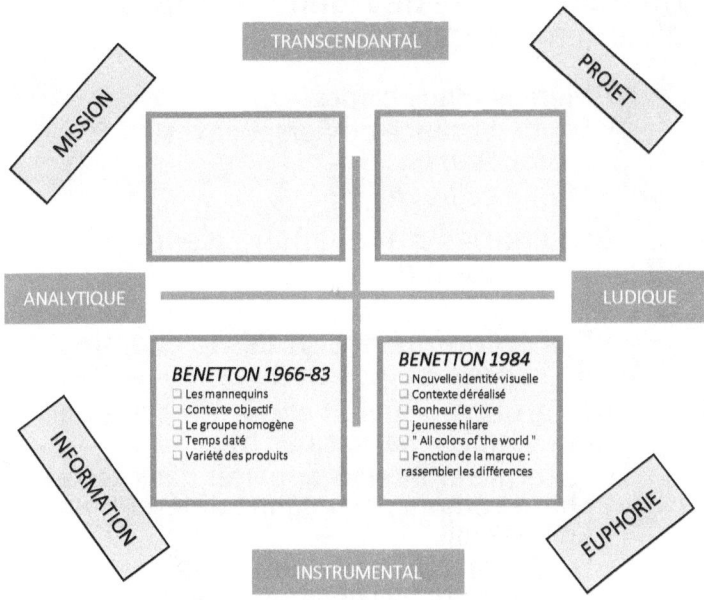

Le cas Benetton

- Nous arrivons à la phase 3 qui occupe le quadrant du *projet* et qui se situe dans les années 1985-90.
- C'est la phase où la communication Benetton commence à soulever des polémiques.
- Du point de vue de l'identité visuelle peu d'éléments changent :
    - Mêmes fonds blancs
    - Même absence de perspectives et de profondeur
    - Même cadrage.
- Ce qui a changé en revanche c'est le discours de fond de la marque :
    - Elle emprunte désormais le chemin de la prise de position.
    - Le groupe disparaît et est remplacé par des couples, parfois des trios.
    - Le terme *différence* apparaît dans cette phase comme *polémique* : différent est un ennemi.
    - Le discours de la marque ne se contente plus de faire coexister des identités différentes, mais non conflictuelles, elle veut maintenant assurer la cohabitation de deux identités opposées, elle veut abattre les barrières et assurer le dialogue : la marque passe de la valorisation des différences équivalentes à la négation des différences conflictuelles. Son projet est maintenant l'intégration des opposés.

Le cas Benetton

Le cas Benetton

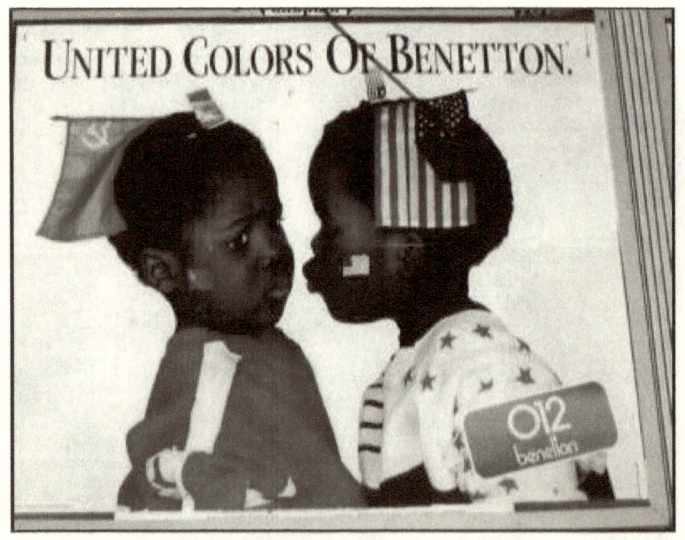

Le cas Benetton

Le cas Benetton

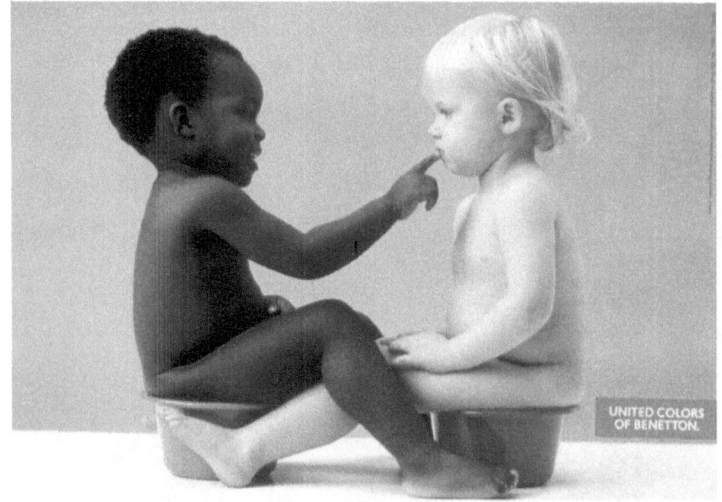

Le cas Benetton

Le cas Benetton

Le cas Benetton

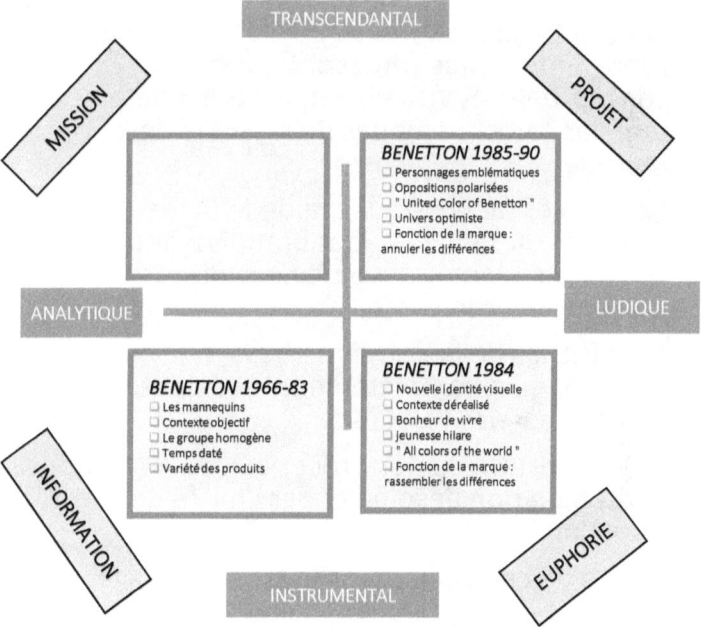

Le cas Benetton

- L'entrée nette et explicite dans la culture de la *mission* commence à partir de 1991.
- L'élément central qui caractérise la nouvelle évolution de l'identité de marque Benetton est l'abandon de la logique oppositive : abandon qui entraîne un changement dans le discours de fond de la marque.
- Les sujets représentés se diversifient et ne représentent plus cette continuité – conceptuelle et visuelle – qui a été longtemps une des caractéristiques du discours de la marque.
- Les images de la campagne de 1992 (le mourant du sida, le soldat brandissant un fémur, etc.) font preuve d'une rupture évidente avec le passé.
- Les affiches de la dernière phase abandonnent complètement le ton optimiste des campagnes jusque-là.
- Elle y substitue le désarroi et la contemplation désolée et pessimiste de l'être humain.
- À côté de cet aspect pessimiste, ces images affichent un côté agressif : elles ne sont pas seulement "négatives" elles se veulent aussi "choquantes". Elles montrent la douleur, le souffrance, la désolation dans leurs expressions les plus crues et les plus directes.

Le cas Benetton

- Ces codifications témoignent d'un tournant dans le discours de la marque :

    - *À l'annulation de la multiplicité qui était son projet de la phase 3, Benetton substitue la recherche de l'unicité, de ce qui est commun à toute l'humanité.*

- Le discours de la marque monte en généralité pour aborder l'insoluble paradoxe de *l'unicité-multiplicité*, de *l'identité-différence*, soit ce substrat par lequel tous les hommes passent à un moment ou un autre de leur existence :

    - *La naissance*, lorsqu'on est encore en deçà de tout conditionnement social
    - *La mort* lorsqu'on est au-delà de ces mêmes contraintes.

- La marque parallèlement à la planétarisation de ses produits et de son enseigne fait donc évoluer son identité vers un nouvel universalisme qui se veut en fait un *nouvel humanisme*.

Le cas Benetton

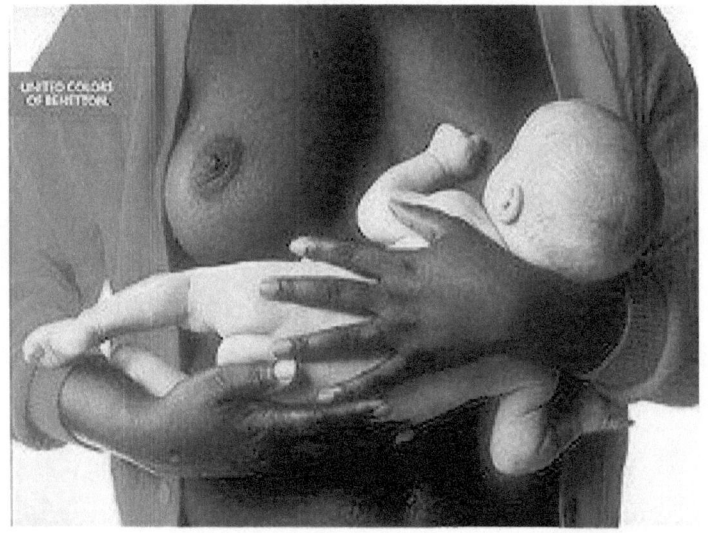

Le cas Benetton

Le cas Benetton

Le cas Benetton

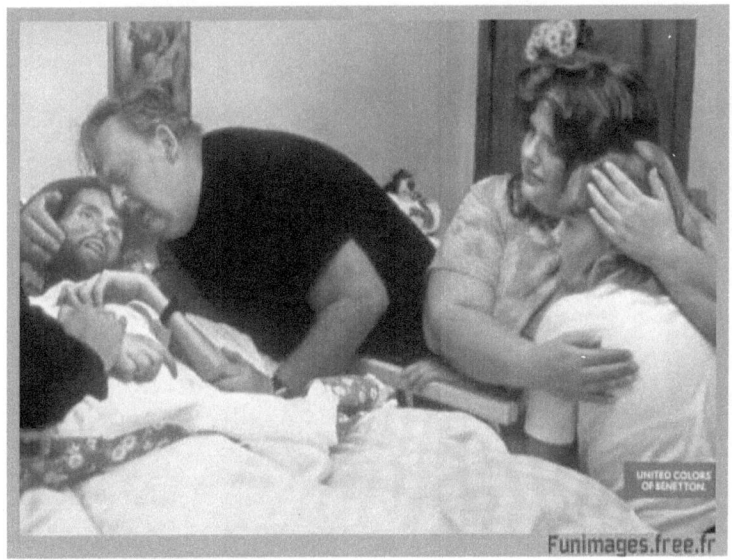

Le cas Benetton

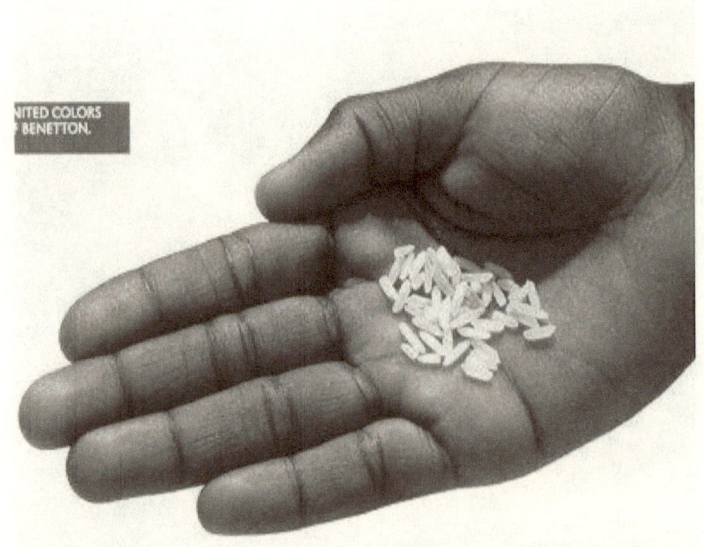

Le cas Benetton

Le cas Benetton

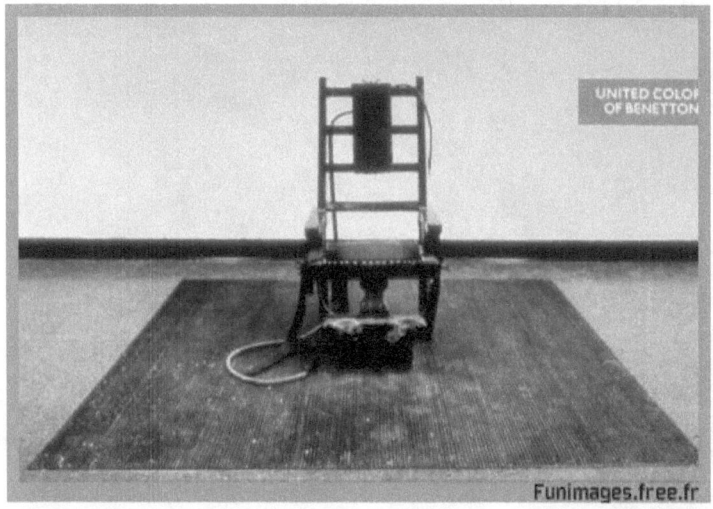

Le cas Benetton

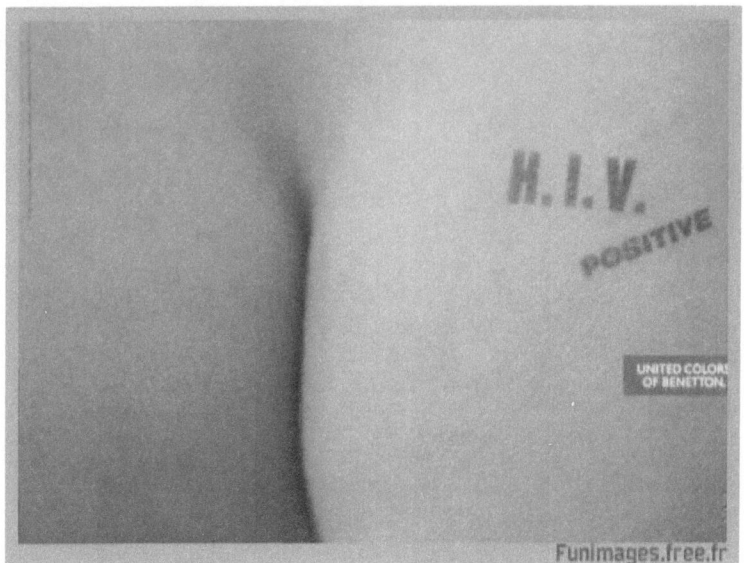

Le cas Benetton

Le cas Benetton

Le cas Benetton

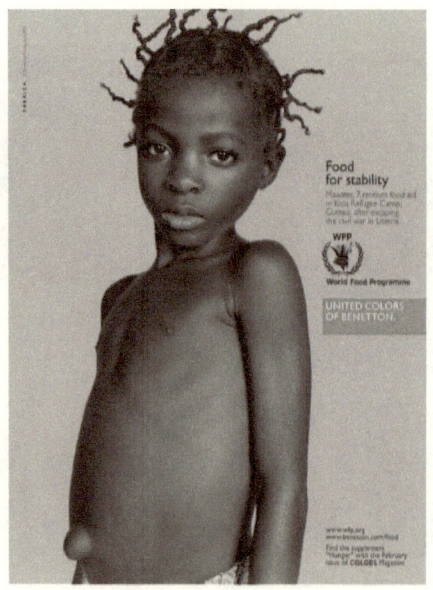

Le cas Benetton

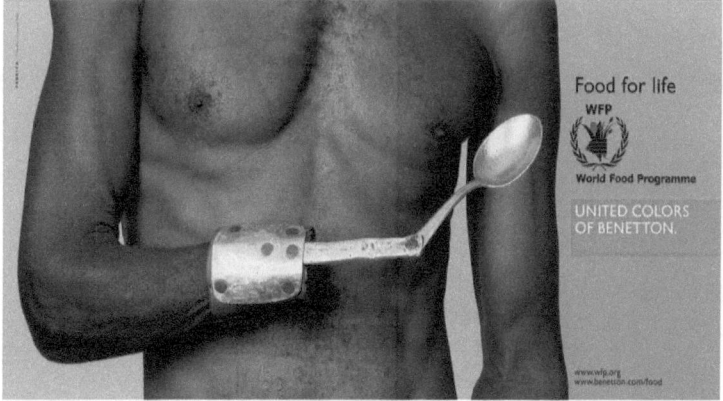

Le cas Benetton

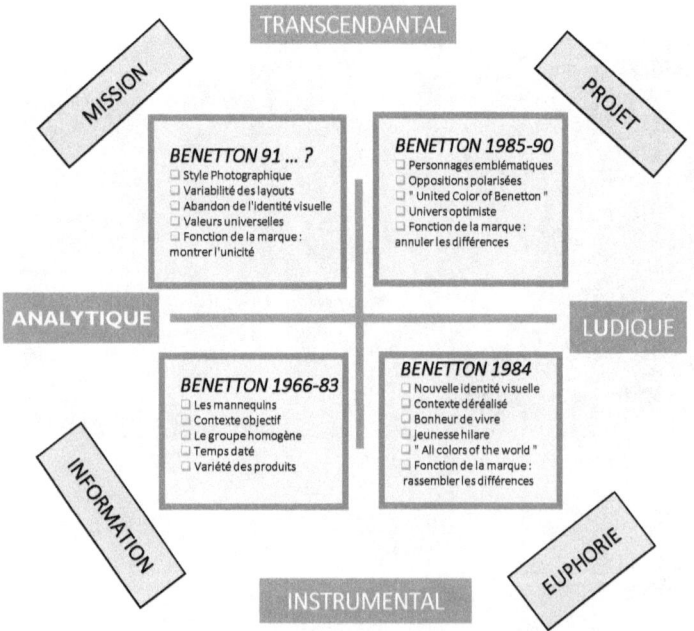

LE DISCOURS
DE LA MARQUE

Le discours de la marque* : identité et valeurs

- On a vu que l'identité de la marque reposait sur un nombre réduit de valeurs de base, qui sont ensuite transformées en narrations et en discours par les différents moyens sémiotiques mis à disposition de la marque et qui constituent pour ainsi dire son arsenal de communication.

- Il est évident que ces moyens de communication auront d'autant plus d'efficacité et de précision qu'ils étaieront de façon synergique le noyau fondateur des valeurs de la marque.

- Les 4 quadrants du maping structurent d'une manière générale 4 systèmes de valorisation différents.

- La détermination de la localisation correcte des valeurs fondatrices d'une marque sur le maping permet de développer de façon cohérente tous les éléments de son mix discursif.

* d'après Andréa Semprini

Le discours de la marque : *le temps*

- La dimension temporelle est une des composantes fondamentales de tout discours de marque.
- Implicitement ou explicitement, chaque marque tient dans sa communication un discours sur le temps.
- Dans certains cas, le temps est seulement une composante de l'architecture discursive d'une marque. Dans d'autres, il peut se trouver carrément parmi les valeurs de base.

Le discours de la marque :
le temps

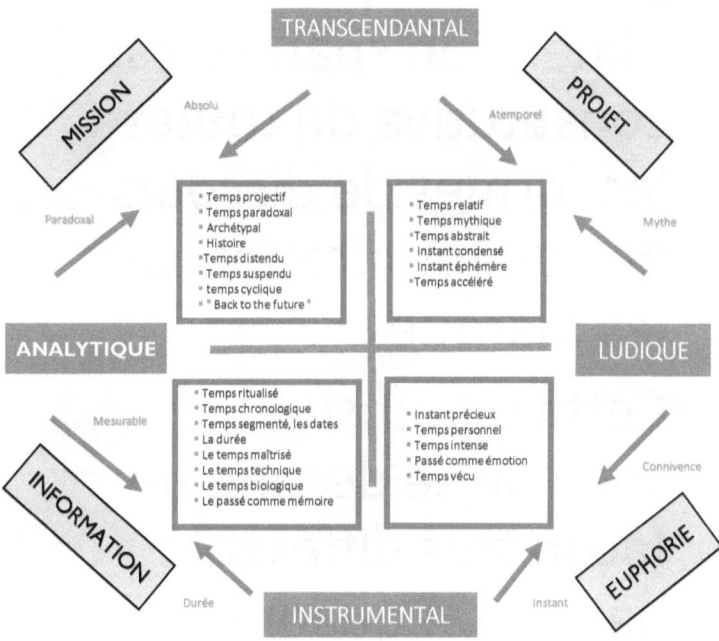

Le discours de la marque : *l'espace*

- De la même façon que pour le temps la dimension spatiale est constitutive de toutes les formes de discours en communication sur les marques.
- Cette dimension spatiale se décline de façon très différente dans les 4 quadrants du maping.

Le discours de la marque : *l'espace*

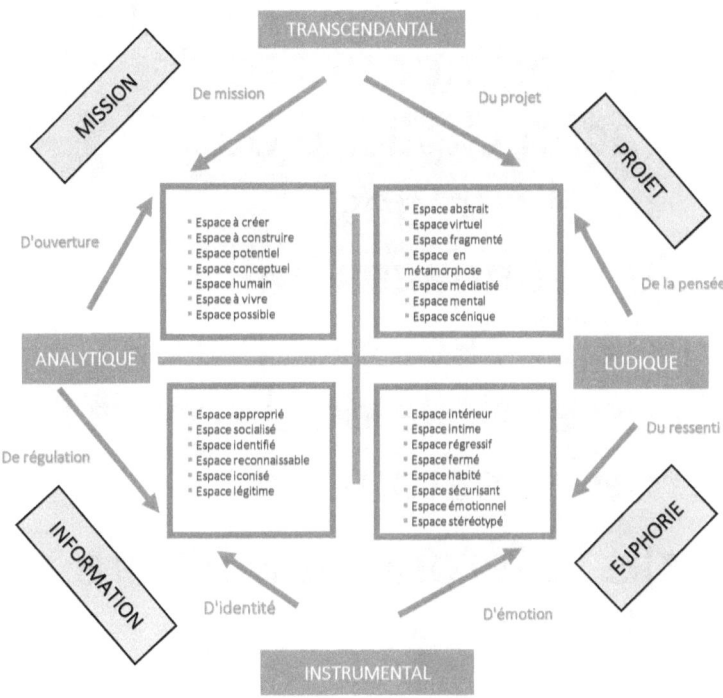

Le discours de la marque : *les acteurs*

- Chaque marque pour s'exprimer utilise de façon explicite ou implicite des personnages qui défendent une partie essentielle du discours de la marque.
- Ils le feront de manière différente selon le quadrant où se positionnera la marque.

Le discours de la marque : *les acteurs*

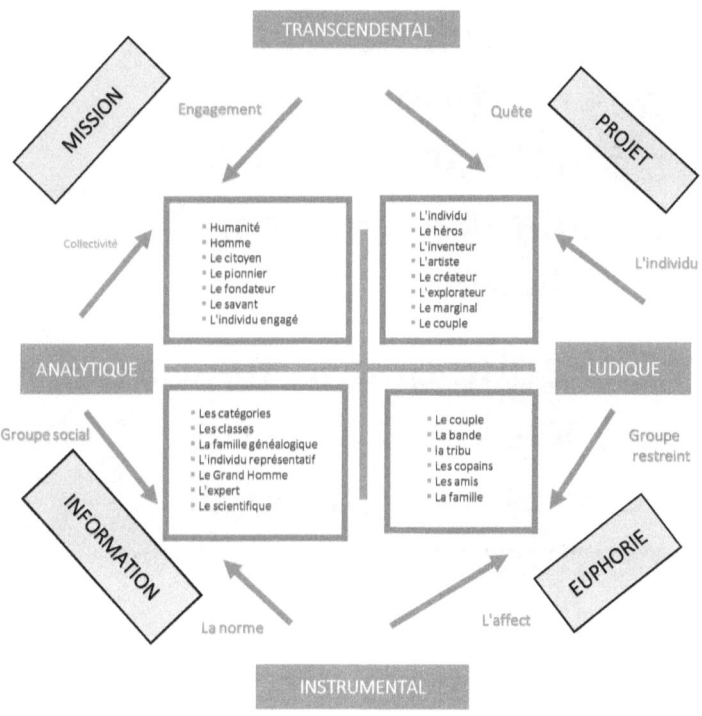

Le discours de la marque : *les relations*

- Le système d'acteurs que nous venons de voir implique naturellement des relations qui s'établissent entre les individus et les groupes d'individus.

- À chaque quadrant sont associé des types de relations propres qui permettent à la marque de s'exprimer et d'acquérir un discours sémiotique en relation avec les autres aspects de ce même discours.

Le discours de la marque :
les relations

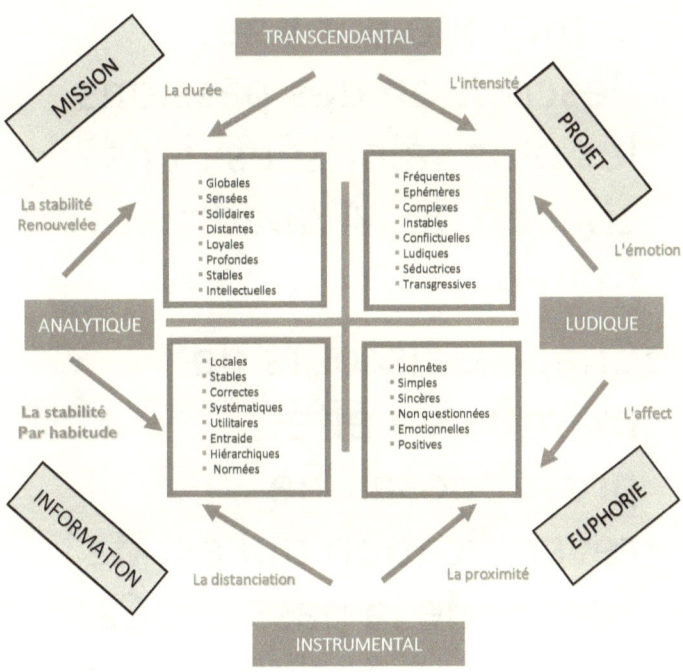

Le discours de la marque : *les passions*

- Nous allons conclure cette partie de notre analyse de la marque par une description des passions les plus valorisées dans chacun des 4 quadrants du maping.

- Chaque discours de marque en effet présuppose une revendication qui est de l'ordre de la passion. Car sans cela pas de marque qui n'obtienne de l'adhésion.

Le discours de la marque : *les passions*

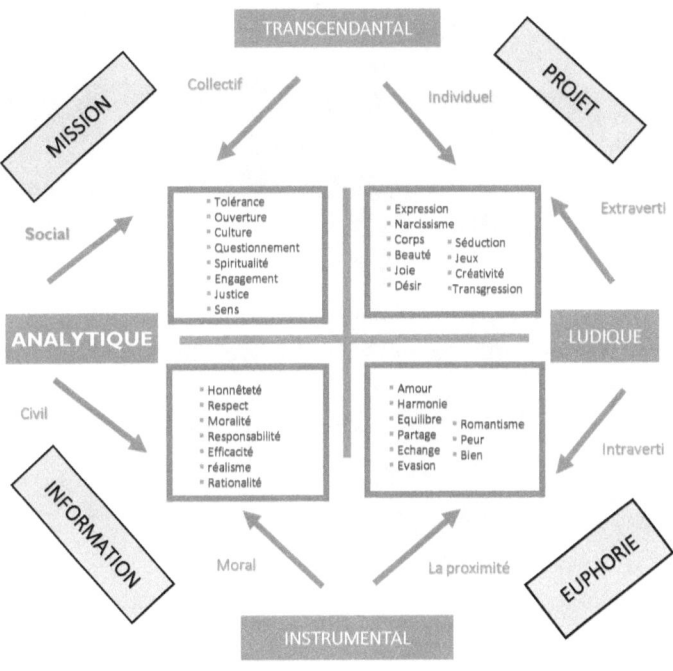

220

6. LES STRATÉGIES D'UN DÉVELOPPEMENT EFFICACE

Gérer son portefeuille de marques
Le co-branding
Internet

LE PORTEFEUILLE PRODUITS

Comment composer un portefeuille produits

- Pendant longtemps les portefeuilles produits étaient composés en fonction des méthodes de production. C'était les outils de fabrication qui déterminaient la nature et le nombre de produits qui se trouvaient dans un portefeuille.
- Beaucoup de magasins sont encore architecturés selon cette logique. Les plans des gondoles reprennent les structurations marchés qui sont des structurations fabrication.
- Désormais un portefeuille produits doit être architecturé en fonction des univers de consommation et donc des comportements consommateurs.
- On peur en effet étendre un portefeuille produit aussi loin que l'univers de consommation le permet si l'on dispose d'une marque élastique.
  - DONC AVANT DE DÉFINIR LE PÉRIMÈTRE DE SON PORTEFEUILLE PRODUITS, ON DOIT DÉCOUVRIR QUELLES SONT LES MOTIVATIONS D'ACHAT DES CONSOMMATEURS DANS UN UNIVERS DONNÉ ET SAVOIR SI OUI OU NON ON Y DISPOSE D'AVANTAGES CONCURRENTIELS VIA LES PLUS PRODUITS.
  - ON DOIT ÉGALEMENT CONNAÎTRE LE STATUT ET L'EXTENSION DE LA MARQUE QUI PORTERA LE/ LES PRODUIT(S).

Définition :
le portefeuille produits

- Pour une marque donnée, on appelle **portefeuille produits l'ensemble des produits qui portent ou porteront le nom de la marque.**

- Plus ce portefeuille sera étendu, plus on prendra de soin de mettre en place une architecture de marque qui **rende lisible pour le consommateur** le **rapport des produits à la marque** et les **relations des produits entre eux**, de même que la **justification de la présence** de tel produit ou tel autre à l'intérieur du portefeuille de produits.

Comment composer un portefeuille produits

- Un portefeuille produits cohérent, pour une marque donnée, en fonction du statut de la marque et de ses possibilités d'extension, **est un portefeuille qui permet à la marque de procéder à son extension maximum sans aller** (cf. tableau de Davidson) **jusqu'à la zone rouge.**
- On le construit en s'inscrivant dans la matrice de Davidson. Voir exemple LIPTON.

Comment composer un portefeuille produits

- Il est clair que les extensions ne se feront que si :

    - Si l'on dispose d'un ou de plusieurs plus produit.
    - Si on dispose d'un ou de plusieurs avantages concurrentiels (Prix, Pression publicitaire, Distribution).

        - C'EST LA RAISON POUR LAQUELLE ON UTILISE LA BONNE VIEILLE TECHNIQUE DES 4P AFIN DE **METTRE EN ÉVIDENCE LA COMPÉTENCE DISTINCTIVE DES PRODUITS** QUE JE VAIS AJOUTER À MON PORTEFEUILLE AFIN DE L'ÉTENDRE AU MAXIMUM.

Rappel de ce qu'il faut aller rechercher dans les 4 P

PRODUIT	PRIX	PROMOTION	DISTRIBUTION
Qualité intrinsèque	Δ prix conso	Packaging (originalité, force)	Canaux de distribution
Gamme de produits	Δ vs indice de la marque concurrente	Publicité	Logistique
Options, tailles, couleurs	PERFORMANCE PRIX DU PRODUIT	Promotion des ventes (thématique /mécanismes)	Merchandising
Garanties		Relations publiques	Force de vente
Service après-vente		Sponsoring et mécénat	AVANTAGE CONCURRENTIEL DISTRIBUTION
Conditionnement		Marketing direct	
PERFORMANCE GLOBALE DU PRODUIT		PERFORMANCE COMMUNICATION	

Communiquer les avantages concurrentiels

- À partir des 4P du produit, il est impératif dans le monde surmédiatisé qui est le nôtre de communiquer sur les avantages concurrentiels de ses produits.
- Il faut **mettre en avant la compétence distinctive :**
    - Les bénéfices tangibles ou Plus Produit.
    - Les valeurs d'imaginaire.
- Tous les supports de communication doivent y contribuer :
    - **Le packaging en premier lieu**
    - Le linéaire où est proposé le produit en utilisant notamment **la PLV.**
    - La **communication média.**
    - La **promotion des ventes** via le choix d'une thématique judicieuse.

Définition :
le portefeuille de marque

- Alors que le portefeuille produits a pour mission d'optimiser le nombre de produits sous une marque donnée, le portefeuille de marque joue son rôle **au niveau d'une activité ou d'une entreprise.**

- La question est de savoir **quel est le nombre optimum de marques dont l'entreprise doit disposer pour assurer à son activité le plus de chance de toucher les consommateurs intéressés par son offre.**

    - Faut-il une plusieurs marques ?
    - S'il en faut plusieurs, pourquoi ?
    - Qu'apporte un portefeuille composé de plusieurs marques dans la conquête du consommateur ?
    - Est-ce que l'on éclaircit mon offre en multipliant le nombre de marques ou bien est-ce qu'on brouille les pistes ?

La solution optimisée de constitution d'un portefeuille de marque

1. Définir à partir de la matrice Étoile de l'identité de la marque son potentiel et son territoire imaginaire.
2. Mettre en exergue les valeurs de la marque.
3. Fixer le statut de la marque et en déduire les conséquences en termes d'élasticité ou d'extension de la marque et donc de couverture produits.
4. Statuer sur l'élasticité de la marque ou le « brand stretching » de façon à éviter soit les sur extensions, soit les sous-extensions.
5. Utiliser la matrice de Davidson pour positionner un maximum de produits.

La solution optimisée

- Disposer d'un nombre restreint de marques (car comme pour l'impôt : *Trop de marques tuent les marques*).

- Mais en disposer suffisamment pour pouvoir être en mesure de toucher un maximum de cibles comportementales de consommateurs en fonction de l'offre que l'on propose.

- Compléter aussi éventuellement des identités de marque défaillantes par des marques au profil complémentaire.

LE CO-BRANDING
ou les stratégies d'alliance de marques

Pourquoi le co-branding ?

- Nous avons constaté avec le tableau de Kotler que nous nous trouvions dans une situation d'offre pléthorique.
- La conséquence de cette situation, c'est que le marché va avoir tendance à s'établir sur 2 axes :
    - Un axe Choix
    - Un axe Prix ou Low cost
- Dans l'axe choix (domaine privilégié du co-branding) on va devoir, outre s'appuyer sur un capital de marque fort, proposer des offres de plus en plus sophistiquées, qui, dans le cadre du permission marketing, devront allier produit + service(s).

Pourquoi le co-branding ?

- Le co-branding n'a d'intérêt que lorsque 2 marques se complètent au niveau de l'identité et s'apportent mutuellement au niveau des produits.

Des identités complémentaires

- Il est important que des marques qui décident de devenir partenaires au niveau du co-branding aient des **identités complémentaires** qui s'enrichissent mutuellement.

- Notamment les cultures et les mentalisations doivent être très proches.

Des identités complémentaires

- Ainsi avant de marier 2 marques, on procédera à une analyse en profondeur des identités de chacune.
- On veillera à ce que les valeurs qu'elles promeuvent (consciemment et inconsciemment) soient les mêmes ou se complètent.

Des identités complémentaires

- On veillera également à ce que le positionnement des marques sur le **maping sémiotique** (et donc le discours que chacune doit tenir) soit en symbiose et vienne enrichir toutes les marques concernées
- Ainsi, après avoir analysé en profondeur les identités, procédera-t-on également à une mise à plat des discours de façon à mettre en évidence leur coordination.

Pourquoi le co-branding ?

- *EXERCICE :*

  - Citer des exemples de propositions co-brandées.
  - Montrer comment les identités de chacune des 2 marques se répondent l'une l'autre ?
  - Montrer que les discours tenus sur les 2 marques se répondent l'un l'autre.
  - Montrer quels en sont les avantages.
  - Relever leurs faiblesses, si elles en présentent.

Forces/Faiblesses du co-branding

- Marier 2 marques entre elles ne présente pas que des avantages.
- Lorsque cela est réalisé avec rigueur, certes on peut assister à un enrichissement mutuel. C'est la raison pour laquelle des tentatives sont lancées régulièrement.
- Néanmoins, il y a de multiples risques, même lorsqu'on prend la peine de faire correspondre les identités de marque.

Forces/Faiblesses du co-branding

- Le premier inconvénient est lié aux difficultés de communication.
    - Dans le monde hyper médiatisé dans lequel nous nous trouvons plus une communication est simple et directe plus elle possède de chance d'être retenue.
- Le second tient au fait que les segmentations comportementales varient d'une marque à l'autre.
    - Les comportements des consommateurs face à une marque résultent certes de son identité et des valeurs qu'elle véhicule, mais beaucoup aussi de son histoire.
    - Or il est fort rare que les histoires de 2 marques se rapprochent. La plupart du temps elles sont très différentes.

Les champs d'application

- Compte tenu de tout ce que nous venons de dire, il est intéressant de faire du co-branding :
    - Lorsque l'on se trouve devant deux offres complémentaires :
        - Un produit + un service
        - Une marque produit/service + une marque de distribution
        - Une marque produit/service + une marque média (presse, TV, radio, etc)
    - Lorsque l'on veut modifier le sens d'une marque mère en lui créant des marques filles :
        - Le cas Renault
        - Voir ce que nous avons dit sur les architectures de marques.
    - Lorsque l'on veut bénéficier de la notoriété d'une marque forte pour pénétrer plus rapidement un marché et accroître sa propre notoriété :
        - L'utilisation de l'architecture marque caution pour lancer une nouvelle marque. Ex Aquarelle lancée par l'appui de la marque Nestlé.

Perspectives

- Compte tenu de l'importance de l'hyper médiatisation à laquelle sont contraints les offreurs :
  - On développe aujourd'hui le co-branding lorsque l'on se trouve devant deux activités complémentaires :
    - Un industriel et un distributeur par exemple.
    - Un groupe de presse et un offreur de services.
  - Ou bien lorsque l'on souhaite monter en notoriété rapidement. Solution Aquarelle.
  - Néanmoins, c'est le cas activité complémentaire qui se développe le plus :
    - POURQUOI ?

LE CO-BRANDING : UN OUTIL PRIVILÉGIÉ DE PARTENARIAT AVEC LA DISTRIBUTION

Le partenariat marque/distribution

- Le partenariat marque/distribution est un vaste champ d'application du co-branding.
  - Lorsque la distribution s'associe à un événement médiatisé qui est une marque (Tour de France).
  - Lorsque la distribution s'attache à promouvoir une offre spécifique qui lui est réservée (Lorina à son lancement, Senséo à son lancement).
  - Lorsque la distribution s'associe à des services (ex Cofinoga).

Exemple de partenariat marque/distribution

Exemple de partenariat marque/distribution

Exemple de partenariat marque/distribution

Exemple de partenariat marque/distribution

Exemple de partenariat marque/distribution

Exemple de partenariat marque/distribution

La partenariat marque/distribution

- Ce partenariat présente de nombreux avantages :
    - Il permet à la distribution de se démarquer de ses concurrents en promouvant une marque qui lui est réservée.
    - Il permet à la distribution de proposer des offres complémentaires à ses clients qui accroissent la fidélisation à l'enseigne.
    - Il permet à la marque de bénéficier de la puissance de mise en avant de la distribution, ce qui lui permet de monter rapidement en notoriété auprès des clients de l'enseigne.
    - Il permet à la marque de bénéficier de tous les supports de communication de la distribution.

MARQUES ET INTERNET

La marque et Internet

- En matière de communication des marques, Internet joue de plus en plus un rôle capital.
- C'est la raison pour laquelle (de même qu'on l'aura fait pour le packaging ou la communication médias) on attachera de l'importance à la façon dont les messages y seront communiqués.
- Dans la Charte de Marque ou dans le Cahier des Charges sera donc exprimés le type de messages qu'on entend voir véhiculé et la façon de le faire, notamment en prenant une grille de lecture basée sur le maping sémiotique.

Site Haribo

Elsève de l'Oréal

Site Senseo

Site Pampers

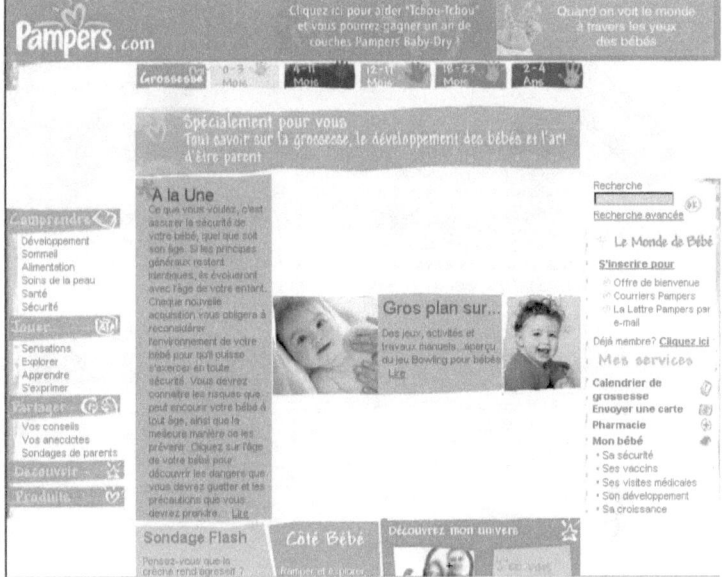

Les types de site en fonction du maping sémiotique

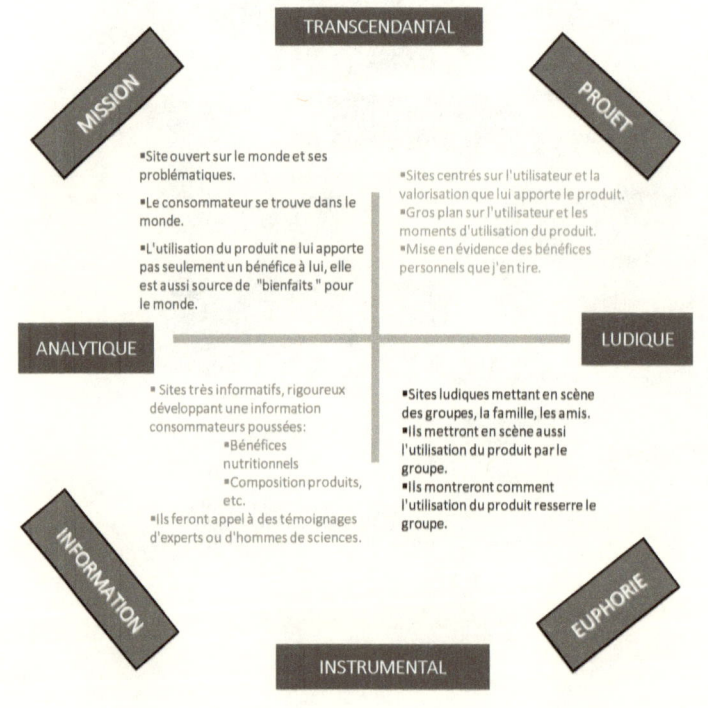

7. L'IMPORTANCE DE LA MARQUE DANS LA COMMUNICATION DE L'ENTREPRISE

Séparer marques et Institution
Affecter les portefeuille produits
en fonction des identités de marque

MARQUES ET INSTITUTION

LE SYSTÈME EIMP*

- Bien souvent marque et entreprise portent le même nom (c'est le cas par exemple de CASTORAMA, RENAULT, CARREFOUR, IBM, NESTLÉ, DANONE, etc.)

- L'Institution en tant que réalité de l'entreprise s'adresse au monde des financiers. Elle a ce faisant des valeurs à promouvoir et un registre de communication particulier, qui peuvent être différents de ceux auxquels s'attachent les consommateurs.

- Tandis que les produits et la marque qui les supporte s'adressent aux consommateurs. Ils ont donc pour mission de communiquer sur la satisfaction des attentes de ces derniers et de parler à leur imaginaire.

* Source : Jean-Noël KAPFERER : Les marques, Capital de l'entreprise

- Cette symbiose entre **Institution, Entreprise, Marque** et **Produits** nécessite une gestion du discours de la marque plus complexe, que lorsque marque et entreprise sont dissociées. On se doit de fonctionner selon une vision systémique des registres du discours.

Les paramètres de cette réalité :

- L'**Institution** est à l'**Entreprise**, ce que la **Marque** est aux **Produits et Services**.
- L'**Institution** comme la **Marque** appartiennent au monde de l'imaginaire, tandis que l'**Entreprise, Produits** ou **Services** se développent à partir du tangible.

Les bases du schéma EIMP

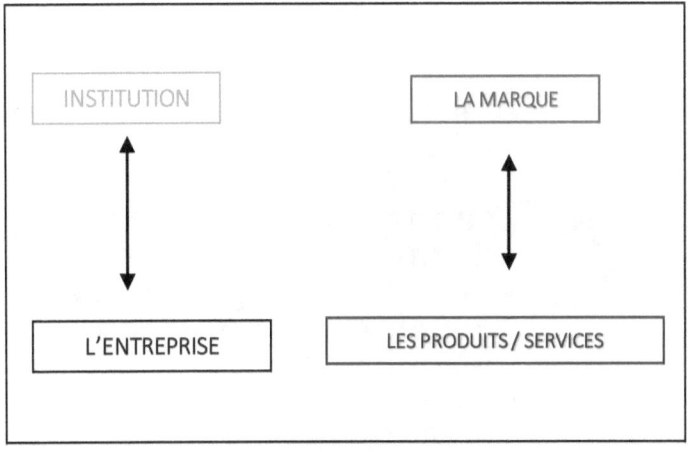

À Partir de ce schéma " dynamique " toute stratégie de communication consistera à choisir le ou les registre(s) sur lequel / lesquels on investira massivement : E.I.M.P.

GÉRER LE SYSTÈME EIMP

- Prenons l'exemple de la Régie Renault pour illustrer notre propos :
    - Le fait que RENAULT ait longtemps été le laboratoire social de la FRANCE a sapé la construction d'une image de marque de qualité (la répétition des grèves et des manifestations n'est pas favorable à cela).
    - Cela a donné à la marque un reflet de marque populaire : l'acheteur ne cherchant pas à se distinguer, mais à se fondre dans la collectivité. Il y avait derrière Renault-Marque une latence égalitariste issue de Renault-institution. Cela segmentait en termes de produits et en termes de cibles son offre.

Le fonctionnement du système EIMP chez RENAULT avant la privatisation :

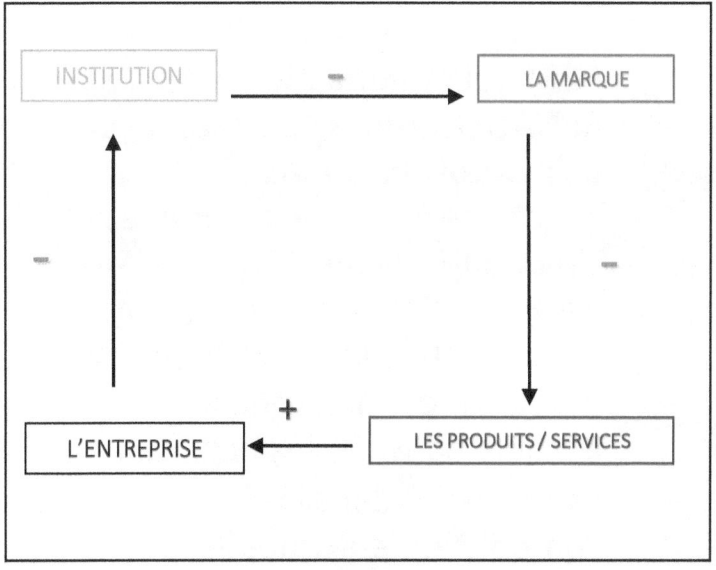

- Malgré de bons produits fabriqués par l'entreprise, leur image était mauvaise.

- Le redressement est venu d'une triple modification de la politique de communication :

    1. L'abandon des R (R5-R9-R11-R25) qui ramenait les produits à RENAULT donc à l'entreprise et à l'Institution, sources négatives en termes d'image. Une politique de **personnalisation des produits** en leur attribuant des **prénoms de marque** : Clio, Mégane, Laguna, Safrane, Espace, etc.
    2. La présence dans la compétition automobile, notamment en Formule 1.
    3. L'acceptation des règles du jeu de la globalisation (accords Renault-Volvo, rachat de NISSAN).

- Si l'on essaye de tracer le schéma de fonctionnement du nouveau système EIMP chez RENAULT, on devrait avoir :

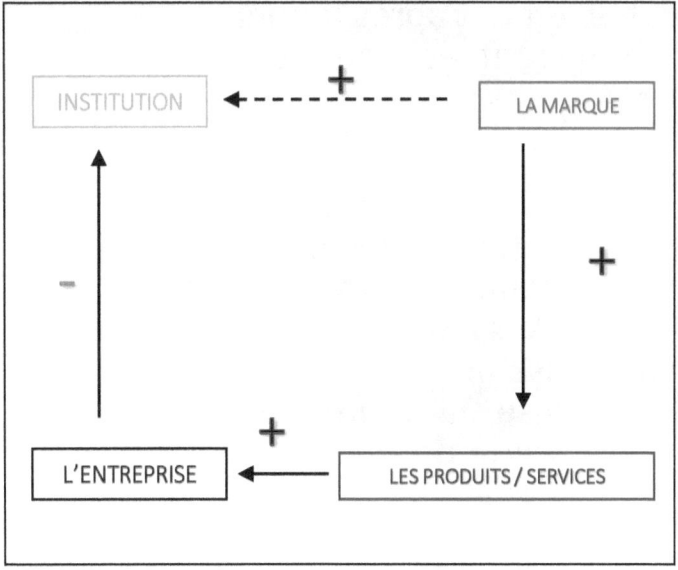

L'ÉTOUFFEMENT DE LA MARQUE PAR L'INSTITUTION

- On le constate avec l'exemple RENAULT, il s'en est fallu de peu que l'Institution et les images négatives qu'elle véhiculait n'anéantissent la marque, puis probablement après rendent inintéressant les produits.

- C'est ce qui faillit également arriver à C_2I Honeywell Bull. Bien que voulu par l'État, comme le fleuron institutionnel informatique de notre État, les nombreuses déconvenues financières de l'entreprise ont eu une image désastreuse sur les produits, allant jusqu'à **priver de sens la marque**.

- Ainsi au milieu des années 80, on aurait pu tracer le schéma de fonctionnement du système EIMP chez Bull comme suit :

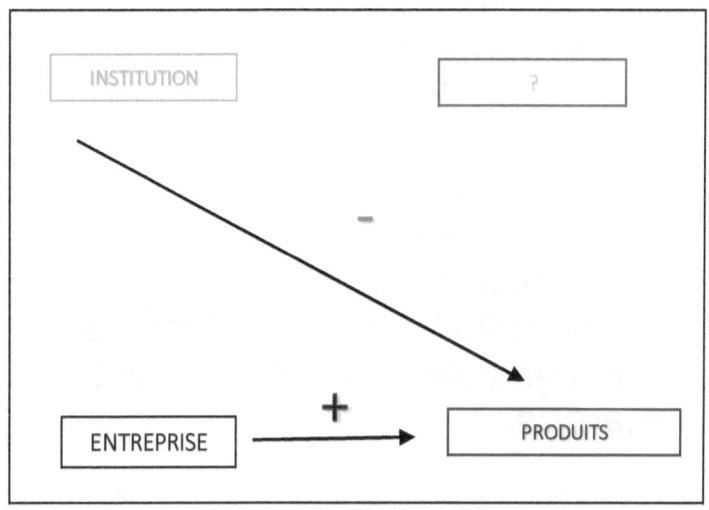

- À partir de ce constat, les dirigeants se sont ingéniés à retourner la situation, en introduisant dans leur communication le concept de l'adaptabilité. C'était un concept fort qui induisait soit un résultat :
    - L'adaptabilité des entreprises clientes aux changements du monde moderne.
    - L'adaptabilité de Bull aux réalités de ses clients.

- La manifestation de ce retournement de stratégie fut l'adoption du symbole de l'arbre (introduit dans le logo) et l'abandon du nom institutionnel C2I Honeywell Bull, au profit de Bull, qui avait tout sémantiquement et en termes d'imaginaire pour devenir une marque.

- Ce faisant le schéma a pu passer à :

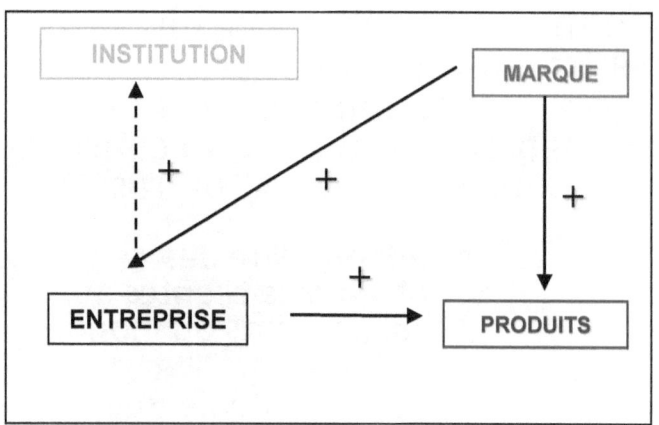

L'ÉTOUFFEMENT DE LA MARQUE PAR LE PRODUIT

- Un autre déséquilibre classique, que l'on rencontre souvent, c'est celui où le produit vide de tout contenu la marque. Alors, la marque ne peut plus fonctionner comme source. Elle est progressivement asséchée par le produit.

- C'était le cas par exemple de la marque NINA RICCI, après le décès de Monsieur Robert RICCI, fils de la fondatrice à la fin des années 80.

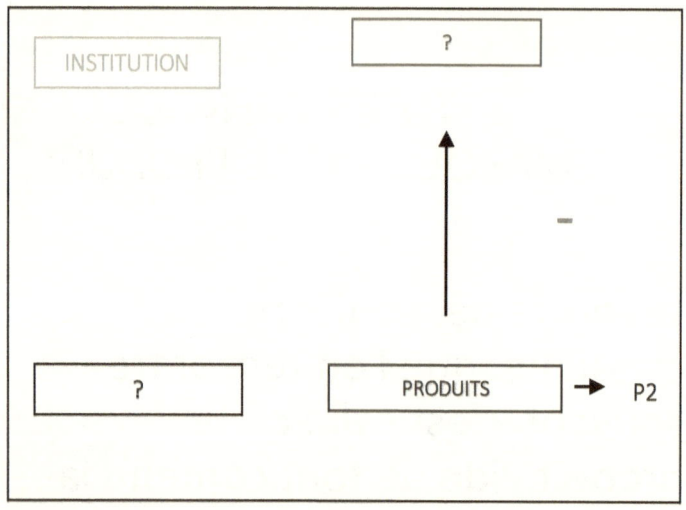

- NINA RICCI n'était plus qu'une **institution** du monde de la Haute Couture.
- **L'entreprise**, bien incapable était-on de dire en quoi elle consistait.
- **La marque** avait disparu, phagocytée qu'elle avait été par son **produit STAR** le parfum des jeunes filles nostalgique *L'air du temps* et par le traitement communicationnel qu'en avait donné David Hamilton, son photographe. Une tentative de désenclavement de la marque avait certes eu lieu avec le lancement d'un nouveau parfum "NINA", mais en pure perte.

- En effet, avoir confié au même David Hamilton, le lancement de ce nouveau produit ne fit que renforcer alors la stature de " l'air du temps ".

- Cette erreur est à comparer avec la sagesse de CACHAREL : LOULOU de CACHAREL sut fort bien se démarquer d'ANAIS ANAIS, tout en respectant certains codes, qui étaient eux-mêmes de la marque.

CET EXEMPLE NOUS RAPPELLE QU'UNE MARQUE DOIT ÊTRE UNE SOURCE ET NE SE DÉVELOPPE QUE PAR LES NOUVEAUX PRODUITS QU'ELLE SUPPORTE.

8 . L'AUDIT DE LA MARQUE

La Matrice d'Optimisation Stratégique (MOS)
Le scoring : mesurer les performances de la marque
Les pistes d'amélioration

Objectifs

- Le scoring de la marque a pour objectif principal de faire un état des lieux chiffré qui permette de comparer une marque A avec une marque B puis C, etc. de façon à ne retenir dans un portefeuille de marques d'une entreprise que celles qui présentent un réel potentiel.
- Par ailleurs, il a comme objectifs secondaires :
    - Mettre en évidence des pistes d'amélioration des marques retenues de façon à mieux communiquer sur elles et à enrichir le portefeuille de produits plus en adéquation avec le cœur identitaire de la marque et ses valeurs.
    - Repositionner une marque retenue en retravaillant son Mix (Packaging, Communication, Distribution) afin de séduire une cible plus en adéquation avec son identité.
    - Servir de base pour constituer la **Charte de Marque** qui sera l'outil à partir duquel les agences seront à même de définir les axes de communication de la marque.

Méthodologie

- Le scoring s'établit à partir d'études :
  - Des **études qualitatives** donnant lieu à des focus groups.
  - Des **interviews** permettant de répondre à des questions fermées et d'approfondir un ressenti via des questions ouvertes complémentaires.

- Le scoring s'établit **également** à partir des résultats obtenus sur les différentes matrices vues (L'Identité, l'Étoile de la marque, son statut, le maping sémiotique etc.)

Les études qualitatives

- Elles sont nécessaires pour l'établissement de l'Étoile de la marque.
- Elles seront effectuées auprès de consommateurs et de non-consommateurs de la marque.
- Un focus particulier sera fait sur le cœur de cible.
  - **RÉSULTAT À OBTENIR : PERMETTRE DE COMPRENDRE QUELLES SONT LES VALEURS QUI GOUVERNENT LA MARQUE.**
  - **PERMETTRE DE TRACER L'ÉTOILE DE LA MARQUE.**

Les interviews

- Ils viendront compléter les études qualitatives auprès des consommateurs.
  - Interroger le **cœur de cible** (de façon statistiquement représentative, soit par exemple avec un échantillon de 200 personnes).
  - Interroger également les **non-consommateurs** (en prenant le soin d'avoir là encore un échantillon représentatif.)
- Ils viendront donner un éclairage sur le ressenti des personnels de l'entreprise.
  - L'enrichir par une interview du personnel en prenant soin d'interroger des collaborateurs de tous les services ou de toutes les directions.

Les Interviews

- L'objet des questionnaires est de faire le point aussi bien **sur sa propre marque** que sur les principales **marques concurrentes** de façon à avoir une vue exhaustive de la situation du marché et de pouvoir mesurer les apports de sa propre marque pour les consommateurs au regard de celles de la concurrence.
- Cela tant pour les questionnaires consommateurs stricto sensu que pour les questionnaires internes à l'entreprise.

La Matrice d'Optimisation Stratégique (MOS)

ITEMS	Identité (Forces des facettes de l'étoile vs l'offre)	Âge	Simplicité de l'architecture (Une seule architecture vs plusieurs)	Notoriété spontanée	Notoriété assistée	Statut de la marque	Co-branding	Megabrand	SCORING
Coefficients	6	4	4	3	1	3	3	4	
Marques ⬇									
La vôtre									
B (Concurrent N°1)									
C (Concurrent N°2)									
D (Concurrent N°3)									
ETC…									

Notation des performances de la marque : 4 = Très Bien, 3 = Bien, 2 = Moyen, 1 = Mauvais,
On multiplie ensuite la note de chaque marque par le coefficient, ce qui donne une nouvelle valeur. La somme des valeurs pour chaque marque donne son scoring. La marque ayant le scoring le plus élevé est celle qui a le plus de potentiel.

Conclusion du séminaire

Références

- Jean- Noël Kapferer :
  Les marques, Le Capital de l'Entreprise.

- Andréa Semprini :
  Le maping sémiotique.

www.ingramcontent.com/pod-product-compliance
Lightning Source LLC
Chambersburg PA
CBHW020631220526
45464CB00001B/101